The Fragmentation of Reason

The Fragmentation of Reason:

Preface to a Pragmatic Theory of
Cognitive Evaluation

Stephen P. Stich

A Bradford Book
The MIT Press
Cambridge, Massachusetts
London, England

First MIT Press paperback edition, 1993

This book was set in 10/12 Palatino by DEKR Corporation and printed and bound in the United States of America.

Library of Congress Cataloging-in-Publication Data

Stich, Stephen P.
    The fragmentation of reason : preface to a pragmatic theory of cognitive evaluation / Stephen P. Stich.
        p.   cm.
    "A Bradford book."
    Includes bibliographical references.
    ISBN 0-262-19293-4 (HB), 0-262-69159-0 (PB)
    1. Knowledge, Theory of. I. Title.
BD161.S75   1990
121—dc20   89-39165
                                                                              CIP

For Becca and Jonah

Contents

Acknowledgments

During the dozen years that this book has been evolving, I've been the beneficiary of enormous amounts of help, support, and encouragement from many people and many institutions. Quite a number of them are mentioned in the text. But for many others, there was no convenient place to record my debt. Also, in many cases, people who are mentioned in the text were helpful in lots of other ways that could not be easily noted. So before beginning, I want to acknowledge my debt and express my thanks to:

Michael Bishop
Keith Campbell
Patricia Churchland
Paul Churchland
Roy D'Andrade
Daniel Dennett
Michael Devitt
Michael Dietrich
Warren Dow
Richard Feldman
Hartry Field
Jerry Fodor
Peter Godfrey-Smith
Alvin Goldman
Cliff Hooker
Ed Hutchins
Norbert Hornstein
Philip Kitcher
Elizabeth Lloyd
Brian Loar
William Lycan
Douglas MacLean
Andrew Milne
Sam Mitchell
Edmund Mulaire

Richard Nisbett
Donald Norman
Christopher Peacocke
William Ramsey
Dudley Shapere
Francis Snare
Kim Sterelny
David Stove
Joseph Tolliver
Bruce Wilshire

Special thanks are in order to Todd Jones, who helped prepare the final version of the manuscript, and to Betty and Harry Stanton, who waited for it with their usual good cheer and gentle encouragement.

My deepest debts are to my wife, Jude, and my children, Jonah and Becca. Without their unfailing love and support the project might never have been finished; indeed, it would hardly have been worth doing at all.

Chapter 1

Something between a Preface and an Introduction

One good way to begin a philosophical essay is to locate the project in philosophical space by saying how the questions to be asked and the answers to be defended relate to the questions and answers that have occupied other writers. Another way to get started, particularly when the views to be defended are at odds with much of received opinion—and mine certainly are—is to say something about the evolution of one's own thinking, in an effort to explain how one arrived at such unorthodox views. In this introductory chapter, I propose to do a bit of both. The autobiographical approach will predominate, not because I imagine the reader will find the details of my intellectual autobiography to be of any intrinsic interest, but simply because it provides a perspicuous way to give an overview of the book and to explain how its various themes come to be linked together. Though issues in the philosophy of mind, the philosophy of language, and the philosophy of psychology will all be center stage at one point or another in the pages to follow, the cluster of questions that motivate the volume fall squarely within the domain of epistemology. So let me start by saying how I view that domain.

1.1 Three Traditional Epistemological Projects

There are, as I see it, at least three interrelated projects that traditionally have been pursued in epistemology, with different authors naturally enough emphasizing different ones. The first of these projects focuses on the evaluation of methods of inquiry. It tries to say which ways of going about the quest for knowledge—which ways of building and rebuilding one's doxastic house—are the good ones, which are the bad ones, and why. Since reasoning is central to the quest for knowledge, the evaluation of various strategies of reasoning often plays a major role in the assessment of inquiry.

There is no shortage of historical figures who have pursued this sort of epistemological investigation. Much of Francis Bacon's epistemological writing is devoted to the project of evaluating and criticizing strategies of inquiry, as is a good deal of Descartes's. Among more modern epistemological writers, those like Mill, Carnap, and Popper, who are concerned with the logic and methodology of science, have tended to emphasize this aspect of epistemological theory. From Bacon's time to Popper's, it has frequently been the case that those who work in this branch of epistemology are motivated, at least in part, by very practical concerns. They are convinced that defective reasoning and bad strategies of inquiry are widespread, and that these cognitive shortcomings are the cause of much mischief and misery. By developing their accounts of good reasoning and proper strategies of inquiry, and by explaining why these are better than the alternatives, they hope others will come to see the error of their cognitive ways. And, indeed, many of these philosophers have had a noticeable impact on the thinking of their contemporaries.[1]

A second traditional epistemological project aims to understand what knowledge is, and how it is to be distinguished from other cognitive states like mere opinion or false belief. For Plato, and for many other philosophers as well, the effort to understand what knowledge is was taken to be an inquiry into the nature of a natural kind. It was the form or essence of the natural kind that the inquiry sought to uncover. With the "linguistic turn" in twentieth-century philosophy, this project has been reconstrued as a quest for the correct definition of the word 'knowledge' or for the correct analysis of the concept of knowledge. Since the publication, in 1963, of Gettier's brief and enormously influential attack on the venerable view that 'knowledge' could be defined as 'justified true belief', the analytic enterprise has grown into a thriving cottage industry.[2]

A third project that has loomed large in epistemology has been elaborating replies to the arguments of those skeptics—real or more often imaginary—who deny that we have knowledge, or certainty, or some other epistemologically valuable commodity, and who often go on to claim that knowledge, certainty, or what have you is impossible to obtain. Answers to the skeptic have been a persistent motif in epistemology from Descartes to G. E. Moore, and right down to the present.[3]

Clearly, these three projects are linked together in a variety of ways. To answer the skeptic, a natural first step might be to develop an analysis of knowledge or certainty so that we can be clear on exactly what it is the skeptic is claiming we don't have or can't get. Moreover, in attempting to say what knowledge is, an epistemological theorist will often find it necessary to give some account of good reasoning or good strategies of inquiry, since whether a given belief will count as an instance of knowledge is often said to depend, in part, on whether the belief was arrived at in an appropriate way.

My own interests are not distributed equally among these three projects. Indeed, for as long as I can remember, I have found the latter two projects to be somewhat dreary corners of philosophy. On the few occasions when I have taught the "analysis of knowledge" literature to undergraduates, it has been painfully clear that most of my students had a hard time taking the project seriously. The better students were clever enough to play fill-in-the-blank with 'S knows that p if and only _____'. They could recognize the force of the increasingly arcane counterexamples that fill the literature, and they occasionally produced new counterexamples of their own. But they could not, for the life of them, see why anybody would want to do this. It was a source of ill-concealed amazement to these students that grown men and women would indulge in this exercise and think it important—and of still greater amazement that others would pay them to do it! This sort of discontent was all the more disquieting because deep down I agreed with my students. Surely something had gone very wrong somewhere when clever philosophers, the heirs to the tradition of Hume and Kant, devoted their time to constructing baroque counterexamples about the weird ways in which a man might fail to own a Ford, or about strange lands that abound in trompe l'oeil barns.[4] But just what had gone wrong I was, at that time, quite unable to say. Though the arguments developed in this book began with concerns far removed from the analysis of knowledge and other epistemic notions, as my position evolved I began to see with increasing clarity what it was that made the project of analyzing epistemic terms seem so wrongheaded. I'll say more on this a bit later in this chapter; my full brief against "analytic epistemology" will be set out in chapter 4.[5]

I have confessed that for about as long as I can remember I have had deep, though largely inarticulate, misgivings about the project of analyzing epistemic notions. I have also long harbored similar concerns about the effort to construct responses to the epistemic skeptic. As I got clearer on what I thought was wrong with the analytic project, I also got clearer about why responding to the skeptic often seems a waste of time. I'll elaborate on this theme, in 1.4.1.1.

Before beginning the work that led to this book, my attitude toward the remaining entry on my list of epistemic projects—the evaluation of strategies of reasoning and inquiry—was much more conventional and benign. The part of the literature I knew seemed far less frivolous than the literature on the analysis of knowledge and far more persuasive than the attempts to reply to the skeptic. Moreover, the issues themselves struck me as important ones with real, practical implications both for the conduct of science and for the governing of one's cognitive affairs in everyday life. But my own philosophical interests had long been centered on the philosophy of language and the philosophy of psychology, and this branch of epistemology seemed quite unrelated to those interests.

1.2 Finding Connections: The Psychology of Reasoning, the Evaluation of Inquiry, and the Analysis of Intentional Content

I began to see that these domains might be more closely related than I had thought when, a bit over a decade ago, my friend and former colleague Richard Nisbett posed an intriguing problem to me. To explain Nisbett's problem, I'll have to back up a bit and fill in some background.

1.2.1 The Empirical Exploration of Reasoning
Nisbett, along with a number of other experimental social psychologists, was exploring the ways in which normal human subjects (well, undergraduates actually) go about the business of reasoning, on quite ordinary problems, in relaxed and unthreatening surroundings. What they found was both fascinating and more than a bit unsettling. On many sorts of problems their subjects, despite being fairly bright, seemed to reason very badly and to do so in more or less predictable ways. Indeed, in some domains the reasoning was so strikingly bad that Nisbett and his colleagues were led to describe the implications of their research as "bleak."[6] In the intervening years, much of this work has become well known, and there are several excellent surveys available.[7] But since the implications of these findings will be a recurrent theme in the pages to follow, I had best set out a few examples for readers who may not be familiar with the literature. Those for whom this is all old hat may wish to scoot ahead to 1.2.2.

1.2.1.1 The Selection Task   One of the most extensively investigated examples of *prima facie* failure in reasoning is the so-called selection task first studied by Wason and Johnson-Laird.[8] In a typical selection task experiment, subjects are presented with four cards like those in figure 1. Half of each card is masked. Subjects are then given the following instructions:

> Your job is to determine which of the hidden parts of these cards you need to see in order to answer the following question deci-

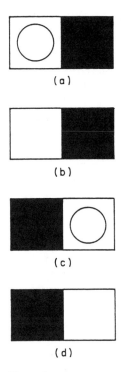

(a)

(b)

(c)

(d)

Figure 1

sively: FOR THESE CARDS IS IT TRUE THAT IF THERE IS A CIRCLE ON THE LEFT THERE IS A CIRCLE ON THE RIGHT?

You have only one opportunity to make this decision; you must not assume that you can inspect the cards one at a time. Name those cards which it is absolutely essential to see.

Wason and Johnson-Laird found that subjects, including very intelligent subjects, typically do very badly on this question. In one group of 128 university students, only *five* got the right answer. Moreover, the mistakes turn out not to be randomly distributed. The two most common wrong answers are that one must see both (a) and (c), and that one need only see (a); subjects find it particularly difficult to understand why (d) must be removed. In the years since Wason and Johnson-Laird's first studies of the selection task, there have been many further studies looking at related tasks that vary from this one in a number of dimensions. Some of those studies have indicated that subjects do a much better job on structurally analogous problems if the subject matter of the problem is more realistic, or more familiar to them, or if it can be fitted into one or another preexisting schema for reasoning. These results have provided a rich data base for theorists trying to understand the cognitive mechanisms underlying this sort of reasoning. Though at present there is no consensus at all about what those mechanisms are.[9]

1.2.1.2 The Conjunction Fallacy   A second example of research revealing apparent deviations from normative standards of inference focuses on the way people assess the probability of logically compound events or states of affairs. It is a truism of probability theory that the likelihood of a compound event or state of affairs must be less than or equal to the likelihood of the component events or states of affairs. If the components are probabilistically independent, the probability of the compound is equal to the product of the probabilities of the components. If the components are not probabilistically independent, matters are more complicated. But in no case will the probability of the compound be *greater* than the probability of any component. There are, however, a number of experiments which demonstrate that people regularly violate this basic tenet of probabilistic reasoning and fall into what has been called "the conjunction fallacy."

In one such experiment Tversky and Kahneman posed a number of questions like the following:[10]

> Linda is 31 years old, single, outspoken and very bright. She majored in philosophy. As a student she was deeply concerned with issues of discrimination and social justice, and also participated in antinuclear demonstrations.
>
> Please rank the following statements by their probability, using 1 for the most probable and 8 for the least probable.
>> (i) Linda is a teacher in an elementary school.
>> (ii) Linda works in a bookstore and takes Yoga classes.
>> (iii) Linda is active in the feminist movement.
>> (iv) Linda is a psychiatric social worker.
>> (v) Linda is a member of the League of Women Voters.
>> (vi) Linda is a bank teller.
>> (vii) Linda is an insurance salesperson.
>> (viii) Linda is a bank teller and is active in the feminist movement.

In this experiment, 89 percent of the subjects ranked (viii) as more likely than (vi). Moreover, the result turns out to be very robust. Concerned that subjects might tacitly suppose that (vi) really meant

Linda is a bank teller and is *not* active in the feminist movement

Tversky and Kahneman replaced (vi) with

(vi') Linda is a bank teller whether or not she is active in the feminist movement

and tried the new material on a second set of subjects. The results were essentially the same. But perhaps subjects were distracted by all the other options and failed to notice the relationship between (vi) and (viii). To test this, 142 subjects were given the original problem with all the alternatives except (vi) and (viii) deleted and asked to indicate which of the two alternatives was more likely. Eighty-five percent said that the conjunction was more likely than the conjunct.

1.2.1.3 Pseudodiagnosticity Suppose we were interested in the effectiveness of a new drug in treating a certain disease, and we have evidence that 79 percent of patients suffering from the disease who have taken the drug recover completely within a month. What should we conclude about the efficacy of the drug? The answer, of course, is that we do not yet have enough information, since we must also know the spontaneous recovery rate—the rate of recovery of people who have not taken the drug. Without such information, there is no saying whether the drug fosters recovery or impedes it. However, there are a number of studies indicating that people often do draw conclusions in cases like this, even when they have no information at all about relevant base rates.[11] Moreover, in one striking study, Doherty, Mynatt, Tweney, and Schiavo showed that subjects are reluctant to seek out diagnostically relevant base rate information, even when it is readily available.[12]

These investigators set subjects the task of determining whether a certain archaeological find had come from Coral Island or from Shell Island. The find was a clay pot, and the subjects were given a list of the pot's characteristics (smooth clay—not rough; curved handles—not straight) and so on for a number of other binary characteristics. The subjects were then given a booklet from which they could get some data about the kinds of pots that had been produced on the two islands. The data were arrayed as follows, with each pair of percentages covered by an opaque sticker as indicated.

On one page of the booklet there were a total of 12 stickers, and in order to get the data they needed, subjects were permitted to peel off any six of them. The most useful or "diagnostic" information would be gleaned only if subjects removed both stickers in a given row, and therefore the optimal strategy would be to select three row-pairs.

	Coral Island	Shell Island
Curved handles	21%	87%
Straight handles	79%	13%
Smooth clay	19%	91%
Rough clay	81%	9%
.	.	.
.	.	.
.	.	.

However, only 11 of 121 subjects removed three pairs; nine removed two pairs, and thirty removed one pair. The remaining 71 subjects (that's 59 percent) removed no pairs at all. Thus, the majority of subjects formed their belief about which island the pot had come from on the basis of "pseudodiagnostic" information. Though it was readily available, they chose not to seek out the information that would be of most use to them.

There might be some temptation to suppose that results like these are artifacts of the rather artificial experimental format. However, as Nisbett and Ross point out, the logic exhibited by these experimental subjects "is suspiciously similar to the logic shown by poorly educated laypeople in discussing a proposition such as: Does God answer prayers? Yes, such a person may say, because many times I've asked God for something and He's given it to me."[13]

1.2.1.4 Belief Perseverance   My final example of a research program that has uncovered apparent irrationality is the work Ross and his colleagues, exploring how people modify their beliefs when the evidence for those beliefs is no longer accepted.[14] One of the experimental strategies used in this work is the so-called debriefing paradigm in which subjects are given evidence that is later completely discredited. But despite being debriefed and told exactly how they had been duped, subjects tend to retain to a substantial degree the beliefs they formed on the basis of the discredited evidence.

In one such experiment, subjects were presented with the task of distinguishing between authentic and inauthentic suicide notes. Some of the notes, they were told, had been found by the police, while others were written by students as an exercise. As the subjects worked on the task, they were provided with false feedback indicating that overall they were performing close to the average level, or (for another group of subjects) much above the average level, or (for a third group of subjects) much below the average level. Following this, each subject was debriefed, and the predetermined nature of the feedback was clearly explained. They were not only told that their feedback had been false but were also shown the experimenter's instruction sheet assigning them to the success, failure, or average group and specifying the details of the feedback that they had been given. Subsequent to this, and allegedly for a quite different reason, subjects were asked to fill out a questionnaire on which they were asked to estimate their actual performance at the suicide note task they had completed, to predict how well they would do on related tasks, and to rate their ability at suicide note discrimination and similar tasks. The striking finding was that, even after debriefing, subjects who had initially been assigned to the success group continued to rate their performance and abilities far more favorably than did subjects in the average group. Subjects initially assigned to the failure group showed the opposite pattern of results. Once again, further experiments suggested that these results reflect a robust phenomenon that manifests itself in many variations on the experimental theme, including some conducted outside the laboratory setting. The phenomenon has been labeled "belief perseverance."

1.2.2 Nisbett's Problems and Goodman's Solution

These were the sorts of experimental findings Nisbett had in mind when he posed a problem to me that went something like this: *When I present these experimental results to various professional audiences and draw the obvious, pessimistic conclusions about the reasoning abilities of the man or woman in the street, people raise various sorts of objections. Some of the objections are about experimental design, "ecological validity" and similar issues. And these I know how to handle. But from time to time someone will challenge my claim that in a particular experiment, subjects who give a certain answer are in fact reasoning badly. These critics demand to know why I get to say which inferences are the good ones and which are the bad ones. They want to know what it is that makes the subject's inference bad and the inference I think they should draw good.* Like Nisbett, I was at the time strongly inclined to say that the subjects, not the experimenters, were the ones who were reasoning badly. But if nothing more than this could be said, the debate between Nisbett and his critics would degenerate into an exchange of raw intuitions about which inferences are good ones. What more could be done, Nisbett asked? How could it be *shown* that the subjects were reasoning badly?

When Nisbett first posed the question to me, I thought I knew the answer. Having been, as an undergraduate, a student of Nelson Goodman's, I had cut my philosophical teeth on what I took to be an elegant, powerful, and entirely persuasive answer to the question of how inferences and rules of inference are to be justified. The way to do it, Goodman had argued, is via a process of mutual adjustment in which judgments about particular inferences and judgments about inferential rules are brought into accord with one another.[15] The justification for rules of inference lies in the accord thus achieved. But as soon as I proposed Goodman's process as a solution to Nisbett's problem, it became clear that this very influential account of inferential justification could not be quite right; there must be a bug somewhere. For, read literally, Goodman's account of what it is for an inference to be justified, when conjoined with a plausible extrapolation of the empirical data about actual inferential practice, seems to entail that some very strange inferences are justified. At the time, the bug did not strike me as a major one. All that was needed, it seemed, was a bit of fine tuning of Goodman's picture of inferential justification. And after a few months of discussion, Nisbett and I thought we knew just how that fine tuning should go. We published our proposal in Stich and Nisbett (1980).

Even before that article was in print, I had come to realize that our fine tuning was going to need some fine tuning. For our story, no less than Goodman's, had some very curious counterintuitive consequences. Further infelicities were noted by Conee and Feldman in their critique of our paper.[16] Still, I was reasonably confident that, with a bit more effort and a bit more thought, I would find a way to patch up Goodman's account so that it would not sanction what seemed to be patently unjustified inferences. Indeed, I even supposed I had an argument of sorts demonstrating that there *must* be a way to repair Goodman's account. (This is the argument I attribute to the "neo-Goodmanian" in 4.4.) It took about four years of trying intermittently and failing consistently before I came to suspect that my lack of success might be symptomatic of something besides my own limited intellectual endowments. But here I'm getting ahead of myself. For while hunting for some variation on Goodman's theme that would avoid counterintuitive consequences, I had a number of other, warmer irons in the fire.

1.2.3 Good Reasoning and Intentional Content: The Davidson/Dennett Argument That Bad Reasoning Is Impossible

As I became better acquainted with the data on human inference collected by psychologists like Tversky, Kahneman, Ross, Nisbett, and others and with the conclusions these authors wanted to draw from those data about the often questionable quality of everyday reasoning, I began to realize that these conclusions sit very uncomfortably with certain aspects of Donald Davidson's much-discussed theories in the philosophy of language and with some kindred ideas in the philosophy of mind developed by Daniel Dennett—ideas that were just then attracting a great deal of attention. Davidson and Dennett, both inspired by Quine, have offered accounts of how we go about interpreting, or assigning "intentional content," to a person's utterances and to the mental states that they presumably express. While differing in a variety of ways, both accounts require a high degree of rationality as a prerequisite for intentional interpretation. People's beliefs must be mostly true, and the inferences they draw must be mainly the right or normatively appropriate ones. If they are not, Davidson and Dennett maintain, it will be impossible to assign any interpretation to their verbal output or ascribe any content to their mental states. But acoustic output that admits of no interpretation is not language at all, and mental states without content can not be beliefs or thoughts. It follows that inference which is seriously and systematically irrational is a conceptual impossibility. For inference is a process in which beliefs are generated or transformed. But without a high level of rationality and truth there can be no belief, and without belief there can be no inference. Thus it is simply incoherent to suggest that people reason in ways that depart seriously and systematically from what is rational or normatively appropriate. If Davidson and Dennett are right, the psychologists who claim to have evidence for extensive irrationality in human inference must be mistaken. No evidence could possibly support such a conclusion, since the conclusion is conceptually incoherent.

This is a type of doctrine for which I have never had much sympathy. Philosophy has a long history of trying to issue a priori ultimatums to science, decreeing what must be the case or what could not possibly be the case. And those a priori decrees have a dismal track record. *Pace* Kant, space is not Euclidean, nor are the laws of physics Newtonian. *Pace* Hegel, there are nine planets, not seven. But underlying my distrust of the a priori arguments against the possibility of systematically defective reasoning, there was more than a general skepticism about philosophy's attempts to constrain science. For at the time I first saw the conflict between the theories advanced by Davidson and Dennett and the thesis about widespread human irrationality defended by various psychologists, I was working out the details of my own account of intentional interpretation or "content ascription."[17]

My account agreed with Davidson and Dennett that there is indeed a link of sorts between rationality and content and thus that significant departures from rationality make the ascription of content difficult or impossible. Moreover, unlike Dennett's story, or Davidson's, my account of content ascription tries to make it clear *why* content and good reasoning are linked; it offers an *explanation* of the connection. But it seemed to me that if my account of content ascription was on the right track, and my explanation of the link between rationality and content was even roughly right, it would undermine the conclusion of the Davidson/Dennett argument. For it follows from my account that the distinction between those mental states to which content can be comfortably ascribed, and those to which it can be ascribed either tenuously or not at all, is a distinction entirely bereft of theoretical interest. It is a parochial, observer-relative, context-sensitive distinction that marks no significant psychological boundary.

If this is right, then the sort of impossibility that the Davidson/Dennett argument might establish is simply not worth worrying about. For at best, what that argument shows is that systematically irrational people cannot engage in "real" inference at all but only in "inferencelike" mental processes. These processes don't count as inference, properly so-called, because they generate and transform mental states that cannot be intentionally described and thus do not count as "real" beliefs. But if, as I maintain, the distinction between "real" beliefs and those "belieflike" mental states that are not intentionally characterizable is a vague and parochial one that marks no significant psychological boundary, then the same is true of the distinction between "real" inference and contentless "inferencelike" processes. And we hardly need worry about the fact that seriously irrational people don't infer at all, if they do something that is like inference except in ways that are of no psychological interest.

Setting out a detailed defense of all of this was my first major project after finishing the book in which my account of content ascription was developed. Most of the work was done at the Center for Advanced Study in the Behavioral Sciences in Stanford. The Center provided me with a year free of teaching and administrative obligations and a study whose floor-to-ceiling window offered a spectacular view of San Francisco Bay. For both, I remain deeply grateful.[18] A first pass at defending my views on rationality, content, and the Davidson/Dennett argument was published in Stich (1984a), though I have since come to think that parts of that article are less than satisfactory. Chapter 2 of this volume is a revised—and I hope improved—version of that material.

1.2.4 The Varieties of Cognitive Pluralism

While working on the original version of that paper, I began to see, if
only dimly, the outlines of what would ultimately become one of the
more radical theses of this book. To explain the thesis, let me introduce
a pair of claims, each of which might plausibly be labeled *cognitive
pluralism*. To set them apart, I'll call one *descriptive cognitive pluralism*
and the other *normative cognitive pluralism*.[19] The descriptive claim is
one that has been much debated by social scientists and, more recently,
by historians of science. What it asserts is that different people go
about the business of cognition—the forming and revising of beliefs
and other cognitive states—in significantly different ways. For example, it has been urged that people in certain "primitive" or preliterate
societies think or reason very differently from the way modern, western, scientifically educated people do.[20] Closer to home, it has been
suggested that different individuals in our own society solve cognitive
problems in markedly different ways—ways that indicate differences
in underlying cognitive processes.[21] These claims are, or at least they
appear to be, empirical claims—the sort of claims that might be supported by various sorts of observations, experiments, and historical
research. The denial of descriptive pluralism about cognition is *descriptive monism*, the thesis that all people exploit much the same cognitive
processes. Clearly, the distinction between descriptive monism and
descriptive pluralism is best viewed not as a hard and fast one but as
a matter of degree. No one would deny that people differ from one
another to some extent in the speed and cleverness of their inferences,
nor would it be denied that in attempting to solve cognitive problems,
different people try different strategies first. But if these are the only
sorts of cognitive differences to be found among people, descriptive
monism will be vindicated. If, on the other hand, it should turn out
that different people or different cultures use radically different "psy-
cho-logics," or that the revising and updating of their cognitive states
is governed by substantially different principles, pluralism will have
a firm foot in the door. The more radical the differences, the further
we will be toward the pluralistic end of the spectrum.

Normative cognitive pluralism is not a claim about the cognitive
processes people do use; rather it is a claim about *good cognitive processes*—the cognitive processes that people *ought to* use. What it asserts
is that there is no unique system of cognitive processes that people
should use, because various systems of cognitive processes that are
very different from each other may all be equally good. The distinction
between normative pluralism and normative monism, like the parallel
distinction between descriptive notions, is best viewed as a matter of

degree, with the monist end of the spectrum urging that all normatively sanctioned systems of cognitive processing are minor variations of one another. The more substantial the differences among normatively sanctioned systems, the further we move in the direction of pluralism.

Historically, it is probably true that much of the support for normative pluralism among social scientists derived from the discovery (or putative discovery) of descriptive pluralism, along with a certain ideologically inspired reluctance to pass negative judgments on the traditions or practices of other cultures. But normative pluralism was certainly not the only response to descriptive pluralism among social scientists. Many reacted to the alleged discovery of odd reasoning patterns among premodern peoples by insisting on monism at the normative level and concluding that the reasoning of premodern folk was "primitive," "prelogical," or otherwise normatively substandard.[22] I don't have a good guess as to whether normative monism or normative pluralism is more widespread among contemporary social scientists. But among philosophers, both historical and contemporary, normative cognitive pluralism is very clearly a minority view. The dominant philosophical view is that there is only one good way to go about the business of reasoning or, at most, a small cluster of similar ways. Good reasoning, philosophers typically maintain, is rational reasoning, and in the view of most philosophers, it is just not the case that there are alternative systems of reasoning differing from one another in important ways, all of which are rational.

When, in response to Nisbett's query, I began thinking seriously about the issue of cognitive or epistemic virtue—about what it is that makes a strategy of inference or reasoning a good one—I unquestioningly fell in with the prevailing prejudice and assumed that normative monism was correct. It was only as I repeatedly tried to give a monistic normative account, and repeatedly failed, that I began to suspect normative pluralism might be the better view. The account of cognitive virtue I have come to defend is floridly pluralistic. Moreover, it is relativistic as well, since it entails that different systems of reasoning may be normatively appropriate for different people. For a long time I was rather embarrassed to hold such a view, since it aligns me with a small minority among philosophers and an even smaller minority among philosophers whose work I most respect. By and large, I'm afraid, the writings of my fellow relativists are more than a bit obscure and scruffy. But I am convinced that it is possible to be a cognitive relativist without being muddleheaded, which is a good thing, since that is where the arguments lead.[23]

I said earlier that I first began to worry about cognitive pluralism while at work on my response to the Davidson/Dennett argument for the impossibility of irrationality. Let me take a moment to note how those issues are interwoven.[24] Suppose that normative cognitive monism is right—that in matters cognitive, the good is one rather than many. Then, if the Davidson/Dennett line is defensible, and serious departures from good reasoning are indeed conceptually impossible, it follows that *descriptive* cognitive monism is true as well. For if all genuine cognitive systems must be largely rational, and all rational systems are minor variations on a common theme, then all actual cognitive systems must be very similar to one another. This is, on the face of it, a quite astounding result since both descriptive monism and its denial, descriptive pluralism, *appear* to be empirical theses. But the argument just sketched for descriptive monism and against descriptive pluralism is not an empirical argument at all. One of its premises (the Davidson/Dennett thesis) purports to be a conceptual claim, while the other is a normative claim. So if the argument works, I suppose we would have to conclude that, contrary to appearances, descriptive monism and pluralism are not genuine empirical theses. This is, near enough, the view urged by Davidson in his argument against "the very idea of [alternative] conceptual schemes," and his argument, though characteristically illusive, seems to have some points in common with the one I have sketched.[25] However, the argument I've sketched is not one with which I have sympathy, and I shall argue that both of its premises are mistaken. The argument against the Davidson/Dennett thesis developed in chapter 2, and while there is a sense in which the entire book mounts an argument against normative monism, the issue is center stage in chapter 6.

The initial motive for my concern about the Davidson/Dennett thesis that rationality is a prerequisite for cognition was that it threatened to undermine the empirical explorations of irrationality that were producing, and have continued to produce, surprising and unsettling insight into human cognition. A second concern, one that became increasingly important as work on this volume proceeded, was that if the thesis were true, then much of the urgency would be drained from the project of assessing strategies of reasoning and inquiry. The interest and vitality of this branch of epistemological research can be traced, in significant measure, to the practical worries it addresses: People out there are reasoning badly, and this bad reasoning is giving rise to bad theories, many of which have nasty consequences for people's lives. But if Davidson and Dennett are right, then these concerns are overblown. Cognition *can't* be all that bad. Perhaps the reasoning of the man and woman in the street (or the jury box, or the legislature) is not quite normatively impeccable, but we need not worry about them departing in major ways from the normative ideal. This Panglossian doctrine reduces the normative evaluation of inquiry to a rather bloodless, scholastic preoccupation. We can still, if we wish, try to say what it is that makes good reasoning good. But the project can hardly be infused with the reformer's zeal, since we know in advance that there is nothing much to reform.

1.2.5 The Evolutionary Argument that Bad Reasoning Is Impossible
The conceptual argument suggested by Davidson and Dennett is not the only route to Panglossian optimism about human cognition. There is another argument for much the same conclusion hinted at by Dennett and by many other authors as well. It maintains that *biological evolutior.* guarantees that all normal cognitive systems will be rational, or nearly so, since organisms whose cognitive systems depart too drastically from the normative standard will run a very high risk of becoming posthumous before they have had a chance to pass on their genes to offspring. In saying that the evolutionary argument is "hinted at" by many authors, I chose my words quite deliberately, since I have been able to find nothing in the literature that amounts to anything even close to a full-dress argument. So to explore the plausibility of the view, I set about trying to build an argument myself. A first attempt was included, and criticized, in Stich (1985), and subsequent versions were tried out in front of a number of audiences from Adelaide to Helsinki. From their many helpful suggestions I have cobbled together, in chapter 3, what I believe to be the most detailed and plausible version of the evolutionary argument yet offered.[26]

That argument divides into two parts, one of which maintains that evolution produces organisms with good approximations to optimally well-designed systems, while the other maintains that an optimally well-designed cognitive system is a rational one. But, as I try to establish in chapter 3, the second part is very dubious. The first part is worse. It simply can't get off the ground without the help of a cluster of serious though widespread misunderstandings about evolution and natural selection. Though I had long realized that there is something very wrong with that part of the argument, its problems came into sharp focus only after I joined the philosophy department of the University of California at San Diego in 1986. At UCSD, I had the singular good fortune to have Philip Kitcher as a colleague and mentor on these matters. My critique of the evolutionary argument, set out in detail in chapter 3, borrows frequently from Kitcher's work and has benefited enormously from his good advice.

1.2.6 Competence, Performance, and Reflective Equilibrium: Cohen's Argument That Bad Reasoning Is Impossible

The Davidson/Dennett argument and the evolutionary argument conclude that widespread departures from normative standards of reasoning are impossible or unlikely. Thus, they challenge the conviction, widely held by psychologists who study reasoning, that the cognitive processes of ordinary men and women could be significantly improved. But the empirical literature on reasoning was not center stage in the research agendas of Davidson, Dennett, or others who urged versions of these arguments. So the conflict between those arguments and the usual interpretation of the empirical results went largely unnoticed.[27] But to L. J. Cohen, those results were both salient and paradoxical. Many of the undergraduates who serve as subjects for the experiments, Cohen noted, will go on to become leading scientists, jurists, and civil servants. How could they be so successful, Cohen asked, if they do not know how to reason well?

The answer that Cohen urged was that the subjects *do* know how to reason well.[28] Indeed, he argued, the suggestion that they don't is demonstrably incoherent. Central to Cohen's argument is the distinction between *competence* and *performance* that has loomed large in recent linguistics. In the linguistic domain, a person's competence is typically identified with his tacit knowledge of the grammatical rules of his language. In the domain of reasoning, Cohen urged, a person's competence can be identified with his tacit knowledge of his "psychologic"—the rules he exploits as he goes about the business of reasoning. The crucial, and enormously clever, step in Cohen's argument is his demonstration that if we adopt something like Goodman's account of what it is for an inferential rule to be justified, it follows that the rules constituting a person's reasoning competence will inevitably be justified. Thus in the domain of inference, people's competence must be normatively impeccable. In 4.2, I'll set out a detailed sketch of Cohen's argument. At the time I first heard Cohen's argument, Nisbett and I had already become convinced that the version of Goodman's normative account needed for Cohen's argument to work would have to be rejected. Thus yet another argument for the inevitability of rationality came to grief.

1.3 The Search for a Theory of Cognitive Evaluation: Clearing the Ground

From time to time I have jokingly described my efforts in chapters 2 and 3, and in my critique of Cohen, as an attempt to make the world safe for irrationality. The point is not, of course, that irrationality is a good thing or that bad reasoning is to be encouraged. But if bad cognitive processing were either conceptually or biologically impossible, it would make nonsense of the empirical exploration of reasoning and its foibles. It would also turn the effort to articulate and defend a normative theory of cognition into an arcane academic exercise of no particular practical importance. This second consequence of the irrationality-is-impossible thesis came to seem doubly unwelcome to me since, while working on chapters 2 and 3, I was also investing considerable time and effort trying to rework Goodman's proposal into a defensible criterion for distinguishing good inferential strategies from bad ones.

1.3.1 Goodman's Project Might Turn Out to Be Impossible

This work was not going at all well, however. As time passed, I accumulated a substantial collection of variations on Goodman's idea and an even more substantial collection of arguments showing that none of them worked. Some of those variations, and the arguments against them, are assembled in chapter 4.

At about the time I was getting thoroughly discouraged with my neo-Goodmanian quest, two lines of argument began to take shape in my mind. The first of these suggested that the Goodmanian project might very well turn out to be impossible. Initially at least, that struck me as a most unwelcome conclusion, since I had long thought that Goodman's approach to building a normative theory of cognition was by far the most promising one available. The conclusion followed from a cluster of considerations all of which shared a common theme: The Goodmanian approach tacitly presupposes a number of empirical theses, and each of these stands in some serious risk of turning out to be false. To see these empirical presuppositions, it helps to back up a bit and get a broader view of what Goodman was up to.

Goodman had sketched a procedure or test, that a system of inferential rules should pass if it is to count as rational or justified. Others, including Nisbett and I, had argued that Goodman's test was inadequate and had proposed a variety of modifications. But what counts as getting the story right here? What is the relation between rationality and the right test supposed to be, and why is the fact that a system of inference passes some test or other supposed to show that the system is rational? I think the most plausible answer for a Goodmanian to give is that the right test, when we discover it, will be an *analysis* or *explication* of our ordinary concept of rationality (or some other commonsense concept of epistemic evaluation).[29] The test—which will be a tidied up version of the procedures we actually follow in evaluating the merits of an inferential system—provides necessary and sufficient conditions for rationality because it unpacks our concept of rationality; it tells us what that concept comes to.

Now for this sort of answer to be defensible, it must be the case that our commonsense concept of rationality is univocal and more or less coherent and that it is structured so as to admit of an analysis or explication in terms of necessary and sufficient conditions. It must also be the case that the procedures we use for deciding whether a system is rational exhausts the content of the concept. None of this can safely be supposed a priori. The conclusion to be drawn from these considerations is not that our commonsense concepts of epistemic evaluation *do not* admit of the sort of explication that Goodman's project seeks—the evidence needed to settle that is far from in—but merely that they *may* not. The feasibility of the Goodmanian project is very much hostage to the psychological facts. Moreover, as argued in chapter 4, what little we know about the mental representation of concepts gives scant reason for optimism.

1.3.2 The Irrelevance of Analytic Epistemology

These ominous thoughts had taken shape during the year I spent at the Center for Advanced Study in the Behavioral Sciences. At the end of that year I took my forebodings with me to Australia, where I was to spend a year as visiting professor at the University of Sydney. There, perhaps influenced by the refreshing Australian iconoclasm of my colleagues and students in the Department of Traditional and Modern Philosophy, a second line of argument began to come into focus, one that was both more radical and more liberating. This second line began as yet another critique of the Goodmanian project. But it soon became evident that its real target was much larger. If the argument is right, it undermines the entire analytic epistemology tradition, a tradition that has been dominant in the English-speaking world for the last quarter century or more. It is a hallmark of that tradition to seek criteria of cognitive evaluation in the analysis or explication of our ordinary concepts of epistemic evaluation. However, one of the conclusions that drops out of this second line of argument is that, for almost anyone who takes the project of evaluating cognitive processes seriously, analytic epistemology is going to be a hopeless nonstarter. If the analytic strategy were the only one around, this conclusion would be as disheartening as it is radical. However, the argument that undermines analytic epistemology also highlights the virtues of a very different strategy for cognitive evaluation.

The starting point for the argument against analytic epistemology is the observation that if descriptive cognitive pluralism is true—if different people go about the business of reasoning in significantly different ways, some of which may be substantially better than others—then much of this divergence is likely to be traceable to cultural differences, though genetic factors and idiosyncratic differences in individual experience may also play a role. In attempting to evaluate these divergent strategies and in deciding which of them we ought ourselves to use, we are trying to decide among a variety of cultural products. The analytic epistemologist proposes to evaluate these differing cognitive processes by explicating our intuitive notions of cognitive evaluation, and then exploring which inferential processes fall most comfortably within the extention of those notions. But these intuitive notions of cognitive evaluation are themselves local cultural products, and there is no reason to think that they won't exhibit just as much intercultural and interpersonal variation as the cognitive processes that they evaluate. In light of this, it is hard to see why most people would *care* very much whether a system of cognitive processes falls within the extension of some ordinary notion of epistemic evaluation—why, for example, they would care whether their reasoning falls within the boundaries of the intuitive notion of rationality—unless of course there is some reason to think that falling within the extension of one of these concepts correlates with something else we do care about.

To be sure, there may be some exceptions here. It is not unthinkable for a person to find intrinsic value in having cognitive processes sanctioned by our culturally inherited concepts of epistemic evaluation, just as a person might find intrinsic value in adhering to the traditional social practices of his ethnic group. In each case the person recognizes that the concepts or practices in question are just one set among many that people might or do exploit. Yet he values his own, and does so for no further reason. He values them for their own sake. At one time I thought it was clear that this was the position embraced by David Stove, the most outspoken of my Sydney colleagues and a man whom I came to regard as one of the most acute, and most conservative, cultural critics of our time. However, Stove has protested that this is a hopeless caricature of his view. The reader may wish to read Stove (1986) and judge for him- or herself.

Some writers have been tempted by the Wittgensteinian idea that epistemic assessments must come to an end with the criteria embedded in our ordinary concepts of cognitive evaluation. But surely this is nonsense. Both our notions of epistemic evaluation and (more important) our cognitive processes themselves can be evaluated *instrumentally*. That is, they can be evaluated by how well they do at bringing about states of affairs that people do typically value—states of affairs like being able to predict or control nature, or contributing to an interesting and fulfilling life. The idea of viewing cognitive processes as mental tools, to be evaluated as we might evaluate other sorts of tools, has its roots in the pragmatist tradition, and it came to play a quite central role in my thinking, once I had finally persuaded myself that the Goodmanian strategy, and the analytic tradition in which it was embedded, were of no use to the project of evaluating cognitive strategies.

1.3.3 An Attack on Truth

In rejecting the appeals to our ordinary notions of epistemic evaluation—appeals to rationality, justification, and the rest—as final arbiters in our efforts to choose among competing strategies of inquiry, I was, in effect, denying that rationality or justification have any intrinsic or ultimate value. At that juncture, a natural question to ask was whether there was any other paradigmatically epistemic feature of our cognitive lives that might be taken to be intrinsically valuable. And when the question was posed in this way, there was an obvious candidate: *truth*. However, from my earliest work in the philosophy of language, I had harbored a certain skepticism about the utility, indeed even the intelligibility, of the notion of truth.[30] And in the process of polishing the argument against analytic epistemology, I came to suspect that there was a largely parallel argument to be mounted against truth.[31] Thus I came to think that neither being rational nor generating truth would turn out to be an intrinsically valuable feature for cognitive processes to have. If the argument about the value of truth could be sustained, the natural upshot for the normative theory of cognition would be a thoroughgoing pragmatism which holds that all cognitive value is instrumental or pragmatic—that there are no intrinsic, uniquely cognitive values. And this, indeed, is the position I finally came to defend. But once again I have let my story get ahead of itself. So let me go back and retrace the steps that led me to reject truth as a cognitive virtue.

The path that led me to the surprising conclusion that truth is not to be taken seriously as a cognitive virtue begins with the observation that Goodmanian analyses of notions of cognitive evaluation are only one approach in the analytic epistemology tradition. Another well-explored idea is that the rationality or justifiedness of a set of cognitive processes can be explicated by appeal to the success or failure of the processes in producing true beliefs. There are lots of variations on this "reliabilist" theme, but all of them offer analyses on which the normative status of a cognitive process is at least in part a function of how well it does in producing true beliefs.[32] An advocate of reliabilism might be tempted to think that this sort of analysis blunts the conclusion of the argument against analytic epistemology. To be sure, the reliabilist might concede, the mere fact that a cognitive process is sanctioned by some socially transmitted notion of epistemic evaluation or other is no reason to favor that process. But if the evaluative notion can be explicated along reliabilist lines, the situation is very different. For then processes that fall within the extension of the notion do a good job of producing true beliefs. And for most people, having true beliefs *is* intrinsically valuable.

Now it surely is the case that many people, if asked, would profess to value having true beliefs. But most of these same people would be hard pressed to say anything coherent about what it is for a belief to be true and thus would be quite unable to explain what it is that they value. This is not to suggest that there is nothing to be said on that score, however. Quite the opposite. In recent years philosophers, particularly those concerned with issues in the philosophy of mind and the philosophy of language, have lavished considerable attention on theories of mental representation (or "psycho-semantics") whose central concern is to explain how psychological states like beliefs could come to have semantic properties—properties like being true or being false, being about (or referring to) a particular person, and so forth. The strategy I pursued in exploring whether we might undermine the conviction of those who think they take true belief to be intrinsically valuable was to extract, from some of the more plausible and well–worked out of these theories of mental representation, an account of just what it is, on those theories, for a belief to be true. With such an account in hand, we can have people ponder the following question: If *that* is indeed what it is for a belief to be true, do you really care whether your beliefs are true? Do people really value having true beliefs once they are offered a clear view of what having a true belief comes to? The result of this exercise, at least in my own case (and I don't think my values are idiosyncratic here), was a consistently negative answer. Moreover, the negative judgment was most firm in just those cases where the account of true belief was clearest and most explicit. The argument on this point is developed in chapter 5, and while it is not an argument that admits of a comfortable summary, the following brief remarks may help a bit in anticipating what is to come.

Let's start with beliefs. What sorts of things are they? On one widely held view, the so-called token identity theory, belief tokens (like my current belief that Princeton is south of New Brunswick) are brain states—no doubt fairly complex ones. If we accept this view, the next question to ask is how a brain state could possibly have semantic properties: how could a complex neural event have a truth value? A variety of plausible answers begin with the idea that there is a function

(I'll call it the "interpretation function") that maps belief-brain-states to a class of entities that are more comfortably semantically evaluable—entities like propositions, or truth conditions, or situations, or possible states of affairs. According to theories of this sort, a belief is true if and only if the proposition to which it is mapped is true (or if and only if the possible state of affairs obtains, etc.). But of course mappings or functions are easy to come by. If there is one function from belief-brain-states to propositions, then there are indefinitely many. Obviously, not just any mapping will do. Which function is the right one?

This last question may be read in two different ways. On one reading it is a request for a detailed story about the right interpretation function, a story that specifies which belief-brain-states the theorist would map to which propositions. In the literature on mental representation, there is much careful discussion, and no shortage of debate, about how the interpretation function is to be constructed. On another reading, the question is not a request for details but rather a request for a criterion of what it is to get those details right. Suppose a pair of theorists offer competing detailed stories about the function from brains states to propositions. How would we go about deciding which one is the right one? On this issue there is relatively little discussion in the literature. However, as I argue in chapter 5, it is clear from the sorts of arguments that theorists use in defense of their proposed interpretation functions that one strong constraint on getting the mapping right is that it must generally capture our intuitive judgments about the content or truth conditions of the mental states in its domain. Absent special circumstances, a function that assigns counterintuitive truth conditions is the wrong function.

But now what is so special about those intuitions? Why do they get to have such a significant say in deciding which interpretation function is the right one? Presumably the intuitions theorists exploit are a socially acquired set of judgments that may well vary from one individual or culture to another. Just as it is hard to see why the intuitive, socially shaped notions of epistemic evaluation that prevail in a culture should command such commitment, so too it is hard to see why anyone would take our intuitively sanctioned interpretation function to be special or important, unless of course there is some reason to believe it correlates with something else that is more generally valued. But recall that, on the accounts of mental representation in question, a belief is true if and only if it is mapped to a true proposition *by the intuitively sanctioned mapping function*. If it is granted that there is nothing uniquely special or important about that intuitive function—that it is simply one mapping among many—it would seem to follow that there is nothing special or important about having true beliefs. One could still find true beliefs to be intrinsically valuable, of course. But in light of these considerations, it seems a curious, culturally local value, on a par with finding intrinsic value in the cultural practices of one's ethnic group. Alternatively, one could give up on the intrinsic value of true beliefs and urge, instead, that true beliefs and the cognitive systems that tend to produce them are instrumentally valuable because they foster our pursuit of other goals. This last idea is considered at some length in chapter 5. Though I have no knockdown argument against it, I try to show that making a case even for the instrumental value of true beliefs is, to put it mildly, no easy matter.

1.4 Epistemic Pragmatism

On more than one occasion, when recounting my none too sanguine views about the notions of rationality and truth, I have been accused of intellectual vandalism—defacing established structures and offering nothing positive to replace them. And I must admit that from time to time, particularly when the shortcomings of various traditional doctrines were coming clearly into focus while the outlines of a defensible alternative were still very hazy, I began to wonder whether the charge might not be justified. But as work progressed, I became increasingly convinced that a pragmatic account of cognitive evaluation could avoid the difficulties that scuttle analytic and truth-linked accounts.

Central to a pragmatic account is the very Jamesian contention that *there are no intrinsic epistemic virtues*.[33] Rather, for the pragmatist, cognitive mechanisms or processes are to be viewed as tools or policies and evaluated in much the same way that we evaluate other tools or policies. One system of cognitive mechanisms is preferable to another if, in using it, we are more likely to achieve those things that we intrinsically value. At the beginning of chapter 6, I try to show why this sort of pragmatic account of cognitive evaluation is suggested by the shortcomings of other accounts. I then go on to explore some of the problems to be expected when we unpack the notion of one cognitive system being more likely than another to enable us to achieve those things that we intrinsically value.

1.4.1 Objections to Pragmatism
Though the attractions of a pragmatic account of cognitive evaluation were fairly easy to see, it took me a long time to take pragmatism seriously. For along with the virtues of the view, there were a pair of obvious objections, each of which initially seemed quite overwhelming. The first objection is that pragmatism leads to relativism. And

relativism, I had long thought, is to be avoided at all costs in matters epistemic. The second objection is that pragmatism is viciously circular, since there is no way we could show that our cognitive system is pragmatically preferable without using the very system whose superiority we are trying to establish. The more I thought about these objections, however, the less objectionable they came to appear.

1.4.1.1 Relativism   It can hardly be denied that a pragmatic account of cognitive evaluation is relativistic, since the pragmatic assessment of a cognitive system will be sensitive to both the values and the circumstances of the people using it. Thus it may well turn out that one cognitive system is pragmatically better than a second *for me*, while the second is pragmatically better than the first *for someone else*. But while it is obvious that pragmatism is relativistic, I gradually came to realize that it is not at all obvious why this is a bad thing. Indeed, despite the widespread prejudice against relativism, I found it surprisingly hard to find any plausible, published arguments aimed at showing why epistemic relativism would be unwelcome. Since serious arguments were in such short supply in the literature, I set about quizzing philosophical friends about the grounds of their antipathy toward the view.

The charge that I heard most often was that relativistic accounts of cognitive assessment play into the hands of epistemic nihilists because they abandon any serious attempt to separate good cognitive strategies from bad ones. For both the relativist and the nihilist, it was said, "anything goes." But this, as I argue in 6.2.2.1, is just a mistake as far as epistemic pragmatism is concerned. The pragmatic assessment of cognitive strategies is certainly relativistic, but it is no more nihilistic than the pragmatic assessment of investment strategies or engineering techniques.

A second accusation was that relativism, or indeed any version of normative pluralism, leads to skepticism by driving a wedge between good reasoning, on the one hand, and truth, on the other. If significantly different systems of reasoning may be preferable for different people, and if these systems generate significantly different beliefs on the basis of similar sensory input, then presumably different people may end up with different beliefs even though they have much the same evidence and are all invoking normatively sanctioned systems of reasoning. Under those circumstances, however, it is hard to see how we could ever defend the view that good reasoning is likely to lead to truth. And, of course, one of the classic worries of the skeptic is that no matter how good our reasoning may be, it will not lead us to the truth.

When I first began thinking about how an epistemic pragmatist might respond to this challenge, my goal was to find some weakness in the argument; and as we'll see in 6.2.2.2, they are not all that hard to find. After finding them, however, it occurred to me that I had a more powerful, and more radical, reply available, one which was not hostage to the success or failure of various possible strategies for shoring up the weaknesses in the argument. For even if we grant that a relativistic account of cognitive evaluation will make it impossible to show that good reasoning generally leads to truth, this should be no cause for concern unless we have some reason to *want* our cognitive systems to produce true beliefs. And the burden of my argument in chapter 5 is that most of us have no such reason. Epistemic skepticism generally simply assumes the importance or desirability of the commodity it claims to be beyond our reach—be it certainty, or truth, or justification. And for the most part those who have done battle with the skeptic have shared this assumption. But on my view, the best first response to the skeptic who maintains that we cannot achieve certainty, truth, knowledge, or what have you, is not to argue that we can. Rather, it is to ask, so what? There is no point in worrying about whether our cognitive system can generate beliefs with a given property unless we think such beliefs would be of some value. So before investing any effort in the skeptic's argument, we should demand some explanation of why it matters whether our beliefs are true. And if the arguments in chapter 5 are on the right track, that explanation is not going to be easy.

1.4.1.2 Circularity   While working on relativism, I realized that truth-linked accounts of cognitive evaluation are also typically relativistic, though the critics of truth-linked accounts rarely make much of it.[34] By contrast, critics are forever protesting that truth-linked accounts are unacceptable because they are circular. And this, it turned out, was a great convenience for my project, since both the accusations and the responses are much the same when the targets of the circularity complaint are pragmatic accounts rather than truth-linked accounts. Even more convenient was the fact that Goldman's admirable, systematic defense of truth-linked theories had recently appeared (1986), and in that volume he set out some of those responses in a singularly clear and persuasive way. Thus, when it came time for me to defend pragmatic accounts against the charge of circularity, in 6.3, I simply adapted Goldman's arguments and added a few bells and whistles of my own.

1.4.2 *The Empirical Study of Human Reasoning: Pragmatism Applied*

The line of thought that ultimately led me to advocate epistemic pragmatism had begun, almost a decade earlier, with Nisbett's worry about replying to critics who insisted that in many experiments which allegedly demonstrated that people reason poorly, the subjects were in fact reasoning quite well. Having convinced myself of the merits of a pragmatic account of cognitive evaluation, the obvious next step was to apply that account to the disputed cases. But when I set out to do so, I was in for a pair of surprises. The first surprise was that the pragmatic story, as I had developed it to that point, did not really address the question of whether the subjects were reasoning well or badly. For, as I tell the story, the pragmatic account is a *comparative* account—it tells us whether one system is better than another (for a given person, at a given time). It does not tell us whether any given system is a good one (for a person, at a time) full stop. To address this question, it's tempting to say that a system is a good one if it is pragmatically at least as good as any possible alternative. But this leaves us with the problem of saying just how we are to understand the notion of a "possible alternative," and that, it turns out, is far from trivial. For, as Christopher Cherniak has argued, if we follow a venerable tradition in epistemology and take "possible" to mean "logically possible," then many of the "possible alternative strategies" are going to be *vastly* beyond anything that brains like ours could use. And it seems simply perverse to judge that subjects are doing a bad job of reasoning because they are not using a strategy that requires a brain the size of a blimp. It seems, then, that in deciding whether a person is doing a good job of reasoning, we should compare his cognitive system not to all logically possible alternatives but only to the *feasible* alternatives. But which ones are these?

One way to approach this question would be to adopt the standard strategy of analytic philosophy: We try to set down necessary and sufficient conditions for feasibility, and then test these conditions against our intuitions about a host of particular cases. But that strategy looked singularly unappealing. For, as I argue in 6.4, what we take to be feasible is going to depend on the purposes at hand and on the technologies available. Thus there is no clear sense to questions about the goodness or badness of a given inferential strategy when asked abstractly. Before trying to answer such questions, we have to get clear on what William James would call the "cash value" of the question; we have to ask what sorts of actions would be suggested by one answer or another.

While there are many projects that might involve an evaluation of people's cognitive processes, one that has played a central role in epistemology from Descartes to Popper and Goldman is the project of *improving* people's cognitive performance. If that is our goal in assessing existing cognitive systems, then the relevant class of feasible alternatives are those that we could actually get people to use. Which those are is not something we can discover without some serious empirical exploration. Though from the work of Cherniak, Harman, and others, we can be pretty certain that some very demanding cognitive strategies, like those that require the elimination of all inconsistencies or those that require us to keep track of the evidence for all of our beliefs, are well beyond the reach of brains like ours. The result of all this—and this was my second surprise—is that it is not at all clear that Nisbett's critics were wrong, since it is far from obvious that the subjects were reasoning badly. To show that they were, we would have to show that there is a pragmatically superior alternative and that people can actually be taught to use it. But surprisingly little is known about the effectiveness of various techniques aimed at altering people's cognitive processes. Until we know more, we often won't be able to say whether Nisbett's subjects, and those who reason like them, are reasoning well or badly.

It is a consequence of the sort of epistemic pragmatism I advocate that a pair of venerable epistemological concerns—the assessment of people's cognitive performance and the improvement of people's cognitive performance—become inextricably interwoven with empirical explorations of psychological feasibility. Those explorations are in turn dependent on the advancing state of the art in the various technologies which help to determine what is feasible. There is a long tradition in epistemology which would reject out of hand any proposal that makes epistemological questions dependent on empirical findings or technological developments. But that is a tradition which I, in the company of a growing number of philosophers, take to be sterile and moribund. Another, younger tradition in epistemology, tracing to James and Dewey, finds nothing untoward in the suggestion that epistemology is inseparable from science and technology. From the perspective of that tradition, the doctrines defended in the pages to follow hardly look radical at all.

Chapter 2

Good Reasoning and Intentional Content: How Irrational Can We Be?

In this chapter my concern will be to explore, and ultimately to dismiss, a cluster of influential arguments aimed at showing that there are *conceptual constraints* on how badly a person can reason. These arguments maintain that it is simply incoherent to suppose a person's cognitive processing could deviate without limit from the standards of rationality. If the arguments are convincing, there will be limits to the "bleak implications" that might emerge from the empirical exploration of human reasoning. Moreover, if the conceptual constraints are tight and possible deviations from rationality are small, then there is little pressing work for the reform-minded epistemologist to do. If it is impossible for people to deviate very far from ideal standards of good reasoning, then there is not much we can do to improve the way we go about the business of cognition.

In arguing that there are conceptual constraints on how irrational a person can be, it might be thought that a natural first step would be to specify in some detail just what the standards of rationality are. However, in the literature in this area detailed accounts of rationality are conspicuously lacking. What we get instead are assertions that one or another pattern of cognitive processing is clearly rational (or clearly irrational), buttressed by appeals to our intuitions. In subsequent chapters, we will find abundant reason to be suspicious of such appeals to intuition. But for the present, I propose to let them go unchallenged. The deeper defects in these "conceptual" arguments for limited irrationality lie elsewhere.

Though the doctrines I will disparage differ in detail, they all have as their common ancestor a brief but enormously influential passage in Quine's *Word and Object*. Section 2.1 will be devoted to an analysis and interpretation of this Quinean ur-text. Though it takes some doing, I think it is possible to tease from Quine's text a plausible argument for the claim that there are conceptual constraints on how badly a person can reason. The central step in the argument is to show that there is a conceptual connection between being rational, on the one hand, and having "contentful" or intentionally describable cognitive states, on the other. If this is right, then a person who is insufficiently rational will have no intentionally describable cognitive states. But beliefs, it is urged, are of necessity intentionally describable, and reasoning is a process in which beliefs are formed and modified. It follows that without the requisite degree of rationality, a person could not reason at all. And, of course, a person who cannot reason at all cannot reason badly. The argument I will reconstruct in 2.1 is, like Quine, notably noncommittal on the question of *how much* rationality is required for intentional description. Or, to put the question in a slightly different way, just how far can a person get from perfect rationality before he no longer counts as having any beliefs at all? In 2.3, I will take up this topic and defend a minimal rationality requirement against a pair of more stringent alternatives. If there is indeed an interdependency between belief and rationality, one would like to know just why it obtains. In 2.4, I'll review and reject a pair of explanations and offer one of my own. Finally, in 2.5, we will get back to the central question of how irrational it is possible to be. My theme there will be that Quine's followers have won the battle and lost the war.

2.1 Quine's Argument and Beyond

In *Word and Object*, Quine spends some pages pondering how we would go about translating the logical locutions of an exotic tongue.[1] His reflections on this theme lead him to take a dim view of what he calls the "doctrine of 'prelogical mentality'":

> To take the extreme case, let us suppose that certain natives are said to accept as true certain sentences translatable in the form 'p and not p'. Now this claim is absurd under our criteria [for translating logical connectives]. And, not to be dogmatic about them, what criteria might one prefer? Wanton translation can make natives sound as queer as one pleases. Better translation imposes our logic upon them, and would beg the question of prelogicality if there were a question to beg. . . . (58)

> The maxim of translation underlying all of this is that assertions startingly false on the face of them are likely to turn on hidden differences in language. . . .

> The common sense behind the maxim is that one's interlocutor's silliness, beyond a certain point, is less likely than bad translation—or, in the domestic case, linguistic divergence. (59)

In this passage, Quine's quaint behaviorist scruples make him reluctant to invoke the ordinary, folk psychological vocabulary of belief and inference. His squeamishness on this score is twice unfortunate. First, it makes it hard to see what this argument has to do with belief or reasoning. Second, it makes the argument exasperatingly difficult to interpret and thus obscures what I think is a quite fundamental insight about the link between intentional ascription and rationality. To bring out this insight, let me raise some puzzles about how Quine's text should be read and say how I think they are best resolved. My goal, I should stress, is to draw from Quine's words an argument that is both plausible and reasonably clear. Whether or not the argument I end up with is faithful to Quine's intentions is a question I happily leave to others.

To begin, consider the "commonsense" precept which Quine tells us lies behind his maxim of translation: "One's interlocutor's silliness, beyond a certain point, is less likely than bad translation—or linguistic divergence." Just what kind of silliness does Quine have in mind? His behaviorist predilection for talking about verbal behavior might incline one to think that it is the silliness of what one's interlocutor says. If what you say is too silly, then I should suspect bad translation. But this, surely, is an unhappy interpretation. Common sense sanctions no precept about the silliness of what a person may *say* but only about the silliness of what he may *believe*. In my own household, where a taste for verbal play prevails, it is a rare day that does not see the utterance of at least a dozen patent absurdities before breakfast. But none of this verbal play inclines any of the participants to suspect hidden linguistic divergence, since it is clear that those uttering absurdities do not believe what they say. They are just joking. In addition to humor and word play, there are many other situations—from sarcasm to testing microphones—in which the utterance of patently false or outrageously silly sentences engenders no suspicion of linguistic divergence. It is only if we have good reason to think that a speaker believes what he says that we begin to worry when what he says is absurd. And this is because it is silly *belief*, "beyond a certain point," that common sense takes to be unlikely.

There is a closely related problem in interpreting what Quine might have in mind when he talks about assertions and accepting sentences as true. Once again, Quine's behaviorist sympathies might lead one to think that asserting and accepting as true are bits of behavior of the sort that a behaviorist might straightforwardly detect and record. But if we read Quine in this way, what he says is clearly false. The mere fact that I assert some sentences that are "startlingly false on the face of them," or that I nod in vigorous assent, is no reason to think that there is some hidden difference in language lurking, for I might just be joking. To set us off looking for some hitherto unsuspected difference in language, it takes more than the assertion or acceptance of something which is patently absurd, where assertion and acceptance are construed as behaviorally manifest. What it takes is what I shall call *sincere assertion* or *sincere assent*, by which I mean the kind of assertion or assent that accurately reflects the speaker's beliefs. Or we might characterize sincere assertion and assent the other way around: S's sincere assertion or acceptance of a sentence, 'q', along with the fact that the translation of 'q' into our language is 'p', entails that S believes that p. *Mere* assertion or assent, in contrast with the sincere variety, sanctions no such inference. None of this is offered by way of criticism of Quine; my current project is sympathetic interpretation. The point I am urging is that for Quine's "maxim of translation" to be at all plausible, we must understand him as talking about sincere assertions, and sincere assertion is not the sort of notion that admits of any straightforward definition in terms of behavior.

It is clear how Quine's commonsense precept about silliness, read in the way I am proposing, supports his maxim of translation. For suppose that our interlocutor, S, sincerely asserts a sentence, 'q'. From this we can infer S believes that p, where 'p' is replaced by the sentence which we take to be the (possibly homophonic) translation of 'q' into our language. Now let us further suppose that 'p' is so patently false that believing that p would be absurdly silly. Quine's precept against silly belief tells us that silliness of this magnitude is very unlikely. But if it is so very unlikely that S believes that p, we have no option but to impugn our translation.

All this works, of course, only if we take it as given that S's assertion of 'q' was a sincere assertion. In any actual case of absurd utterance, there would be a pair of options available to us: either the translation or the sincerity of the assertion might be called into question. It is something of a myth, or a simplifying idealization if you prefer, to suppose that the sincerity of an assertion can ever be taken as given. But it is a useful myth, since it enables us to view a subject's verbal behavior as a transparent window on his beliefs. As will soon become apparent, we can exploit this idealization to explore the conceptual relation between the rationality of a subject's beliefs and the intentional characterization of these beliefs, in a particularly straightforward and illuminating way. Before elaborating on this point, however, I want to note an important parallel between the myth that we can take the sincerity of an assertion as given and another myth that has recently been invoked in discussions of the content or intentional characterization of beliefs.

2.1.1 The Parallel between Sincere Assertions and Mental Sentences Stored in the "Belief Box"

The widely shared *language of thought* paradigm in contemporary cognitive psychology maintains that many mental processes are best viewed as manipulations and transformations of internalized, sentencelike representations. The manipulations and transformations are formal, in the sense that they are sensitive only to the syntactic properties of mental sentences. For theories which cleave to the computational paradigm, the holding of a propositional attitude like a belief or a desire is identified with having an appropriate mental sentence stored in an appropriate mental location.[2] If one takes this model of the mind seriously, and many do, one can be led to wonder just what it is about sentences in the head in virtue of which they admit of the intentional characterizations we use to describe them. Why is one mental sentence (a token of) the belief that Socrates is wise, while another is (a token of) the belief that if you scratch poison ivy it will get worse?

Of course, those philosophers and psychologists who worry about such issues all suppose that if there really are tokens of mental sentences in the head, they are inscribed in some currently unknown neurochemical code. But in thinking about the assignment of content to mental sentences, it proves enormously useful to adopt the myth that mental sentences are inscribed in some readily recognizable orthography. For example, Stephen Schiffer, who has made particularly vivid use of this myth, asks that we imagine a person who is psychologically quite ordinary, save for the fact that he has a huge, transparent head in which two boxes are plainly visible—one marked "Beliefs," the other "Desires." In these boxes are an enormous number of sentence tokens in some unfamiliar but easy-to-recognize orthography.[3] Having adopted this myth, we can go on to ask just how we would go about interpreting or determining the content of the various mental inscriptions in our hypercephalic subject's Belief Box. How must a mental inscription be related to other mental sentences, to behavior, and to objects and events outside the head in order for the sentence to count as a token of the belief that Socrates is wise?

A bit later in this chapter I will offer an outline of the answer to this question that I favor, and a similar answer will be sketched in much greater detail in 5.3. However, my present purpose is simply to stress the strong parallel between this question about the interpretation or intentional characterization of mental sentences and Quine's concern with the translation of a speaker's utterances. We have seen that in order to render Quine's claims about the translation of "startlingly false" assertions plausible, we must suppose that he is talking about sincere assertions—the kind that accurately reflect what the speaker believes. But, of course, in attempting to say what a person believes, his sincere assertions in a language that we do not yet understand play a role that is formally analogous to his mental inscriptions in an orthography that we cannot interpret. In both cases, they provide a theoretically idealized window into the workings of the mind, though neither a total catalogue of the inscriptions in the Belief Box nor a total list of the sentences to which a person would sincerely assent will suffice to tell us what he believes. In each case we also need a theory that will enable us to interpret or translate the unfamiliar inscriptions or utterances. In light of the strong parallelism between the project of translating a speaker's sincere assertions and the project of interpreting or intentionally characterizing his mental sentences, it should come as no surprise that the principles governing and constraining translation will be mirrored by principles governing and constraining intentional interpretation. Indeed, I think the most illuminating reading of the passage from Quine quoted in 2.1 is to view it not only as a contribution to the theory of translation but also, and more fundamentally, as an attempt to set out some conditions constraining the intentional characterization of a speaker's beliefs. With this perspective in mind, let me return to the job of trying to extract a plausible argument from the passage—one that will throw some light on the thesis that belief presupposes rationality.

2.1.2 Extending Quine's Stricture against Silliness

I have already argued that the commonsense precept that lies behind Quine's maxim of translation is best understood as a claim about beliefs: silliness of belief, beyond a certain point, is exceedingly unlikely. The example of silliness that Quine gives us is belief in a flat-out contradiction. But it is clear that this is not the only sort of silliness that Quine and common sense would take to be unlikely. If it is implausible that anyone would have the belief that Socrates is wise *and* Socrates is not wise, it is equally implausible, or nearly so, that anyone would have the belief that Socrates is wise and also have the belief that Socrates is not wise. This silliness, in turn, is not much more egregious than the silliness of the person who believes and sincerely asserts that p, believes and sincerely asserts that if p then q, and fails to believe that q (where 'p' and 'q' are replaced by perspicuous, logically uncomplicated sentences). There is every reason to think that Quine would and should find a translation scheme, which led us to ascribe these *patterns* of belief to be as suspect as the scheme which led us to ascribe a single contradictory belief. What is more, it is not just silly beliefs and silly patterns of belief which would and should impugn our scheme of translation. Silly inference would do so as well. Thus, for example, suppose that our translation manual (or our scheme for interpreting mental sentences) leads us to attribute to a person the belief that if p then q (where again 'p' and 'q' are replaced by perspicuous sentences). Suppose further that some perceptual experience causes the person to believe (and perhaps sincerely assert) that p. And suppose finally that from these two beliefs he infers (or is led to believe) that *not*-q! We are not likely to rest content with the translation or interpretation scheme that entails these intentional characterizations of our subject's sincere assertions and beliefs. If, moreover, our subject as we interpret him *regularly* infers in this silly way, our discontent with our scheme of interpretation will grow even more acute.

The conclusion I would draw from all this is that Quine's stricture against silliness ought to be construed much more broadly than his single illustration of a blatantly contradictory belief suggests. Our schemes of translation or interpretation are called into question not only when they lead us to ascribe single silly beliefs but also when they lend us to ascribe silly sets of beliefs and/or silly inferences. Our interlocutor's silliness, beyond a certain point, in any of these respects should lead us to be suspicious that there is something wrong with the intentional characterizations we have imposed on his words and beliefs. You may, if you prefer, take this to be more of a generalization than an explication of Quine's stricture on silliness, though I think there is abundant textual evidence suggesting that Quine had something very much like this in mind.

2.1.3 The Grounds of Quine's Stricture against Silliness
Up to this point I have been following Quine's lead and writing as though the stricture barring silly beliefs and inferences was simply a matter of probability. Quine seems to be telling us that we should not accept a scheme of translation that leads us to attribute silly beliefs to people, because it is very unlikely that anyone would be so silly. If we read Quine in this way, however, we lay him open to the charge of begging the question against the proponents of "prelogicality." How, after all, has Quine determined that startlingly false beliefs and silly inferences are unlikely? He may, perhaps, have substantial inductive evidence for the rarity of absurd beliefs among his compatriots. But, of course, those who think that irrational or prelogical strategies of inference prevail in other cultures would also insist that people in other cultures reason very differently from the way we do. We could no more show that this claim is false by arguing inductively from the domestic case than we could show that people in other cultures don't

eat ants by demonstrating the rarity of ant eating close to home. Indeed, there is a worse problem for the inductive likelihood construal of Quine's antisilliness precept. For even in the domestic case it is hard to see how we might go about collecting our evidence. To know whether a compatriot reasons absurdly, we must interpret his words; to interpret his words, we need a translation manual; and to write an acceptable manual, Quine tells us, we must eschew the ascription of silly belief. So it looks like any inductive attempt to support Quine's precept will beg the question. In order to gather inductive evidence in favor of the precept, we must presuppose that it is true.

There is, I think, a clear path out of this morass, though whether it is what Quine had in mind I will leave for others to argue. What our recent reflections seem to demonstrate is that the doctrine that bars interpretations leading to the ascription of wildly implausible beliefs and inferences could not be based on inductive evidence. The alternative is to view the doctrine as a species of conceptual truth, an a priori constraint on the business of translation and interpretation. Writers who have pursued this line sometimes make it sound as though the antisilliness principle were a sort of conventionally imposed post hoc filter. First we go about constructing our translation or interpretation, and then when we are done we put it to the antisilliness test. But I think matters run much deeper. Underlying the stricture against absurdity is a cluster of conceptual constraints on just what is required of a belief for it to qualify for a given intentional description.

The point is easiest to see if we adopt the myth of the transparent head and focus on the link between intentional description and inference. Suppose that in the course of studying the inscriptions in our imagined subject's Belief Box we note a number of them of the form '#p' and a number of others of the form 'p * q', where the 'p's and 'q's are inscriptions that also sometimes occur alone or in other compounds. Suppose further that we note certain regularities in the changing pattern of our subject's beliefs:

(a) 'p' and '#p' are never to be found in the Belief Box at the same time, though sometimes 'p' will be removed to be replaced by '#p', and vice versa;

(b) if 'p * q' is already in the Belief Box and 'p' is added, typically this is followed by 'q' being added also;

(c) if 'p * q' is already in the Belief Box and '#q' is added, typically this is followed by '#p' being added also.

The discovery of these regularities might incline us to conclude that an inscription of the form 'p * q' is a token of a conditional belief, which we might characterize as the belief that if P then Q, and that an inscription of the form '#p' is a token of a negative belief which we might characterize as the belief that not-P (where 'P' is replaced by the intentional characterization of 'p' inscriptions and 'Q' is replaced by the intentional characterization of 'q' inscriptions.) The regularities (a)–(c) do not, of course, constitute a conclusive case for this scheme of intentional interpretation, and it is easy to imagine further regularities that would bolster our confidence in the scheme.

But now suppose that our observations of our subject's Belief Box had revealed a rather different set of regularities:

(a') 'p' and '#p' often occur simultaneously, and there is no systematic connection between the appearance of one and the removal of the other;

(b') if 'p * q' is already in the Belief Box and 'p' is added, this is not typically followed by 'q' being added;

(c') if 'p * q' is already in the Belief Box and 'q' is added, this is typically followed by 'p' being added also.

Under these circumstances, we would surely feel strongly inclined to *reject* a scheme of intentional interpretation which treated '#p' as a negation and 'p * q' as a conditional.

Why would the former regularities incline us to accept the proposed intentional characterizations, while the latter ones would incline us to reject them? A first pass at the answer might go like this: It is part of what it is to be a belief with a given intentional characterization, part of the concept of such a belief, if you will, to interact with other beliefs in a rational way—a way which more or less mirrors the laws of logic. This sort of interaction with other beliefs is a conceptually necessary condition for being the belief that not-p or for being the belief that if p then q. Thus if a belief fails to manifest the requisite interactions with other beliefs, *it just does not count* as the belief that not-p or the belief that if p then q.

A similar conceptual connection links the intentional description of a belief with the sorts of sensory experiences that may give rise to the belief. Thus suppose that in observing the doings of our subject's Belief Box we notice that the inscription '!@ |^EE*%^' (I'll call it 'E' for short) appears when and only when an elephant ambles into our subject's view, and that the inscription's departure regularly coincides with the elephant's. Such a pattern would encourage our interpreting 'E' as a token of the belief that there is an elephant in front of one. But the same pattern would count heavily against the thought that 'E' might be interpreted as the belief that an elephant has just left, or as the belief that one has just been attacked by a puma. The generalization that would appear to cover both this case and the inference case is that in order to be a belief that p, a mental state must manifest suitable rational interactions, both with sensory input and with other mental states. A mental state whose interactions depart too drastically from what would be rational for a belief that p does not count as a belief that p.

I have been writing as though the rationality requirement might be applied to mental states one at a time. But, of course, this is not the case. For in order to know whether a given state counts as the belief that p, we must trace its pattern of interactions with other states. And in order to know whether that pattern approximates what would be rational for the belief that p, we must have intentional characterizations for the other states as well. Thus the rationality constraint is best viewed as applying to *systems* of intentional interpretation or *systems* of translation. In order for any given mental state to count as the belief that p, there must be a system of interpretation which assigns it and its fellows intentional characterizations on which the interactions of p with sensory input and with its fellow mental states are what we would rationally expect of the belief that p. It is in this wholly unmysterious sense that the business of intentional interpretation is "holistic."

The view I have been urging in the last several paragraphs is that Quine's stricture against silliness is best viewed not as an empirical generalization but as a conceptual point about the intentional characterization of mental states. Quine himself would no doubt be uncomfortable with this reading of his commonsense principle, since he is suspicious of conceptual analysis and reluctant to indulge in the vocabulary of folk psychology. However, those who have seen Quine as speaking to the issue of how badly it is possible to reason generally do not share his behaviorist squeamishness. And among them, I think, there would be wide agreement with the conceptual point I have wrung from Quine's text. But the price of that agreement is a certain vagueness on a quite fundamental point. I have said that to count as a belief that p, a mental state must interact in a "suitably rational" way. But I have not said just how much rationality is suitable. On this question, there is quite substantial disagreement, with some writers insisting that intentional description presupposes perfect rationality, others claiming that only a bare minimum of rationality is required, and still others opting for an intermediate view. In 2.2 I will elaborate on each of these views and argue that of the three the minimalists have much the strongest case.

2.2 The Case for Minimal Rationality

Let us take it as established that the intentional description of a person's mental states requires some degree of rationality in the way the states interact with perceptual stimuli and with each other. The question before us is how much.

2.2.1 Perfect Rationality, "Fixed Bridgeheads," and Minimal Rationality

One answer, which has been urged most notably by D.C. Dennett, is that intentional description requires "perfect rationality." On Dennett's view, "there is no coherent intentional description" of a person who "falls short of perfect rationality and avows beliefs that either are strongly disconfirmed by the available empirical evidence or are self-contradictory or contradict other avowals he has made."[4] As Dennett himself has stressed, it is no trivial matter to say just what the requirement of perfect rationality comes to. It might be thought that in the domain of inference, a standard logic text would provide at least a set of necessary conditions on full rationality. But, as Gilbert Harman is fond of pointing out, the laws of logic do not tell us how we ought to go about revising our beliefs.[5] Suppose that you already hold beliefs of the form 'if p then q' and 'not-q', and suppose further that as a result of your observations you come to believe that p. Logic suggests that something will have to go. But what? Should you change your belief on q? or give up your belief in the conditional? or perhaps conclude that despite appearances p is false? The laws of logic offer no guidance. Nor is there any other well-established theory to which we can turn. But even without a detailed account of what the requirement of perfect rationality comes to, we can stipulate some conditions that seem clearly in the spirit of the requirement. Though we may not know just how we should avoid logical inconsistencies, it seems clear that an ideally rational cognitive agent should avoid them one way or another. Also, it seems plausible to insist that a perfectly rational agent would believe all of the logical consequences of what he believes. And, indeed, Dennett himself proposes both of these as conditions on perfect rationality.[6] So let us take these two conditions—consistency and closure under logical implication—to be necessary (or nearly necessary) features of perfect rationality. While far from a full explication of the notion, these will be enough to argue that perfect rationality is not a necessary condition for intentional description.

One way to weaken the requirement of perfect rationality is to insist that there is some special class of inferences and stimuli-induced beliefs which a subject must manifest if his mental states are to admit of any intentional description at all. This view concedes that subjects may indeed infer irrationally but insists that there are limits to that irrationality. A mental state that fails to manifest the special subset of essential inferences will not admit of an intentional description—for no sentence p will it count as the belief that p. The most notable defender of this sort of view on the relation between rationality and intentional description is Martin Hollis. On Hollis's view, "The identification of beliefs requires a 'bridgehead' of true and rational beliefs."[7] What is more, Hollis contends that this is a "fixed" rather than a "floating" bridgehead, in the sense that there are some specific inferential principles and stimulus-belief links that are presupposed by all efforts at translation and interpretation.[8] These, according to Hollis, are "universal among mankind," or at least among that portion of mankind whom we can understand and interpret at all. They are a priori universals, in the sense that they are a conceptual precondition for any possible interpretation.

In arguing for his view, Hollis follows closely in Quine's footsteps. But Quine, unlike Hollis, is very cagey on the question of whether there are any *specific* beliefs or inferences which absolutely must be held or made by anyone whom we can translate at all. It is not entirely clear how Hollis thinks he can wring the conclusion of a "fixed bridgehead" from Quine's reflections on translation. Nor, unfortunately, is it clear just exactly *which* beliefs and inferences Hollis thinks people absolutely must have. But I will not pause here to ponder these matters since, as I will shortly argue, the fixed bridgehead view is false. Intentional description presupposes neither specific beliefs nor specific stimulus-belief links nor specific patterns of inference.

A third, and still weaker, view on the relation between rationality and intentional description is what, following Christopher Cherniak, I will call the "minimal rationality" view. On this view, there is no one inference nor any specific set of inferences that a person's mental states must manifest in order to qualify for an intentional description. Rather, what is required is that the mental states manifest some reasonably substantial subset of the inferences that would be required of a perfectly rational cognitive agent. The minimal rationality idea can be elaborated in two rather different ways. The first is to suppose that questions about the intentional characterizability of mental states always admit of a clear answer, at least in principle. On this view, it would be possible to say, for any cluster of inferences, whether they were rich enough to pass the minimal rationality test—with an affirmative answer indicating that a person whose beliefs manifested these inferences would satisfy a necessary condition for intentional description. The second idea would be to reject the notion that questions of intentional characterizability always have a clear yes or no answer. On this view, intentional characterizability, like baldness, is a matter of degree. As the distance between perfect rationality and the rationality displayed by the system at hand increases, the intentional characterizability of the system decreases. While there will be many clear cases, there will also be many unclear cases—cases where all we can say, even in principle, is that intentional characterization is less appropriate than it would be if the system were inferentially better and more appropriate than it would be if the system were inferentially worse. Writers who opt for the minimal rationality view generally do not distinguish between these two alternatives, though, as I shall urge in the following section, it is the latter alternative that is closer to the mark. Perhaps the most prominent advocate of the minimal rationality view is Donald Davidson, although this reading of his work is not an entirely comfortable one. There are a number of passages in which Davidson sounds instead like an advocate of the perfect rationality view, and Cherniak, another defender of the minimal rationality account, takes Davidson to be an adversary. Among the others who opt for the minimal rationality view are Lukes and possibly Loar.[9]

2.2.2 A Pair of Arguments against the Perfect Rationality and Fixed Bridgehead Views

As I have already indicated, I think it is the second—sliding scale—version of the minimal rationality view that is closest to the truth. In 2.3, I will try to explain why it is true. But before getting to that, I should say why I reject the perfect rationality and fixed bridgehead views. Since these are claims about the workings and implications of the concepts underlying our commonsense intentional locutions, the most obvious way to test them is to see how well they comport with our intuitive judgments about various cases.[10] In a number of places, I have myself set out cases which, I think, cast serious doubt on the perfect rationality and fixed bridgehead views.[11] But the cleanest and most persuasive arguments in the literature have been developed in a series of papers by Christopher Cherniak and collected together in his recent book *Minimal Rationality*.[12]

The central point in Cherniak's argument against the perfect rationality view is the observation, supported by both theory and common sense, that for all of us some inferences are harder than others. Indeed, for each person there will be a class of inferences which are so long and complex, or otherwise difficult, that they will be beyond the person's ability altogether. The existence of such limits is readily explained by what Cherniak calls the "finitary predicament." Our brains and our lifetimes are lamentably finite, and we would expect that any finite system will be able to handle at best a finite number of inferences. But that, of course, leaves most of the (infinitely many) valid inferences beyond our grasp. The existence of such limits to our inferential acumen is, I would hope, not terribly controversial. But this is enough to show that intentional descriptions do not presuppose *perfect* rationality. For, as we have seen, perfect rationality requires closure under logical implication, which in turn requires that we draw all logically valid inferences from our beliefs. Since this is impossible for creatures in the finitary predicament, it follows from the perfect rationality view that none of us, nor anything else in the universe, has intentionally characterizable mental states. And that, surely, is absurd.

A second argument Cherniak develops can be neatly turned against the fixed bridgehead view. The argument begins with the banal fact that for each of us some inferences are harder than others. We can well imagine that with a bit of effort experimental psychologists might construct a partial ordering of inferences in terms of their psychological feasibility for a given person or class of people. Such an ordering would no doubt classify the inference from 'p and q' to 'p' as easier (more feasible) than the inference from 'not-q → not-p' to 'p → q'; and it would classify this latter inference as easier than the inference from '$(\exists x)(y)(Fx \rightarrow Gy)$' to '$(x)Fx \rightarrow (x)Gx$'. Cherniak asks that we imagine a variety of hypothetical people whose inference feasibility ordering is very different from our own. The most radical case is one in which the hypothetical subject's feasibility ordering is inverted. Consider the set consisting of all inferences from the least difficult ones for some normal subject (say, me) through the least difficult ones that are practically unfeasible for me. Now imagine a person whose feasibility ordering for this set of inferences is inverted, so that, for him, inferring 'Socrates is male' from 'Socrates is an uncle' and 'If Socrates is an uncle, then Socrates is male' would not be possible, though inferences like determining the independence of the axiom of choice "would be an easy task, performed reliably and without prolonged investigation."[13] Cherniak claims, and I am inclined to agree, that despite the peculiarity in the inferential behavior of this imaginary subject, we would not find it totally beyond the bounds of intuitive plausibility to translate his sentence 'If Socrates is an uncle, then Socrates is male' homophonically, and to view the belief state which underlies his sincere assertion of that sentence as the belief that if Socrates is an uncle, then Socrates is male. We would, in short, feel no overwhelming intuitive resistance to a scheme of intentional characterization for this subject which paralleled the one we use on less exotic folk. But, of course, the inferences our imagined subject finds impossibly difficult are just the ones Hollis would surely count among the bridgehead inferences, since they are the ones which are trivially obvious for more normal subjects.

In the papers in which Hollis defends his fixed bridgehead view, and indeed in much of the literature in this area since Quine, considerable stress is placed on the problems that would be confronted by a field investigator trying to interpret the sayings and doings in an exotic culture. Against the background of this concern, one can well imagine Hollis protesting that if we were actually to come upon a person or a race whose feasibility ordering were inverted in the way Cherniak imagines, we would never succeed in translating their language since, as a practical matter, we have little alternative but to start with simple bridgehead inferences and stimulus-belief links. Without the aid of the fixed bridgehead, the field investigator would never *discover* which native constructions to translate as conjunctions, conditionals, and so forth.

I think we must certainly concede here that the field investigator's job would be monumentally more difficult with subjects whose feasibility ordering is significantly different from our own. Whether, as a practical matter, it would be entirely impossible seems to me to be less clear. There may be no easy step-by-step discovery procedure by which an investigator could construct his translation. But, of course, much the same is true in most other areas of science. Coming up with a good theory, in physics or in anthropology, may require bold and creative speculation. The fundamental point to be made here, though, is that this is a battle which the opponent of the fixed bridgehead view *need not fight.* For on the interpretation that makes it relevant to our current concerns, the fixed bridgehead view is a claim about the conceptual connection between intentional characterizability and the disposition to draw certain specific inferences. If it is agreed that the proposed intentional characterizations for subjects with exotic feasibility orderings, like those imagined by Cherniak, comport reasonably well with intuition, then the fixed bridgehead view is mistaken. Questions about how we might discover this interpretation in the first place are irrelevant to the issue at hand.

2.3 Why Does Intentional Description Presuppose Rationality?

Let's pause for a moment to see where we've gotten to. In 2.1, I argued that from Quine's ruminations on "prelogicality" we can coax a pretty persuasive argument to the effect that intentional description presup-

poses at least some degree of rationality. When the pattern of inferences a person manifests deviates too drastically from the rational
ideal, the person's mental states simply do not admit of an intentional
description at all. In 2.2, we asked *how much* rationality is required for
intentional description, and we found good reason to reject views that
insist on either perfect rationality or some fixed set of inferences. The
view we are left with is that intentional description requires the disposition to draw some reasonable subset of the inferences that would
be expected of an ideally rational cognitive agent. The question I want
to explore in the current section is *why*? Why should there be this
curious conceptual interdependency between rationality and intentionally characterizable belief?

2.3.1 *The Principle of Charity and the Principle of Humanity*
In *Word and Object*, and in many of the papers prompted by that book,
there was considerable discussion of a so-called principle of charity
which governed translation and intentional interpretation. This principle required that we translate a speaker's language in such a way
that most of his sincere assertions turn out to be true and most of his
inferences turn out to be rational. Davidson, who frequently invoked
the principle of charity, insisted that "charity is not an option, but a
condition on having a workable theory [of translation]."[14] But it is not
likely that we will find in the principle of charity an answer to our
current question, since what underlies that principle is the very fact
we hope to explain. If, as Davidson insists, "charity is forced on us,"[15]
this is because there is a conceptual link between truth and rationality
on the one hand and intentional description on the other. What we
want to know is *why* this conceptual link obtains.

At this point a critic might be tempted simply to reject the question
as inappropriate. It is, she might insist, just a brute fact that there is
a conceptual connection between rationality and intentional description: that just happens to be the way our concepts are put together.
There may, perhaps, be some historical explanation for the fact. But
apart from that there is just no further explanation. I am prepared to
admit that the critic might be right. There is certainly no a priori
guarantee that we can find a deeper explanation. Still, I think the critic
would be a bit too hasty in concluding that explanation has come to
an end. There is a richer story to tell.

As a way into this story, let us consider Richard Grandy's efforts to
patch the principle of charity and to explain why it holds.[16] Grandy
construes the principle as an admonition to choose a translation that
maximizes agreement between ourselves and our interlocutors, at
least on obvious truths. But as Grandy sees it, this principle misses

the mark. He urges that we substitute what he calls "the principle of humanity," which holds that in choosing a translation we should prefer the one on which "the imputed pattern of relations among beliefs, desires, and the world be as similar to our own as possible" (443). Often, as Grandy notes, the principles of charity and humanity will coincide in their counsel. There are, however, cases in which the two principles pull apart.

> Suppose Paul has arrived at a party and asserts "The man with the martini is a philosopher." And suppose the facts are that there is a man in plain view who is drinking water from a martini glass and that he is not a philosopher. Suppose also that in fact there is only one man at the party drinking a martini, that he is a philosopher, and that he is out of sight in the garden. Under the circumstances the charitable thing to do would be to take Paul's remark at face value (homophonically), since that is simple and makes his remark true. But the natural thing to do is to understand him as having said something false, or at least to view the situation as one in which his utterance shows he has a false belief. That is what is predicted by the principle of humanity. . . . Since no reason could be given as to why Paul would have a belief about the philosopher in the garden, it is better to attribute to him an explicable falsehood than a mysterious truth. . . .
>
> The principle of humanity directs us to bear in mind that the speaker is a person and has certain basic similarities to ourselves when we are choosing between translations. (445)

On Grandy's view, the principle of humanity itself is rooted in certain pragmatic considerations dealing with the purposes of translation and the limited information available to us as we pursue those goals. The purpose of translation, Grandy assumes, "is to enable the translator to make the best possible predictions and to offer the best possible explanations of the behavior of the translatee" (442). Sometimes our interest is in predicting and explaining the translatee's verbal behavior, but often our concern lies in predicting various kinds of nonverbal behavior.

> The actual use of translation in this prediction process is only one of the intermediate steps. We translate verbal behavior into our own language and use this to determine what the person's beliefs and desires are, and then use that information to predict actions. The combination of reported desires and beliefs . . . do not suffice to determine the expected behavior. Instead we must have some model of the agent that we use to assist us in making a prediction.

> In theory one could (perhaps) elicit the total belief-and-desire structure and use mathematical decision theory to arrive at the prediction, but this is not what we do in practice. . . . The most obvious alternative is that we use ourselves in order to arrive at the prediction: we consider what we should do if we had the relevant beliefs and desires.
>
> Whether our simulation of the other person is successful will depend heavily on the similarity of his belief-and-desire network to our own. It would be desirable to base our simulation on all of the other person's beliefs and desires, but this is not possible. Thus, it is of fundamental importance to make the interrelations between these attitudes as similar as possible to our own. If a translation tells us that the other person's beliefs and desires are connected in a way that is too bizarre for us to make sense of, then the translation is useless for our purposes. So we have, as a pragmatic constraint on translation, the condition that the imputed pattern of relations among beliefs, desires and the world be as similar to our own as possible. This principle I shall call the *principle of humanity.* (442–43)

Much of what Grandy says seems to me to be both right and important. He is clearly correct in his contention that it is the principle of humanity rather than the principle of charity that captures our judgment about the correct belief to ascribe in the "man with the martini" case. Also, he is on to something important in his suggestion that we use ourselves as models when we attempt to predict another person's behavior on the basis of our very limited knowledge of his beliefs and desires. Introspectively, it often seems that when we try to anticipate another person's behavior we ask ourselves what we would do if we had those of her goals and beliefs we know about and if we were in the situation she is in.[17] Occasionally, though, we depart quite explicitly from this strategy. In games, and also in more serious matters, we sometimes set traps for our opponents in the expectation that they are not clever enough to infer the consequences of their moves as clearly as we have.

Where I think Grandy goes wrong is in his contention that our reliance on the principle of humanity is a pragmatic matter which can be traced to our limited knowledge of another person's beliefs and desires. Though he is not entirely clear on the point, he seems to be saying that the principle of humanity is mandated by the strategy of using ourselves as models and that this strategy is forced upon us by our inevitably limited knowledge of the other person's beliefs and desires. Were it not for this practical limitation on our knowledge,

Grandy suggests, we might use some other strategy for predicting behavior—mathematical decision theory perhaps—and, in so doing, we would free ourselves from the constraints imposed by the principle of humanity. If this is Grandy's view, then I think it is pretty clear that he is mistaken.

To see why, reflect for a moment on the idea that with full enough knowledge of a subject's belief and desire structure we might use mathematical decision theory to generate our predictions of his behavior rather than using the commonsense strategy of imagining ourselves in his shoes. Would this really free us from the constraints of the principle of humanity? The answer, I maintain, is no. For in order to employ mathematical decision theory, we must have an *intentional characterization* of the subject's beliefs and desires: we must be able to identify certain of his beliefs as conditionals and others as disjunctions; we must be able to say that certain of his beliefs are (or are not) about elephants; we must be able to determine whether eating chocolate ice cream is the object of one of his desires. None of this is possible, however, unless the subject's beliefs and desires, and the pattern of causal interactions with each other and with stimuli, are reasonably similar to our own. The argument here is a straightforward generalization of the one developed in 2.1.3. If a subject's mental state does not interact with other mental states in a pattern which approximates the pattern exhibited by our own conditional beliefs, *it does not count as a conditional belief.* Similarly, if a subject's mental state is not caused by stimuli similar to the ones which lead me to believe that there is an elephant in front of me, and if it does not interact with other mental states in a way similar to the way mine would, then *it does not count as a belief that there is an elephant in front of him.* An analogous sort of argument would show that a substantial degree of similarity in *what* is believed is necessary for intentional description to get off the ground. If we imagine a person acquiring a growing collection of "startlingly false" beliefs about elephants, it grows increasingly unclear that he counts as having any beliefs about elephants at all. One can't believe that elephants are liquid, that they are prime numbers, and that they are speech acts.[18] It follows that, far from offering a way of avoiding the principle of humanity, predicting behavior by using mathematical decision theory presupposes the principle. Moreover, the same is true of any strategy for predicting behavior which requires an intentional characterization of the agent's beliefs and desires. I conclude that Grandy's attempt to ground the principle of humanity in pragmatic considerations forced upon us by our limited knowledge is misguided. It is not because we use beliefs and desires to predict behavior under conditions of limited information that we must respect

the principle of humanity. Rather, adherence to the principle is required if we are to exploit intentional descriptions at all in characterizing a person's mental states.

Despite the failure of his pragmatic account, however, I think that
Grandy has provided us with an enormously important clue to use in
answering the question with which 2.3 began: Why do intentional
description and rationality come in the same package? The lesson to
be learned from Grandy is that the link between rationality and intentionality is a by-product of a more general constraint on intentional
characterization: For a person's cognitive states to be intentionally
characterizable, the states, the interactions among them, and their
interactions with the environment must all be similar to our own. The
minimal rationality condition follows from this, if we add the assumption that we ourselves are passingly rational in our inferences.

2.3.2 Why Does Intentional Description Presuppose Similarity to Ourselves? An Account of Intentional Description

It now appears that we have traded one puzzle for another. We began
by wondering why intentional description was linked to rationality,
and we have explained this link by noting that intentional description
requires similarity to ourselves. But why should this be? The answer,
on my view, is to be found in an account of just what we are doing
when we give intentional descriptions of cognitive states. In several
earlier publications, I have tried to develop such an account, inspired
by this brief, richly suggestive passage in Quine.

> In indirect quotation we project ourselves into what, from his
> remarks and other indications, we imagine the speaker's state of
> mind to have been, and then we say what, in our language, is
> natural and relevant for us in the state thus feigned. An indirect
> quotation can usually expect to rate only as better or worse, more
> or less faithful, and we cannot even hope for a strict standard of
> more or less; what is involved is evaluation, relative to special
> purposes, of an essentially dramatic act. Correspondingly for
> other propositional attitudes, for all of them can be thought of as
> involving something like quotation of one's own imagined verbal
> response to an imagined situation.
>   Casting our real selves thus in unreal roles, we do not generally
> know how much reality to hold constant. Quandaries arise. But
> despite them we find ourselves attributing beliefs, wishes and
> strivings even to creatures lacking the power of speech, such is
> our dramatic virtuosity. We project ourselves even into what from
> his behavior we imagine a mouse's state of mind to have been,

dramatize it as a belief, wish, or striving, verbalized as seems relevant and natural to us in the state thus feigned.[19]

My elaboration of this Quinean idea runs roughly like this.[20] When we use a sentence of the form 'S believes that p', we are making a pair of interrelated claims about S. First, we are attributing to S a kind of cognitive state, a belief. This category of state can be distinguished from other categories by the role such states play in the subject's overall cognitive economy. Beliefs are the sorts of states which interact with desires, perceptions, and behavior in certain systematic ways. Thus intentional description presupposes that the cognitive economy of the organism whose states we are describing can be carved more or less smoothly into categories of states which play belieflike and desirelike roles.

Second, we are using the content sentence, 'p', to identify the particular belief we are attributing. The way this works, I argue, is by first picking out a hypothetical belief state that we ourselves might have—the one which in this setting we would express by uttering 'p' and then by attributing to S a belief state which is similar to this one. To say 'S believes that p', then, is to say S has a belief state similar to the one which would underlie my own assertion of 'p' were I (just now) to have uttered 'p' in earnest. Of course, any two things will be similar to one another in some respect or another. On my account, as on Quine's, both the relevant respects and the requisite degree of similarity are largely determined by context, though in typical contexts similarity of inferential pattern and similarity of the surrounding set of beliefs are of great importance. Plainly this account of intentional description requires a fair amount of polishing to make it precise and a fair amount of argument to make it plausible. I have attended to both tasks at some length elsewhere.[21] For current purposes this brief sketch should suffice.

What is important for our present concerns is that something akin to Grandy's principle of humanity is a direct consequence of my Quinean account of the strategy of intentional description. If what we are doing in offering an intentional characterization of a person's cognitive state is identifying it by way of its similarity to a hypothetical state of our own, then we would expect that as subjects get less and less similar to us in salient respects, we will increasingly lose our grip on how their cognitive states might be intentionally characterized. We would also expect that there will be no comfortable intentional characterization for the cognitive states of subjects whose inference patterns, or stock of beliefs, are radically different from our own. And as we noted in 2.1.3 and 2.3.1, this is just what happens when we reflect on subjects with unfamiliar patterns of inference and belief.[22] Looked at in one way, this constitutes an argument in favor of my Quinean analysis, particularly since other accounts offer no explanation of why intentional description breaks down as subjects become increasingly dissimilar to us. Looked at the other way around, we have succeeded in answering the question posed at the beginning of 2.3. The minimal rationality condition is a by-product of the principle of humanity; and that latter principle obtains because in intentional description we characterize other people's cognitive states via their similarity to our own.

2.4 The Argument for Limits to Irrationality and Why Those Limits Are Uninteresting

The reader graced with a robust memory will recall that this chapter was provoked by the prospect of a conceptual argument imposing a priori constraints on how badly a person might reason. This argument was to show that it is conceptually incoherent to suppose that a person's reasoning might depart without limit from the rational ideal. A central element in the argument was the claim that rationality and intentional describability come in the same package. And we now have that part of the argument pretty firmly in place. The full argument might be set out as follows:

(i) In intentional description we characterize cognitive states via their similarity to actual and possible states of our own. Thus, creatures whose cognitive dynamics are very different from ours are not intentionally describable. Being intentionally describable *requires* having cognitive dynamics similar to our own. (This may be viewed as a relative of Grandy's "principle of humanity," though "the principle of intentional chauvinism" might be a more descriptive label.)

(ii) While we may not be ideally rational, we do a pretty good job at the business of cognition; we are reasonably rational. Thus creatures whose cognitive dynamics are similar to our own will also do a pretty good job at the business of cognition—perhaps a bit worse than us, perhaps a bit better. From this, along with (i), it follows that if a cognitive system is intentionally describable, then it too must be reasonably rational.

(iiⁱ) Beliefs are "contentful" or *intentionally describable* cognitive states; every belief is a belief *that* something or other. A cognitive state that does not admit of an intentional description cannot be a belief. From this, along with (i) and (ii), it follows that creatures that have beliefs must be reasonably rational.

(iv) Reasoning is a process in which beliefs are formed, modified or eliminated. Without beliefs there can be no reasoning. From this, along with (i), (ii) and (iii), it follows that creatures that can reason at all must be reasonably rational. Or, to put it the other way around, a profoundly irrational creature, one that did a very bad job at the business of cognition, would not be capable of reasoning at all.

This argument is rather less threatening than it would be if Dennett's view on the link between rationality and intentionality, or even Hollis's, had been sustained. If Dennett were right, only ideally rational creatures could reason at all. And thus for creatures that do reason, there would be no room for improvement. If Hollis were right, there would be certain specific cognitive errors that no reasoning creature could make. But on the more plausible version that I have set out, the argument does not deny that people may depart from the standards of good reasoning in ways that are both substantial and highly variegated. Thus there is no immediate worry that empirical investigators exploring the foibles of human reasoning, or epistemological reformers who would have us do better, will find themselves out of a job. However, even these relatively flexible limits will be inimical to the perspective of the radical epistemic reformer who, while perhaps conceding that we already do a decent job of reasoning, envisions limitless improvements, some of which would leave us with cognitive strategies utterly unlike those we currently employ. This is a perspective I think we should take very seriously; it will loom large in chapters 5 and 6. Thus it is of some importance that we see just what is wrong with the argument set out in (i)–(iv).

One way to attack that argument would be to challenge premise (iii), which claims that beliefs must be intentionally describable, or premise (iv), which claims that without beliefs there can be no reasoning. In both cases, the most plausible defense of the premises would portray them as conceptual truths specifying part of what we mean by 'reasoning' and 'belief'. And to many ears, mine included, it is less than obvious that our concepts of belief and reasoning are constrained in this way. But this is not a line of attack I am much inclined to pursue since, like many disputes about the contours of commonsense concepts, this one is all too likely to end in a stalemate, with each side brandishing its own linguistic intuitions against the other.

A deeper objection to the argument set out in (i)–(iv) is that the "limit" it imposes on how bad reasoning can be, or how much it can improve, is both Pickwickean and profoundly uninteresting. It is an observer-relative, situation-sensitive constraint that marks no natural or theoretically significant boundary. Rather, it follows the contours of a commonsense concept. And the utility of that concept in day-to-day affairs is not at all dependent on the vague boundaries it generates in regions far from those in which the concept is usually invoked.

To see all this a bit more clearly, note first that premise (i)—the chauvinistic principle of humanity—plays a fundamental role in the argument. It is this principle that generates the basic constraint—the constraint on what is and is not intentionally describable. Subsequent premises extend this constraint to the class of cognitive states that will count as beliefs and to the class of cognitive processes that will count as reasoning. But what premise (i) asserts is that in characterizing a cognitive state intentionally, we are saying it is similar to some actual or possible state of our own. So in intentional description, we ourselves are the measure of all things. Moreover, as Quine observes, the standards of similarity that are relevant are dependent on the context—they are "relative to special purposes."[23] Plainly, the demarcation between states that are intentionally describable and states that are not is going to be vague, context sensitive, and observer relative; it will not be stable, or objective, or sharp.

Nor is it going to coincide, even roughly, with the boundary of any natural or theoretically interesting kind. The distinction between states that are intentionally describable and those that are not is not one that divides nature at its joints. Perhaps the easiest way to emphasize this last point is to adopt the perspective of the computational paradigm, sketched in 2.1.1. Suppose we have a sequence of people whose brains are alike in the following respect: Each exploits the same class of formal structures (that is, they have syntactically identical "languages of thought"), and each manipulates these formal structures in accordance with exactly the same rules. We will suppose that these people differ from one another in only one respect: they have different sentences stored in their Belief Boxes. We may imagine that the first subject in our sequence is me. The second is someone who has all the same sentences in his Belief Box, save for one, where he and I differ. The third person is related to the second as the second is related to me. That is, he differs from me in two mental sentences, and he differs from the second person in only one. And so on. What is interesting about this imaginary sequence is that in each adjacent pair the people are *very* psychologically similar to one another. And from the point of view of a purely formal computational paradigm, there are no interesting or significant discontinuities. There is no natural or theoretically well-motivated way to divide these people up into two classes. But when we attempt to describe these people in intentional terms (in a given context), we will be forced to divide them up into two radically different groups. The ones relatively close to me have intentionally characterizable states; the ones very far away do not. If the computational paradigm in psychology is on the right track, then this distinction, mandated by the chauvinistic principle of humanity, is without any psychological significance. An entirely similar argument can be mounted if we keep the inscriptions in the Belief Box fixed and gradually alter the principles that govern how these inscriptions interact with one another. In this case, too, we get a sequence in which adjacent people are very similar to one another; there are no natural or theoretically well-motivated boundaries. But those people close to us are intentionally describable, while those far away are not.[24]

What I have been arguing, for the last several paragraphs, is that the limits on how badly people can reason, and on how much they can improve, underwritten by the argument in (i)–(iv), are uninteresting because they follow the capricious contours of intentional describability. Another way to see how unimportant these limits are is to see how easy it is to ignore them by simply adopting a less chauvinistic vocabulary. Once again, the computational paradigm helps to make the point. Assume that the sort of cognitive architecture presupposed by commonsense psychology is roughly correct and that (iii) and (iv) are not in dispute. Then, as we saw in the previous paragraph, there may be people whose cognitive systems exhibit the same general cognitive organization that we do, although the inscriptions in their Belief Boxes don't count as "real" beliefs, and the processes that manipulate these inscriptions don't count as "real" reasoning or inference. Still, these systems have "belieflike" cognitive states and "inferencelike" cognitive processes, which differ from real beliefs and real inference in ways that are vague, parochial, and of no psychological importance. A natural move at this juncture is to adopt terminology that is less beholden to the vagaries of ordinary usage. Let us use the term "cognitive state" for both "real" beliefs and for those "belieflike" states that are just like the real McCoy, save for not being intentionally describable. And let us use the term "cognitive processes" for both "real" inferences and for those "inferencelike" processes that manipulate cognitive states which are not intentionally describable. If we describe people's psychological processes in this terminology (as I have done intermittently throughout this chapter), the limits that emerged in (i)–(iv) disappear. People's beliefs, if they are to count as "real" beliefs, and their reasoning, if it is to count as "real" reasoning, must be reasonably similar to our own. But there are no such constraints on people's cognitive states and cognitive processes. For all that the "conceptual argument" has shown, people's cognitive processes may be endlessly different from our own—and endlessly worse or endlessly better. Thus neither the conceptual argument nor the "limits" it imposes need be taken seriously by either empirical psychologists or epistemic reformers.

Chapter 3
Evolution and Rationality

In the previous chapter I considered and rejected a cluster of conceptual arguments which sought to show that human reasoning couldn't be all that bad and couldn't get much better. My principal project in this chapter is to assemble and criticize another family of arguments aimed at showing much the same conclusion. Unlike those in the previous chapter, however, the arguments that concern us here do not maintain that the hypothesis of widespread or systematic irrationality is *conceptually* impossible. Rather, they contend that significant irrationality is *empirically* impossible or unlikely since it is incompatible with well-established theories about the evolution and the processes that underlie it.

Another contrast with the topic of the previous chapter is that the literature arguing for some sort of connection between evolution or natural selection on the one hand and rationality on the other is singularly sparse. There are lots of suggestive hints scattered here and there, and I have often heard these hints endorsed or elaborated in discussion. Perhaps the best known of them is a brief passage in which Quine reminds us that

> creatures inveterately wrong in their inductions have a pathetic but praiseworthy tendency to die out before reproducing their kind.[1]

Here's an example from Dennett:

> Natural selection guarantees that *most* of an organism's beliefs will be true, *most* of its strategies rational.[2]

And another, this one from Fodor:

> Darwinian selection guarantees that organisms either know the elements of logic or become posthumous.[3]

Many other authors have made similar suggestions.[4] However, I know of no sustained, published exposition of any argument from the facts of evolution or natural selection to the conclusion that irrational systems of inference are unlikely or impossible.[5] The lack of a real advocate leaves critics of this line of thought in something of a quandary, for they must invent the opposition before they can refute it. In 3.1, I will explore a pair of paths along which one might try to forge a connection between evolutionary considerations and conclusions about the limits on irrational inference. Then, in the following two sections, I will argue that both of these paths are beset by serious difficulties. Even if successful, my arguments do not, of course, establish that there is no good evolutionary argument for constraints on how badly people can reason. My goal is more modest. I want to make it clear that there are major problems to be overcome by those who think that evolutionary considerations impose interesting limits on irrationality. I will be well satisfied if, by the time I assemble my conclusions in 3.4, I have convinced you that the burden of the argument is with the opposition—that the ball is in their court.

A second project of this chapter, pursued in 3.5 and 3.6, is to consider the prospects for descriptive cognitive pluralism in light of what we know about genetics, evolution, and the acquisition of complex cognitive systems. Here my theme will be that biology poses no threat to pluralism. There is no compelling reason to think that all of our inferential strategies are innate or, indeed, that any are. And if it should turn out that some cognitive processes are innate, this still would not show that descriptive cognitive pluralism is untenable.

3.1 In Search of an Argument

In my experience, most of those who think that evolutionary considerations insure rationality are drawn to this view by a pair of ideas, each of which has a certain *prima facie* plausibility. One of these ideas is that evolution produces organisms with good approximations to optimally well-designed characteristics or systems. The other is that an optimally well-designed cognitive system is a rational cognitive system. The challenge here is to elaborate these ideas into a valid argument whose premises comport with what is known about evolution. To see how such an argument might go, I'll try to expand on each idea as plausibly as possible.

3.1.1 Evolution and Well-Designed Systems
To flesh out the idea that evolution produces good approximations to optimally well-designed systems, we need to address a number of questions. First, just what does it mean, in this context, to say that a characteristic or a system is "optimally well designed"? Second, why

is it that evolution produces close approximations to optimally well-designed systems? Third, how does all of this bear on the question of what our cognitive system is like?

Since natural selection is going to play a central role in the argument, the notion of a well-designed system is going to have to be unpacked in terms of biological fitness. From the point of view of natural selection, it is plausible to say that one system is better designed than a second if an organism having the first would be more fit—that is, more likely to survive and reproduce successfully—than a conspecific having the second. A system is optimally well designed if it enhances biological fitness more than any alternative. This raises some hard questions about which other systems are going to count as "alternatives," a point we'll return to later. Obviously, the goodness of a system's design is relative both to the kind of organisms in question and to their environment. But to simplify matters, I'll ignore this point for a while.

Why should we think that evolution will produce good approximations to optimally well-designed systems? The most plausible answer starts with the claim that evolution is caused or driven by natural selection. Natural selection, for its part, can be counted upon to choose the best-designed—that is the most fitness-enhancing—genetically coded characteristic or system from among those that are available in the gene pool. Over long stretches of time, natural selection will get to choose among a huge and varied set of options that is very likely to include one or more that closely approximate a theoretical optimum. Thus, systems which result from the long periods of natural selection that lead to evolution can be expected to be about as well designed as it is possible to be.

For all of this to have consequences for our own cognitive or inferential system, we need only assume that our cognitive system is itself the product of biological evolution. If this is right, then our cognitive system can be expected to be optimal or very near optimal in the business of enhancing biological fitness.

3.1.2 Rationality and Well-Designed Systems

Consider, now, the second idea—the idea that an optimally well-designed cognitive system is a rational one. Since the notion of a well-designed system has been unpacked in terms of fitness, this idea must here be construed as claiming that a cognitive system that is optimally fitness enhancing is a rational cognitive system. For some purposes, it may be more useful to put the point in comparative terms: if one cognitive system is more fitness enhancing than another, it is also more rational. Why should we accept this claim? Though I know of no one who has argued the point in any detail, I have come across hints at two very different ways in which this idea might be defended.

The first is to argue that it follows directly from the meaning of 'rational inference' (or 'justified inference', 'good reasoning', or some related term of inferential evaluation). On this view, if we analyze what we ordinarily mean when we say that one inferential system is more rational than another (or, perhaps, if we analyze what we mean in an appropriate technical context), we will find we mean that one is more fitness enhancing than the other. So the claim that optimally well-designed cognitive systems are rational is a conceptual truth. The reader may well protest that this account of the meaning of 'rational inferential system' is more than a bit implausible. And on that point there will be no argument from me. However, this is not the place to debate the merits of competing analyses of terms of epistemic or inferential evaluation, since the issue of how such terms should be analyzed and what we can expect from conceptual analyses will be center stage in chapter 4. In this chapter I will let all such claims go unchallenged.

The second way in which one might defend the idea that a fitness-optimizing inferential system is rational starts with a different, and perhaps more plausible, conceptual analysis. On this alternative analysis, the rationality of an inferential system is a function of how well it does at producing true beliefs: a rational system of inference is one that generally produces true beliefs; and one inferential system is more rational than another if it does a better job at producing truths and avoiding falsehoods. This account bears an obvious family resemblance to the so-called reliabilist accounts of epistemic justification offered by such authors as Armstrong, Dretske, and Goldman.[6]

Now suppose it is granted that the rationality (or goodness or justifiedness) of an inferential system is conceptually tied to its tendency to produce true beliefs. How does this forge the link between natural selection and rationality? The answer lies in the further claim that inferential strategies that generally yield true beliefs are fitness enhancing and thus that natural selection will favor them. This, it is urged, is because in general having true beliefs is more adaptive than having false ones. True beliefs enable an organism to cope better with its environment; they enable the organism to find food, shelter, and mates, to avoid danger, and thus to survive and reproduce more effectively. There are exceptions, of course. It is easy to imagine offbeat situations in which a person or animal would be better off acting on false beliefs than on true ones. The diplomat who missed her meeting because she mistakenly believed that it was scheduled for the following day is likely to be more reproductively successful than her colleague who arrived on time, if those at the meeting are taken captive by terrorists. But such cases are obviously rare and exceptional. All the advocate of the current argument need claim is that on the whole and in the long run, organisms will be more fit—they will outcompete their conspecifics—if their ratio of true beliefs to false ones is higher. If this is right, then we can expect that natural selection will prefer one inferential system to a second if the former does a better job of producing truths and avoiding falsehoods. And, on the reliabilist analysis, that amounts to a preference for the more rational system.[7]

3.1.3 Preview of Coming Attractions

We now have a pair of arguments for the claim that evolution and natural selection guarantee at least a close approximation to full rationality in normal organisms, ourselves included. These arguments share the cluster of considerations leading to the conclusion that evolution produces close approximations to optimally well-designed systems. They also share the claim that optimally well-designed cognitive systems are rational. Where they divide is in the defense they offer for this claim. One argument takes it to be a conceptual truth, supported by the analysis of 'rationality' or some related term. The other argument gives a more complicated defense on which the rationality of an inferential system is conceptually tied not to fitness but to truth. It then argues that natural selection will favor one inferential system over another if it has a greater tendency to produce true beliefs.

In the two sections to follow, I'll take a critical look at some of the elements of these two arguments. Since I'm postponing discussion of the analysis or meaning of terms of epistemic evaluation, I will not challenge either of the analyses of 'rational inferential system' invoked in these arguments. However, in 3.2, I will challenge the idea that natural selection prefers "reliable" inferential systems. If that challenge is successful, then the second argument collapses, since the link between well-designed cognitive systems and rational ones will be severed. In 3.3, I will challenge various steps in the argument aimed at showing that evolution always produces organisms with optimally well-designed systems, or something close. I will also raise some questions about the assumption that our inferential system is the product of evolution. If either or both of these theses are mistaken, then both of the arguments we have sketched will collapse. Finally, in 3.5 and 3.6, I will argue that even if human cognitive systems are genetically coded and the product of evolution, there is no good reason to suppose that all normal cognitive systems are alike. This last point is not needed to scuttle the arguments from evolution to rationality.

But the cognitive diversity it makes room for will play a central role in the chapters to follow.

3.2 Truth, Reliability, and Natural Selection

The thesis at hand is that natural selection prefers reliable inferential systems—those that do a good job at producing truths and avoiding falsehoods—to unreliable ones. And it is my contention that this thesis is false. To build my case, a bit of scaffolding will be helpful.

In "The Evolution of Rationality" Elliott Sober distinguishes two different components into which the overall fitness of a gene or complex of genes can be factored.[8] The distinction is clearest if, following Sober and the evolutionary biologist G. C. Williams,[9] we think of the gene as a "cybernetic abstraction" and view an organism's genetic material as analogous to a program of instructions that the organism obeys, much as a computer obeys the instructions in its program. One complex of genes might direct human bodies to begin a sequence of physiological repair activities when an injury of a certain sort is sustained. Another might lead male baboons to attack a predator when the predator attacks a member of the male's herd. In assessing the "fitness" of a computer program in a given environment, or its suitability for the task it was designed to perform, we will want to consider two factors. The first is what sort of input/output relations it determines—how it leads the system to behave in various sorts of environments or circumstances. Other things being equal, one computer program will be more suitable than another if the input/output pairings it effects are more effective in achieving the intended purposes of the program. Analogously, one genetic program will be more fit than another, other things being equal, if the input/output pairings it effects are more conducive to survival and successful reproduction.

The second factor to be considered in assessing the fitness of a computer program will be just what is going on within the computer itself. "A good program will not only generate the right output for the right input, it will do so economically. It will not use up too much of the computer's memory, nor will it be a drain on the energy source on which the computer runs."[10] Similarly, a good genetic program will achieve its effect without making excessive demands on the memory, energy, or other resources of the organism. Sober calls these latter considerations *internal* in contrast with input/output considerations, which he calls *external*. He maintains, plausibly enough, that an organism's genetic instructions, like a computer program, can be evaluated with respect to both internal and external fitness. This distinction between internal and external fitness is not a hard and fast one. Like Sober, I will use it only as a heuristic device, to help focus our attention on the various kinds of factors that contribute to the overall fitness of an organism.

What I propose to argue is this. Let us suppose that there is a pair of genetically coded inferential systems, G_1 and G_2, in some species—either human or nonhuman. Let us further suppose that in the natural environment of this species, G_1 is more reliable; it leads to true beliefs more often, and to false beliefs less often, than does G_2. I contend that it is nonetheless possible that G_2, the less reliable system, will exceed G_1 both in internal fitness and in external fitness. If this is right, and if natural selection always favors more fit systems over less fit ones, then natural selection will prefer G_2 to G_1 despite G_1's greater reliability in generating truths and avoiding falsehoods.

My thesis is easiest to defend for the case of internal fitness. Here the simple point is that strategies of inference or inquiry that do a good job at generating truths and avoiding falsehoods may be expensive in terms of time, effort, and cognitive hardware. These expenses will have to be taken into account in determining the overall fitness of a genetically coded inferential system. If the costs are very high, and if there is an alternative available that does a less good, but still acceptable, job of generating truths, then natural selection may prefer it. Sober makes this point with the nice analogy between selecting an inferential system and selecting the services of a detective. If you need information of a certain sort, you might be led to hire a detective. The more money you pay him, the more he will discover. But typically there will come a point when the added information is not worth the extra expense. There is, as an economist might put it, a declining marginal utility for information, just as there is for most commodities. The upshot of these reflections is that natural selection might well select a less reliable inferential system over a more reliable one because the less reliable one has a higher level of internal fitness. What I must now argue is that a more reliable inferential system may trail a less reliable one in external fitness as well.

To begin, we should note that there are two very different ways in which an inferential system may get the wrong answer. One way is to infer that p is the case when p is not the case. Following standard practice, I will call these mistakes *false positives*. The other way is to infer that p is not the case when in fact p is the case. These are the *false negatives*. The next point to note is that there are many quite ordinary circumstances in which one sort of inferential error may be relatively unimportant to the organism's fitness, while the other sort may be enormously detrimental. Consider, for example, the question of whether a certain type of food is poisonous. For an omnivore living in a gastronomically heterogeneous environment, a false positive on such a question would be relatively cheap. If the organism comes to believe that something is poisonous when it is not, it will avoid that food unnecessarily. This may have a small negative impact on its chances of survival and successful reproduction. False negatives, on the other hand, are much more costly in such situations. If the organism comes to believe that a given kind of food is not poisonous when it is, it will not avoid the food and will run a substantial risk of illness or death. Confronted with such a situation, an inferential strategy that might bring with it a very high level of external fitness would be a highly risk-aversive one that inferred a kind of food to be poisonous on relatively weak evidence. Such a strategy would generate a substantial number of false positives, since the organism would leap to the conclusion that the food in question was poisonous on the basis of weak and inconclusive evidence. But this doesn't matter too much, since false positives in this situation are cheap. By being very quick to conclude that the food in question is poisonous, the strategy would largely avoid false negatives. And that is important, since false negatives are deadly.

To complete the argument, it remains to note that a very cautious, risk-aversive inferential strategy—one that leaps to the conclusion that danger is present on very slight evidence—will typically lead to false beliefs more often, and true ones less often, than a less hair-trigger one that waits for more evidence before rendering a judgment. Nonetheless, the unreliable, error-prone, risk-aversive strategy may well be favored by natural selection. For natural selection does not care about truth; it cares only about reproductive success. And from the point of view of reproductive success, it is often better to be safe (and wrong) than sorry. What we have shown then is that one inferential system may have a higher level of external fitness than another even though the latter, less fit system makes fewer mistakes and gets the right answer more often.

It might be objected that in the situation we are imagining, the optimal solution would be an inferential system that always got the right answer. And indeed, if such an option were available and imposed no great internal costs, it might well be the one preferred by natural selection. But to suppose that such a system is available is to carry evolutionary Panglossianism to absurdity. There typically will be no infallible danger-detecting strategies. And even if there are, they are not likely to remain infallible for long, since predators, pathogens, and parasites are forever in the business of evolving new ways of deceiving the danger-detecting strategies that are available. Since danger detection is always imperfect, the sorts of trade-offs we have been considering between overall-reliability and reliability-when-it-counts-most will often be live options. The argument developed in 3.1.2, linking good (i.e., fitness-enhancing) design with rationality, must assume that overall reliability always wins these contests. That argument comes unraveled when we recognize that overall reliability can easily come in second.

3.3 Evolution and Optimal Design

An essential component in both arguments sketched in 3.1, aimed at showing that evolution will insure rationality, is the claim that evolution produces close approximations to optimally well-designed systems. In 3.1.1, I tried to put together the most plausible argument I could for that claim. In outline, the argument ran roughly like this:

(1) Evolution is caused by natural selection.
(2) Natural selection will choose the best-designed (i.e., that most fitness-enhancing) system available in the gene pool.
(3) Over evolutionary time, a huge and varied set of options will be available for natural selection to choose among, and this set is very likely to include one or more that closely approximate a theoretical optimum.
Therefore,
(4) Systems produced by evolution can be expected to be about as well designed as it is possible to be.

It is my contention that this argument is quite hopeless, since each of the assumptions I have numbered (1)–(3) is either very dubious or known to be false. Moreover, the further assumption needed if this argument is to bear on our own inferential system, namely

(5) Our inferential system was produced by evolution.

is also open to serious question when it is interpreted as it must be for the argument to work.

3.3.1 The Varied Causes of Evolution
In *The Nature of Selection*, Sober notes that contemporary biologists tend to identify the occurrence of evolution in a population with changes in gene frequency in that population.[11] Significant changes in gene frequency lead to the sort of modifications that we commonly associate with evolution. If we adopt this view, then the question "What causes evolution?" becomes "What causes changes in gene frequency in populations?" And the answer to this question is, many different things. Natural selection is only one of the processes that

leads to evolution. Other processes that can lead to changes in gene frequency include mutation (and differential rates of mutation), migration, and random genetic drift.

Among these, perhaps the best studied is random drift, a process that may result in a gene going to fixation in a population, while all of its competing alleles disappear. Random drift is a particularly potent source of evolutionary changes in small populations where random events have a better chance of eliminating all the copies of a given gene. If, as argued by a number of contemporary evolutionary biologists, rapid evolutionary change is often associated with small populations, then it may turn out that drift is a major force in evolution.[12] For our purposes, genetic drift is a particularly important alternative cause of evolution, since drift can lead to the elimination of a more fit gene and the fixation of a less fit one. To get an intuitive feel for this fact, we need only imagine a small, isolated population in which a mutation appears that gives the organisms carrying it a better chance of catching their prey than conspecifics that don't carry the gene. Now imagine that while this gene is still relatively rare in the population, a storm kills all the organisms carrying it. The result will be a population that is less well designed for catching prey than it might have been, had random drift not been a factor in evolution. It might be thought that this would only be a temporary setback, since in the long run the superior gene would appear by mutation again and again, and sooner or later it would succeed in establishing itself. However, as Kitcher argues, this happy result cannot be relied upon.

> Typically the fixation of an allele at one locus will affect the fitness of mutants that arise at other loci. If these mutants arise and become prevalent before the unlucky allele receives its second chance, then the new opportunity may come too late. In the altered genetic environment the previously optimal allele may no longer be superior. The originally less fit allele that displaced it may have armed itself with alleles at other loci, so that the invasion of the unlucky allele is now resisted by selection.[13]

3.3.2 Natural Selection's Limited Options

Even if we ignore the effects of processes other than natural selection, we cannot conclude that evolution will result in systems that are optimally designed (or nearly so) unless we assume that mutations coding for optimal or near optimal design will generally be available. But, as many authors have noted, this is a singularly implausible assumption.[14] It is relatively easy to look at currently existing organisms with the eye of an engineer and generate lots of suggestions for improvements that Mother Nature has never even explored. Modern technology builds prosthetic limbs out of space age alloys and communications systems that transmit messages with the speed of light. It seems very likely indeed that certain organisms would have a real competitive edge if they were born with such limbs, or with nerves that conduct impulses at the speed of light. The fact that there are no such creatures surely does not indicate that the imagined changes would not enhance fitness. Rather, we can be pretty confident natural selection never had the chance to evaluate organisms that utilize such materials.

For a more biologically realistic illustration of the point that natural selection doesn't always have a go at the best option, we need only consider the widespread phenomenon of pleiotropy, in which one gene affects two or more distinct traits or systems. It will sometimes be the case that a gene has positive effects on one system and negative effects on another. In such cases the optimal situation would presumably be to keep the positive and avoid the negative—either by replacing the gene with one which did not have the negative effects or by introducing a second gene that suppresses the harmful effects of the first. There are, however, lots of cases in which this sort of pleiotropic linking of a positive and a negative trait persists in nature. And it is plausible to suppose that in most of these cases there has never been a suitable mutation or suppressor gene available on which natural selection could act. The genes of albinism in arctic animals provide a nice example. The white coats these genes produce are obviously adaptive. However, the same genes typically produce serious eye problems, and albino animals generally can't see as well as their colored conspecifics. The optimal genes would provide albinism without bad eyes. But apparently this has never been an option which natural selection might choose.[15]

Another phenomenon that can lead to the persistence of less-than-optimal organisms in a population despite the operation of natural selection is heterozygote superiority. Here the most fit phenotype is produced by a genotype having different alleles at a given locus. When this is the case, natural selection cannot eliminate the less fit homozygous phenotypes from the population, since half the offspring of the optimal heterozygotes will be suboptimal homozygotes. From a gene's point of view, there is an obvious improvement on this situation—namely, a mutation that produced the optimal phenotype in both heterozygous and homozygous forms. This is easier said than done, however. There is no guarantee that the optimal mutant will ever appear. The best-known example in this area is the gene that leads to sickle-cell disease in humans. People who are homozygous for this gene suffer from a severe anemia that is usually fatal in childhood, while heterozygous individuals generally have no symptoms. However, on the positive side, heterozygotes have a significant level of resistance to malaria. Why hasn't a mutant that affords protection against malaria but does not cause anemia in homozygotes spread through the affected population? The most likely answer is that there has never been one available.[16]

3.3.3 Will Natural Selection Choose the Best-Designed System?

Suppose we ignore the effects of other processes that interact with natural selection in determining the dynamics of gene frequencies in a population. And suppose, also, that we could be sure that genes producing an optimal phenotype will be available in the population. Could we then conclude that this phenotype would spread throughout the population? Philosophers, and not a few biologists, sometimes assume that the answer is yes. But this is simply mistaken. Perhaps the most obvious place to see this point is in the sort of balanced polymorphism just discussed, in which the optimal phenotype is the result of a heterozygous genotype. Another fascinating illustration is provided by the phenomenon of meiotic drive.

In normal meiosis—the process that produces sperm and eggs— half of the gametes produced by heterozygous individuals will contain one allele, and half will contain the other. However, certain genes have the capacity to "cheat" in meiosis and end up significantly overrepresented in the sperm or eggs. This cheating is accomplished by various mechanisms. The best understood case is the SD (*segregation distorter*) allele in the fruitfly, *Drosophila melanogaster*. In the process of sperm maturation, this "killer" allele causes the homologous chromosome to produce dysfunctional sperm. Obviously, such a gene will spread quickly through a population, even if the phenotypic effects of the gene are harmful. And in a number of cases it is known that the cheating genes do produce harmful effects. In house mice, for example, there is a cheating gene that produces tail abnormalities and is highly damaging or lethal in homozygous mice. There has been some speculation that serious human diseases, like cystic fibrosis, are maintained in the population by meiotic drive. It has also been suggested that meiotic drive may have driven some species to extinction. Obviously it is not always the case that natural selection leads to well-designed systems.[17]

As Philip Kitcher has emphasized, there is yet another, and deeper, problem with the idea that natural selection will lead to the fixation of the fittest phenotype. For even when meiotic drive is not a factor, and the best available phenotype is the result of a homozygous genotype, there is still no guarantee that natural selection will spread that phenotype throughout the population. Indeed, it can even happen that natural selection will result in an optimally fit homozygous phenotype disappearing from the population. To illustrate the point, Kitcher, following Alan Templeton, offers this example.

> Suppose that we have a population in which three alleles, A, S, and C, are all initially present. AA is found in virtually every member of the population, and the following conditions hold:
>
> AS is fitter than AA;
> SS is lethal;
> C is recessive to A (that is, AC and AA have the same phenotype and, in consequence, the same fitness);
> CS is inferior in fitness to AA;
> CC is the fittest allelic pair.
>
> What will happen to the population? Answer: C is eliminated; thus the fittest combination, CC, although initially present in the population, not only fails to become fixed but indeed is driven out. . . . Because of the initial preponderance of A alleles, S alleles occur most frequently in AS combinations, and C alleles turn up in AC combinations, which, because C is recessive, display the AA phenotype. The population thus moves toward a balanced polymorphism between A and S, with a few C alleles still present. Once the polymorphism is reached, selection then works to drive out the rare C alleles. This is because the average effect of incorporating a C allele into a zygote is negative: C alleles do no good when they occur in the AC combination, and they are inferior when they turn up in the company of S. So, despite the fact that CC is the best available genotype, natural selection works to displace C from the population.[18]

3.3.4 Are Inferential Strategies the Result of Evolution?
What has been argued so far in this section is that it is simply not the case that evolution inevitably produces close approximations to optimally well-designed systems. What I want to argue now is that, even if it were the case that natural selection is a flawless optimizer and that it is the only cause of biological evolution, it would still not follow that our system of inferential strategies is optimally well designed. That conclusion requires the added assumption that evolutionary factors are the only ones that have shaped our current inferential strategies. And the truth of this assumption is very far from obvious. To say this is not, of course, to doubt that natural selection has played a

very significant role in shaping current inferential strategies. But that is not enough to argue on evolutionary grounds that our current strategies are optimal or near optimal. For if factors largely independent of biological evolution also played an important role in the process leading to our current inferential system (or to the current distribution of systems, if there are more than one), then the prevailing situation may be nonoptimal even if evolution is an inveterate optimizer. To argue from evolution to the optimal or near optimal design of our inferential system, it must be shown that biological evolution was the only major factor involved; and as we shall see, that is a very tall order indeed.

If natural selection is to shape a characteristic, two conditions must obtain. First, the population must exhibit some variation in that characteristic of a sort that affects the reproductive success of organisms in a systematic way. Second, the variance must be under genetic control either directly or indirectly. However, in many cases, only part of the variance with respect to a characteristic will be genetically based. In these situations, natural selection may be simply incapable of spreading the optimal characteristic throughout the population. Moreover, the distribution of such a characteristic in a population can change in striking ways that are quite independent of its contribution to reproductive success. To see all this a bit more clearly, it will be helpful to consider a pair of examples.

Among contemporary humans there is considerable variation in preference for clothing styles. On my campus, some people prefer the Ivy League look, some prefer California casual, and some prefer other styles. There is even a small minority who prefer to wear nothing at all. It would not be surprising to find that a person's preferences in this area have some impact on his or her chances of survival and reproductive success. Nor would it be surprising to find that at least part of the variance in clothing styles can be explained genetically. However, it is obvious that a great deal of the variance is nongenetic. (I once had a pair of students who were identical twins but were easy to tell apart; one preferred the Ivy League look, the other preferred punk.) Since so much of the variance in clothing preference is due to nongenetic factors, it would be quite absurd to expect that the most fitness-enhancing of current clothing preferences will ultimately spread throughout the population. A much more likely prediction is that the best style (whatever it may be) and the preference for it will follow togas and morning coats into near extinction.

Language provides a second example, and one that may be more interestingly analogous to reasoning. There is a great diversity among contemporary humans with respect to the language(s) they speak and understand. But there is little reason to think that any of this variation is genetically based. Had I been born elsewhere, I would now have the ability to speak Lapp or Korean rather than English. It is not obvious whether the capacity to speak some languages is more fitness enhancing than the capacity to speak others. But however this may be, it is clear that the processes via which the capacity to speak some languages spreads and the capacity to speak others declines or disappears are almost entirely independent of biological evolution. Thus, even if one language does accord some fitness advantage over another, there is no reason to expect that the more fitness-enhancing language will drive the less fitness-enhancing one to extinction. The decline of Gaelic and the spread of English in the period from 1600 to 1900 were processes that had little or nothing to do with biological evolution. Moreover, we could well imagine processes having equally little to do with biological evolution leading to a single language being spoken by all humans. It is, alas, all too easy to imagine scenarios in which an Australian aboriginal language, or some other geographically isolated tongue, is the only one left after the next global war.[19]

Now, to see what all of this has to do with the rationality or optimality of our inferential system, the first step is to note that, in light of what little is known on these matters, it is entirely possible that the cognitive mechanisms subserving inference are similar in important ways to the cognitive mechanisms underlying language comprehension. In particular, it may be the case that the strategies of reasoning a person employs, like the language he or she speaks, are determined in large measure by environmental variables and that variations in inferential strategies across persons or societies are largely independent of genetic factors. If inference is analogous to language in this way, then changes in the distribution of inferential strategies in a population may have little or nothing to do with the level of biological fitness that the strategies in question afford. Moreover, even if there is only a single system of inferential strategies in the current human population, we would not be safe to conclude that this system is optimally fitness enhancing. For just as a single language (or a single clothing style) may spread throughout a population as the result of factors that have nothing to do with biological evolution, so too a single inferential system could have become universal for reasons quite independent of how well it does at enhancing fitness. To establish that the current human inferential system (if indeed there is only one) is optimal or near optimal in promoting survival and reproductive success, we would have to know a great deal about how that inferential system came to be the dominant one. Since we have, near enough, no evidence at all on this matter, we cannot conclude that the currently prevailing system of inferential dispositions is optimal or near optimal, even if for argument's sake we grant that there is just one such system, that natural selection is the only cause of biological evolution, and that natural selection is a flawless optimizer.

3.4 Some Conclusions

The analogy between language-processing systems and inferential systems provides a useful backdrop against which a number of points about the potential for pluralism in human cognition emerge with particular clarity. Since this potential diversity will loom large in the chapters to follow, I want to explore the analogy and its implications with some care. But before taking up that theme, I had best sum up where the argument of this chapter has taken us so far.

In 3.1, I reconstructed a pair of arguments that might be offered by those who think that evolutionary considerations underwrite the claim that normal adult humans must be rational. Those arguments are now in shambles. For both of them exploited the claim that evolution could be counted upon to produce systems that were optimally well designed, or close to it. And, as we have seen in 3.3.1, 3.3.2, and 3.3.3, that claim rests on serious misunderstandings about both evolution and natural selection. Both arguments also required the assumption that biological evolution had produced our current inferential system without the intervention of social forces that are largely independent of biology. In 3.3.4, we saw that this assumption is very dubious indeed. The second of the two arguments sketched in 3.1 tried to defend the thesis that well-designed cognitive systems are rational, rather than simply asserting it to be a conceptual truth. But, as we saw in 3.2, that defense is seriously flawed.

The failure of these arguments does not, of course, prove that there are no good arguments from evolution to rationality. What has been shown is that the paths suggested by those who hint there is some argument in the offing are blocked in serious ways, and in more than a few places. Until some quite different argument is put forward, I think we are safe to assume that neither the existence of substantial irrationality nor the prospect of unbounded improvement in cognitive performance is threatened by anything that evolutionary biology has discovered. Neither the psychologist exploring the shortcomings in human reasoning nor the epistemic reformer seeking to improve it need worry about being put out of business by evolutionary biology.

3.5 Innateness, Inference, and the Prospect for Cognitive Pluralism

Let me return now to the analogy between inferential systems and language-processing systems, with an eye toward seeing what it can teach us about the potential for diversity in human cognitive systems. Philosophers sometimes assume that our inferential system must be innate and thus present in all normal humans. Many authors recognize that some sophisticated aspects of a person's inferential system may be learned. But even these authors typically assume that there must be some more basic inferential strategies that are innate, since without some such strategies it would seem impossible to learn the others.[20] However, the analogy with language suggests that this assumption may well be mistaken. All normal humans speak some language or other. But no language is innate. Nor is there any reason to think that any part or fragment of language is innate or universally shared.

About twenty years ago Chomsky and some of his followers did indeed speculate that there might be an innate core shared by all human languages. But this hypothesis has long since been abandoned in favor of the hypothesis that there is a set of "humanly possible languages" to which the language acquisition mechanism is innately restricted. On this latter hypothesis, the acquisition device is built in such a way that it can only output languages in the innately specified set. Though the innately specified, humanly possible languages are a small subset of the logically possible languages, they need not share any common core or any other common features. Moreover, the "small" subset is small only relative to the class of logically possible grammars. In absolute numbers, it will obviously have to be quite large, since we know that there are thousands of different languages actually spoken.[21] The parallel theory for inferential systems would hypothesize a limited set of "humanly possible" inferential systems to which the "inferential-system-acquisition-mechanism" is innately restricted. There need be no common core shared by all systems in that set, and thus there need be no basic inferential strategies that all normal humans share.

It might be thought that this story about inference acquisition still presupposes a basic core of universally shared inference, since the inferential-system-acquisition-mechanism must itself engage in inference. But again the analogy with language shows that this need not be the case. There is no reason to suppose that the language acquisition system reaches its goal by "inferring" anything from "data." The processes it uses to go from the "input" (the child's linguistic experience) to the "output" (an internally represented grammar, on Chomsky's view) need have nothing whatever to do with inference and need be used nowhere else in the child's cognitive economy. Indeed, the view recently urged by Chomsky and his followers posits a system of innately wired "triggers," which enable various features in the experiential input to toggle a series of cognitive switches and thus to locate the correct grammar in a branching tree of possibilities.[22] Similarly, the processes used by an inference-system-acquisition-mechanism to go from its input (presumably some aspect of the child's experience) to its output (an up and running system of inferential strategies, or perhaps a "psycho-logic") need have nothing to do with inference and need be used nowhere else in the child's cognitive economy.

I should stress that the point I am making in this section is a negative one. I do not claim that inferential systems are in fact acquired the way Chomskians maintain that grammars are acquired. Indeed, I think we know next to nothing about the way in which people come to have their inferential systems.[23] What I do claim is that, given what little we know, it might be the case that language acquisition and inferential system acquisition are parallel. If that were true, then it might well turn out that neither our entire inferential system nor any part of it is innate or universally shared among normal humans. The existence of innate inferential strategies is an entirely open, empirical question, as is the extent to which a person's inferential strategies are shaped by his or her cultural surroundings.

It will no doubt have already occurred to the reader that, just as it might turn out that no inferential strategies are innate, so too it might turn out that many different ones are innate and that there are marked innate differences from one individual to another. This is a theme that deserves a section of its own.

3.6 Genetic Diversity and Cognitive Diversity

Let me begin with some elementary biology. There are many, many cases of apparently stable populations that manifest considerable diversity at both the genotypic and the phenotypic level. In human populations, for example, there is genetically based diversity in eye color, hair color, blood type, and a host of other characteristics. There are many possible reasons for the persistence of this diversity. In 3.3.3, we saw that heterozygote superiority can generate a balanced, evolutionarily stable polymorphism. In other cases it may be that the stability is actually an illusion engendered by our limited historical information and that one of the genes at a given locus is gradually headed toward fixation while the others are headed toward extinction. In still other cases, and these are the ones of most interest to us here, it may be that the alleles in question, and the phenotypes to which they lead, are equally conducive to reproductive success.

A generalization of this last-mentioned phenomenon that has been of special interest to population biologists arises when the fitness of a given allele is in part determined by the prevalence of competing alleles in the population. Genetically coded behavioral traits provide some of the most interesting cases. Consider a very oversimplified example in which there is a pair of hypothetical alleles in an asexual species, one of which (call it the hawk gene) disposes an organism to fight with a conspecific over a contested piece of food until the organism wins or is injured too severely to fight further. The other allele (the dove gene) disposes the organism to share if ownership of the food is contested and to run away if challenged. If the existing population is all dove, the hawk mutant will have a distinct advantage, and the hawk gene will begin to spread through the population. However, as hawks become more common and as a result increasingly do battle with other hawks, the chance of injury goes up and the fitness advantage of being a hawk goes down. Under certain circumstances, an evolutionarily stable equilibrium will be reached in which hawks and doves coexist in the population at fixed ratios.[24] The moral I want to draw from this case and from some of the other phenomena mentioned earlier should not be particularly controversial: It will often be the case that there is no one optimally fit gene at a given locus, and it will often be the case that there is no one optimally fit phenotypic characteristic. Thus talk of *the* optimal allele or phenotype will often make no sense. Such talk presupposes uniqueness, and uniqueness is often not to be had.

This same conclusion can be reached by an even more obvious route when we attend to populations in different environments. For even when there is a unique, optimally fit allele and phenotype in a given environment, it will often be the case that some other allele and some other phenotype do better in some other environment. Except when tacitly relativized to an environment, it makes no sense to ask which characteristic is most conducive to reproductive success.

None of this, of course, suffices to show that there is much (or, indeed, any) diversity in human cognitive systems. What does follow is the much weaker contention that even if the cognitive strategies humans invoke are largely under genetic control, there *may* be lots of diversity in the population, and for lots of different reasons. The mere fact that your cognitive processes and mine are innate would not establish that they are the same. Moreover, even if we assume that all cognitive systems are innate and that all innate cognitive systems are optimal from the point of view of natural selection, it *still* would not follow that all normal cognitive systems are the same. For, as the hawk-and-dove example illustrates, there can be a variety of quite different genetically coded cognitive or behavioral strategies that tie for first place in the natural selection sweepstakes.

My theme, in these last two sections, has been that nothing we know about genetics, or evolution, or the acquisition of cognitive systems would even begin to show that descriptive cognitive pluralism is false. It is overwhelmingly plausible that some parts of our inferential system are acquired from the surrounding culture, and it is entirely possible that much or all of the system is a cultural inheritance. Moreover, even if there are parts of our cognitive system that are innate, there is no biological or evolutionary reason to think that those parts do not differ markedly from person to person or from culture to culture. It might, I suppose, be protested that I have been belaboring the obvious. And perhaps I have. My justification for doing so is that, as I see it, it is the prospect of cognitive diversity among normal folk that lends a genuine, almost existential, urgency to the project of cognitive evaluation. If there are lots of different ways in which the human mind/brain can go about the business of ordering and reordering its cognitive states, if different people or different cultures can and do go about the business of reasoning in very different ways, *which way should we use*? If primitive tribesmen or premodern scientists or the neighbor down the street or our own distant descendants think in ways that are quite different from the ways we think, few of us would be inclined to say that all of these ways are equally good. Surely some ways of going about the business of forming and revising our cognitive states are better than others. But what is it that makes one system of cognitive processes better than another, and how are we to tell which system is best? Which cognitive processes are the good ones? These are the questions that will be center stage for the remainder of this book.

Chapter 4

Reflective Equilibrium and Analytic Epistemology

The previous two chapters were aimed at opening up a range of possibilities by dismantling the arguments that threatened to foreclose them. One of these possibilities is that there is considerable diversity in human reasoning, diversity that may derive from biological differences, cultural differences, or individual differences in various combinations. A second possibility is that amid this diversity there may be individuals, traditions, or cultures that do a bad job at the business of cognition and that we ourselves may be doing much less well than we might. There is no guarantee, either conceptual or biological, that our own reasoning is good reasoning, or even a close approximation. Thus neither the empirical investigators who are concerned to characterize cognitive shortcomings nor the epistemic reformers who hope to improve cognitive performance need worry that they have embarked on an impossible project.

Oddly, though the debates in the last two chapters were concerned with the possibility of departures from normative standards for cognition, there was little discussion of what those standards are, nor of how the standards themselves might be discovered or defended. These are the issues that motivate the current chapter and the two that follow. In this chapter I'll begin, in 4.1, by setting out a particularly influential account of how normative principles of cognition are to be discovered and defended. The account is due to Nelson Goodman, and, as I will interpret it, it proposes to ground an account of the justification of cognitive norms in an *analysis* or *explication* of the commonsense notion of justified inference. Goodman's account has been put to many uses. One of the more intriguing of these is an argument developed by L. Jonathan Cohen, which aims to show—yet again!—that systematically irrational cognition is impossible. In 4.2, I will sketch Cohen's ingenious argument.

Cohen's argument, however, is only as good as Goodman's account of the justification of normative standards of cognition, and in 4.3, I'll offer some reasons for thinking that neither Goodman's account nor various variations on Goodman's theme have succeeded in capturing anything very close to the commonsense notion of justification. If this is right, then Cohen's argument collapses. Still, it might be thought that while available variations on Goodman's theme fall short of the mark, there must be some suitable explication of the commonsense notion of justification, and that if we were to find it, we would have an acceptable account of what the justification of cognitive processes comes to. This hope gives rise to what I'll call the "neo-Goodmanian project" whose aim is to add some further bells and whistles to Goodman's explication. The appeals of that project—and they are considerable—will be advertised in 4.4. Yet despite its attractions, I think the neo-Goodmanian project should be rejected. Some of the reasons for this conclusion focus on the empirical feasibility of providing the sort of explication that the neo-Goodmanian seeks; these reasons are set out in 4.5. But there is a more basic reason for rejecting the neo-Goodmanian project. For, as I shall argue in 4.6, even if it were empirically feasible, most people will find the sort of analysis or explication that the neo-Goodmanian seeks to be completely useless in deciding whether and how their own cognitive processes, or those of others, might be improved. If the arguments in 4.6 are persuasive, they will threaten much more than Goodman's project. For, as I will try to show, a great deal of epistemological theorizing during the last four decades has shared the Goodmanian assumption that cognitive assessment can be grounded in the analysis or explication of our ordinary evaluative concepts. If this assumption is mistaken, then the entire analytic tradition in epistemology will be undermined.

4.1 *Reflective Equilibrium as a Criterion for Assessing Cognitive Processes*

What is it that makes one system of cognitive processes better than another, and how are we to tell which system or systems are best? The answer I want to explore, and ultimately to reject, was first suggested about three decades ago when, in one of the more influential passages of twentieth-century philosophy, Goodman described a process of bringing judgments about particular inferences and about general principles of inference into accord with one another. In the accord thus achieved, Goodman maintained, lay all the justification needed, and all the justification possible, for the inferential principles that emerged. Other writers, most notably John Rawls, have adopted a modified version of Goodman's process as a procedure for justifying moral principles and moral judgments. To Rawls, too, we owe the term 'reflective equilibrium', which has been widely used to characterize a system of principles and judgments that have been brought into coherence with one another in the way that Goodman describes.[1]

It is hard to imagine the notion of reflective equilibrium explained more eloquently than Goodman himself explains it. So let me begin by quoting what he says at some length.

> How do we justify a *de*duction? Plainly by showing that it conforms to the general rules of deductive inference. An argument that so conforms is justified or valid, even if its conclusion happens to be false. An argument that violates a rule is fallacious even if its conclusion happens to be true. . . . Analogously, the basic task in justifying an inductive inference is to show that it conforms to the general rules of *in*duction. . . .
>
> Yet, of course, the rules themselves must eventually be justified. The validity of a deduction depends not upon conformity to any purely arbitrary rules we may contrive, but upon conformity to valid rules. When we speak of *the* rules of inference we mean the valid rules—or better, *some* valid rules, since there may be alternative sets of equally valid rules. But how is the validity of rules to be determined? Here . . . we encounter philosophers who insist that these rules follow from some self-evident axiom, and others who try to show that the rules are grounded in the very nature of the human mind. I think the answer lies much nearer the surface. Principles of deductive inference are justified by their conformity with accepted deductive practice. Their validity depends upon accordance with the particular deductive inferences we actually make and sanction. If a rule yields inacceptable inferences, we drop it as invalid. Justification of general rules thus derives from judgments rejecting or accepting particular deductive inferences.
>
> This looks flagrantly circular. I have said that deductive inferences are justified by their conformity to valid general rules, and that general rules are justified by their conformity to valid inferences. But this circle is a virtuous one. The point is that rules and particular inferences alike are justified by being brought into agreement with each other. *A rule is amended if it yields an inference we are unwilling to accept; an inference is rejected if it violates a rule we are unwilling to amend.* The process of justification is the delicate one of making mutual adjustments between rules and accepted inferences; and in the agreement achieved lies the only justification needed for either.

>All this applies equally well to induction. An inductive infer-
>ence, too, is justified by conformity to general rules, and a general
>rule by conformity to accepted inductive inferences.[2]

There are three points in this passage that demand a bit of interpretation. First, Goodman claims to be explaining what justifies deductive
and inductive inferences. However, it is not clear that, as he uses the
term, *inference* is a cognitive process. It is possible to read Goodman
as offering an account of the justification of rules of logic that are
intended to assess the steps in logical derivations. Read in this way,
Goodman's account of justification would be of no help in the assessment of cognitive processes unless it was supplemented with a suitable
theory about the relation between logic and good reasoning. But as
several authors have lately noted, that relation is much less obvious
than one might suppose.[3] It is also possible to read Goodman as
offering an account of the justification of rules that assess cognitive
processes and thus speaking directly to the question of how we should
go about the business of reasoning. This is the reading required for
Cohen's argument, as set out in 4.2, and it is the reading I propose to
adopt.

A second point that needs some elaboration is just what status
Goodman would claim for the reflective equilibrium test he describes.
It is clear Goodman thinks we can conclude that a system of inferential
rules is justified if it passes the reflective equilibrium test. But it is not
clear *why* he thinks we can conclude this. Two different sorts of answers are possible. According to one answer, the reflective equilibrium
test is *constitutive* of justification or validity. For a system of inferential
rules to be justified just *is* for them to be in reflective equilibrium.
Another sort of answer is that if a set of inferential principles passes
the reflective equilibrium test, this counts as good *evidence* for their
being valid or justified. But, on this second view, being in reflective
equilibrium and being justified are quite different. One is not to be
identified with the other. I am inclined to think that it is the former,
constitutive view that best captures Goodman's intentions. But since
my concern is to criticize a view, not an author, I don't propose to
argue the point. Rather, I will simply stipulate that the constitutive
reading is the one I'm stalking.[4]

The third point of interpretation concerns the status of the claim
that reflective equilibrium is constitutive of justification. On this point,
there are at least three views worth mentioning. The first is that the
claim is a *conceptual truth*—that it follows from the meaning of 'justification' or from the analysis of the concept of justification. Like other
conceptual truths, it is both necessarily true and knowable a priori. If

we adopt this view, the status of the claim that reflective equilibrium is constitutive of justification would be akin to the status of the claim that being a closed, three-sided plane figure is constitutive of being a triangle, though the claim about justification is, of course, a much less obvious conceptual truth. A second view is that the claim is a nonconceptual necessary truth that is knowable only a posteriori. This would accord it much the same status that some philosophers accord to the claim that water is H_2O.[5] Finally, it might be urged that the claim is being offered as a stipulative proposal. It is not telling us what our preexisting concept of justification amounts to, nor what is essential to the referent of that concept. Rather, in a revisionary spirit, it is proposing a new notion of justification. Actually, the divide between the first and the last of these alternatives is not all that sharp. For one might start with an analysis of our ordinary notion and go on to propose modifications in an effort to tidy up the notion a bit here and there. As the changes proposed get bigger and bigger, this sort of explication gradually shades into pure stipulation. So long as the changes an explication urges in a preexisting concept are motivated by considerations of simplicity and don't result in any radical departures from the ordinary concept, I'll count it as a kind of conceptual analysis. I think a good case can be made that Goodman took himself to be providing just such a conservative explication.[6] But again, since it is a view rather than an author that I hope to refute, I will simply stipulate that the conceptual analysis or conservative explication interpretation is the one to be adopted here.

As I propose to read him, then, Goodman is proposing an explication of our ordinary notion of a justified inference: to be justified is to be sanctioned by a set of inferential rules that pass the reflective equilibrium test. The first complaint I will press against Goodman's view is that it does not succeed in capturing anything close to our commonsense notion of justification. But before elaborating on this theme, I want to sketch Cohen's argument for the impossibility of irrationality. Cohen follows Goodman in accepting reflective equilibrium as a test for justification. So, for argument's sake, let us assume for a while that Goodman's explication is correct.

4.2 Cohen's Argument

Central to Cohen's argument is the idea of an underlying mental or psychological *competence*, a notion which has played a large role in recent linguistics. Theories that invoke the notion of competence attempt to explain actual behavior in a given domain (or to explain "performance" as the jargon would have it) by viewing it as resulting from the activities of a number of separate, though interacting, underlying mental systems. One of these systems, the one that is identified with the subject's competence in the relevant domain, stores a rich body of information (or "tacit knowledge") about the domain. The other systems are brought into play when this knowledge is used to accomplish some cognitive task.

For example, in the case of language, speakers can be prompted to make a wide range of "intuitive" judgments about various grammatical properties and relations of sentences and their parts. English speakers, when questioned, will judge that

Tom went to the store.

is grammatical and that

Tom the store to went.

is not; they will judge that

Mary hugged Alice.

and

Alice was hugged by Mary.

are related as active and passive; and they will make similar sorts of judgments about an enormous number of sentences. These judgments (or "linguistic intuitions," as they are often called) count as part of their linguistic performance. To explain this performance, it is hypothesized that speakers have a mentally represented grammar—a complex system of rules that specifies the grammatical properties and relations of all the sentences in the speaker's language. It is further hypothesized that when a speaker makes judgments about sentences, the internalized grammar interacts with the perceptual system, the attention system, the motivation system, a short-term memory buffer, and perhaps other cognitive systems as well.

On certain occasions one or another of the systems with which the internalized grammar interacts may be responsible for the speaker reporting a judgment that does not reflect the information encoded in the grammar. For example, the sentence the speaker is being asked to judge may be so long or multiply embedded that it overtaxes the resources of the short-term memory buffer. On another occasion, a mistake may be caused by the speaker's attention being momentarily diverted from the task at hand. These cases are often called *performance errors* as a way of indicating that the judgments the speakers are reporting do not correctly reflect their own underlying grammatical competence.

In linguistics, a common method for attempting to discover a speaker's underlying competence is to study the judgments the speaker makes about the grammatical properties and relations of a large and varied sample of sentences. To a first approximation, the goal is to construct a set of generative rules that will entail the same judgments about sentences that the speaker actually makes. However, since performance errors are possible, not all of the speaker's judgments will accurately reflect his or her underlying competence. Thus, in constructing the grammar for a speaker's language, the linguist must engage in a bit of judicious idealization. The grammar will be allowed to depart from the data of linguistic intuition in those cases where the theorist suspects that memory limitations, failure of attention, or other performance factors may be implicated. And occasionally the theorist will ignore a speaker's judgment simply because the judgment is incompatible with a rule that is particularly well confirmed or well entrenched, even though the theorist may have no idea why competence and performance are diverging in this particular case. All of this might be summarized in a way that should sound more than a bit familiar: *A grammatical rule is amended if it entails an intuition speakers are unwilling to accept; an intuition is rejected if it violates a rule we are unwilling to amend. The process of discovering the rules of a grammar is the delicate one of making mutual adjustments between rules and intuitions.*

The parallel between the process of discovering the rules that constitute an underlying competence and Goodman's account of justifying rules of inference plays a central role in Cohen's argument. But to make the argument work, we must add one final ingredient: the notion of *cognitive* or *inferential competence.* The basic idea is that in reasoning, as in grammar, we may try to explain performance by positing an underlying competence that interacts with other systems. In this case the underlying competence would consist of rules of inference rather than grammatical rules. They might be thought of as the subject's "psycho-logic"—the internalized rules that guide the subject's reasoning and his intuitive judgments about reasoning.[7] To discover the rules constituting a given subject's inferential competence, we would proceed just as we would in grammar. We would collect data on the subject's intuitions about the acceptability or unacceptability of a large and varied class of inferences and try to construct a system of inferential rules that captures those intuitions. Since performance errors are possible, the theorist will not insist that the psycho-logic match the subject's intuitions perfectly but will instead engage in a bit of judicious idealization. In general, a rule will be accepted if it accords with the inferences the subject actually makes and sanctions. But occasionally a subject's judgment may be rejected if it violates a particularly useful or well-confirmed rule—"a rule we are unwilling to amend."

We now have all the pieces of Cohen's argument in place. According to Cohen, it is impossible for a person's inferential competence, his underlying psycho-logic, to be anything other than normatively impeccable. For the subject's inferential competence is the set of inferential rules we get by collecting his intuitions about particular inferences and building an idealized theory to capture them. But to discover the *correct* or *justified* set of inferential rules—the rules that are in reflective equilibrium for the subject—we would proceed in exactly the same way. Thus, the rules that constitute the subject's cognitive or inferential competence will be identical to those that pass the reflective equilibrium test.

> [W]here you accept that a normative theory has to be based ultimately on the data of human intuition, you are committed to the acceptance of human rationality as a matter of fact in that area, in the sense that it must be correct to ascribe to normal human beings a cognitive competence—however often faulted in performance—that corresponds point by point with the normative theory.[8]

It is important to realize that Cohen's view does not entail that people never reason badly or that they never judge a bad inference to be a good one. Cohen readily acknowledges that people make inferential errors of many sorts under many circumstances. But he insists that these errors are performance errors, reflecting nothing about the reasoner's underlying, normatively unimpeachable competence. If Cohen is right, then the prospects for both the psychologist concerned to study inferential shortcomings and the epistemic reformer concerned to remedy them are much more limited than they might have thought. The psychologist can study performance errors, and the reformer can explore ways of avoiding them. But neither need worry about the internally represented system of inferential rules that lies at the heart of the reasoning process. For these could not possibly be defective.

Of course, all of this follows only if the normative story that Goodman and Cohen tell is the right one—only if we do "accept that a normative theory has to be based ultimately on the data of human intuition," and based on those data in something like the way Goodman describes. In the section to follow, I'll argue that Cohen's Goodmanian account of what it is for an inference to be justified or rational is very wide of the mark. If I'm right, then Cohen's argument for the inevitable rationality of our psycho-logic or cognitive competence will come unglued.

4.3 Does the Reflective Equilibrium Account Capture Our Notion of Justification?

Goodman, as I propose to read him, offers the reflective equilibrium test as an account of what our concept of justified inference comes to.[9] How can we determine whether his analysis is correct? One obvious strategy is to ask just what systems of inferential rules result from the process of mutual adjustment that Goodman advocates. If the inferential systems generated by the reflective equilibrium process strike us as systems that a rational person ought to invoke, this will count in favor of Goodman's analysis. If, on the other hand, the reflective equilibrium process generates what we take to be irrational or unjustified inferential rules or practices, this will cast doubt on Goodman's claim to have captured our concept of justification. Since we are viewing conceptual explication as a kind of analysis, we should not insist that Goodman's account coincide perfectly with our intuitive judgments. But if there are lots of cases in which Goodman's account entails that a system of inferential rules is justified and intuition decrees that it is not, this is a symptom that Goodman's explication is in serious trouble.

In a paper published some years ago, Nisbett and I exploited the strategy just described to argue that the reflective equilibrium account does not capture anything much like our ordinary notion of justification.[10] On the basis of both controlled studies and anecdotal evidence, we argued that patently unacceptable rules of inference would pass the reflective equilibrium test for many people. For example, it appears likely that many people infer in accordance with some version of the gambler's fallacy when dealing with games of chance. These people infer that the likelihood of throwing a seven in a game of craps increases each time a nonseven is thrown. What is more, there is every reason to think that the principle underlying their inference is in reflective equilibrium for them. When the principle is articulated and the subjects have had a chance to reflect upon it and upon their own inferential practice, they accept both. Indeed, one can even find some nineteenth-century logic texts in which versions of the gambler's fallacy are explicitly endorsed. (In a delightful irony, one of these books was written by a man who held the same chair Goodman held when he wrote *Fact, Fiction, and Forecast.*[11]) Moreover, as we saw in 1.2.1, this example is only the tip of the iceberg. It has been shown that many people systematically ignore the importance of base rates in their probabilistic reasoning, that many find the principle of regression to the mean to be highly counterintuitive, that many judge the probability of certain sequences of events to be higher than the probability of components in the sequence, and so forth. In each of these cases, and in many more that might be cited, it is very likely that, for some people at least, the principles that capture their inferential practice would pass the reflective equilibrium test. If this is right, it indicates there is something very wrong with the Goodmanian analysis of justification. For on that analysis, to be justified *is* to pass the reflective equilibrium test. But few of us are prepared to say that if the gambler's fallacy is in reflective equilibrium for a person, then his inferences that accord with that principle are justified.

Now of course each example of an infelicitous inferential principle that allegedly would pass the reflective equilibrium test is open to challenge. Whether or not the dubious principles that appear to guide many people's inferential practice would stand up to the reflective scrutiny Goodman's test demands is an empirical question. And for any given rule, a Goodmanian might protest that the empirical case has just not been made adequately. I am inclined to think that the Goodmanian who builds his defenses here is bound to be routed by a growing onslaught of empirical findings. But the issue need not turn on whether this empirical hunch is correct. For even the *possibility* that the facts will turn out as I suspect they will poses a serious problem for the Goodmanian story. It is surely not an a priori fact that strange inferential principles will always fail the reflective equilibrium test for all subjects. And if it is granted, as clearly it must be, that the gambler's fallacy (or any of the other inferential oddities that have attracted the attention of psychologists in recent years) could possibly pass the reflective equilibrium test for some group of subjects, this is enough to cast doubt on the view that reflective equilibrium is constitutive of justification as that notion is ordinarily used. For surely we are not at all inclined to say that a person is justified in using any inferential principle—no matter how bizarre it may be—simply because it accords with his reflective inferential practice.

Faced with this argument, the friends of reflective equilibrium may offer a variety of responses. The one I have the hardest time understanding is simply to dig in one's heels and insist that if the gambler's fallacy (or some other curious principle) is in reflective equilibrium for a given person or group, then that principle is indeed justified for them. Although I have heard people advocate this line in conversation, I know of no one who has been bold enough to urge the view in print.[12] Since no one else seems willing to take the view seriously, I won't either.

A very different sort of response is to urge that the notion of reflective equilibrium is itself in need of patching—that some bells and whistles must be added to the justificatory process Goodman describes. One idea along these lines is to shift from narrow Goodmanian reflective equilibrium to some analog of Rawls's "wide reflective equilibrium".[13] Roughly, the idea here is to broaden the scope of the intuitions and principles that are to be brought into coherence with one another. Instead of attending only to our intuitions about inferences, wide reflective equilibrium also requires our system of inferential rules to cohere with our semantic or epistemological or metaphysical or psychological views. Just how various philosophical or psychological convictions are supposed to constrain a person's inferential principles and practice has not been spelled out in much detail, though Norman Daniels, whose papers on wide reflective equilibrium are among the best around, gives us a hint when he suggests, by way of example, that Dummett's views on logic are constrained by his semantic views.[14] It would also be plausible to suppose that the classical intuitionists in logic rejected certain inferential principles on epistemological grounds.

A rather different way of attempting to preserve a reflective equilibrium account of justification is to restrict the class of *people* whose reflective equilibrium is to count in assessing the justification of inferential principles. For example, Nisbett and I proposed that in saying an inferential principle is justified, what we are saying is that it would pass the (narrow) reflective equilibrium test for those people whom we regard as experts in the relevant inferential domain.[15]

A dubious virtue of both the wide reflective equilibrium and the expert reflective equilibrium accounts is that they make clear-cut counterexamples harder to generate. That is, they make it harder to produce actual examples of inferential rules which the analysis counts as justified and we do not. In the case of wide reflective equilibrium, counterexamples are hard to come by just because it is so hard to show that anything is in wide reflective equilibrium for anyone. ("Would she really continue to accept that rule if she thought through her epistemological and metaphysical views and reached some stable equilibrium position?" Well, God knows.) In the case of the expert reflective equilibrium account, the dubious but reflectively self-endorsed inferential practice of the experimental subject or the Las Vegas sucker just don't count as counterexamples, since these people don't count as experts.

But though clear-cut cases involving actual people may be harder to find, each of these elaborations of the reflective equilibrium story falls victim to the argument from possible cases offered earlier. Consider wide reflective equilibrium first. No matter how the details of the wide reflective equilibrium test are spelled out, it is surely not going to turn out to be impossible for a person to reach wide reflective equilibrium on a set of principles and convictions that includes some quite daffy inferential rule. Indeed, one suspects that by allowing people's philosophical convictions to play a role in filtering their inferential principles, one is inviting such daffy principles, since many people are deeply attached to outlandish philosophical views. The expert reflective equilibrium move fares no better. For unless experts are picked out in a question-begging way (e.g., those people whose inferential practices are in fact justified) it seems entirely possible for the expert community, under the influence of ideology, recreational chemistry, or evil demons, to end up endorsing some quite nutty set of rules.[16]

4.4 A Neo-Goodmanian Project

At this point, if the friend of reflective equilibrium is as impressed by these arguments as I think he should be, he might head off to his study to work on some new bells and whistles—some further variations on the reflective equilibrium theme that will do better at capturing our concept of justification. Despite a string of failures, he might be encouraged to pursue this project by a line of thought that runs something like the following. I'll call it the neo-Goodmanian line.

> It can hardly be denied that we do something to assess whether or not an inferential practice is justified. Our decisions on these matters are certainly not made at random. Moreover, if there is some established procedure that we invoke in assessing justification, then it must surely be possible to describe this procedure. When we have succeeded at this we will have an account of what it is for an inferential practice to be justified. For, as Goodman has urged, to be justified just is to pass the tests we invoke in assessing an inferential practice. Our procedures for assessing an inferential practice are constitutive of justification. Granted, neither Goodman's narrow reflective equilibrium story nor the more elaborate stories told by others has succeeded in capturing the procedure we actually use in assessing justification. But that just shows we must work harder. The rewards promise to repay our efforts, since once we have succeeded in describing our assessment procedure, we will have taken a giant step forward in epistemology. We will have explained what it is for a cognitive process to be justified. In so doing we will have at least begun to resolve the problem posed by cognitive diversity. For once we have a clear specification of what justification amounts to, we can go on to ask whether our own cognitive processes are justified or whether, perhaps, those of some other culture come closer to the mark.

There is no doubt that this neo-Goodmanian line can be very appealing. I was myself under its sway for some years. However, I am now persuaded that the research program it proposes for epistemology is a thoroughly wrongheaded one. In the remainder of this chapter, I will try to say why. My case against the neo-Goodmanian project divides into two parts. First I shall raise some objections that are targeted more or less specifically on the details of the neo-Goodmanian program. Central to each of these objections is the fact that the neo-Goodmanian is helping himself to a healthy serving of empirical assumptions about the conceptual structures underlying our common-sense judgments of cognitive assessment, and each of these assumptions stands in some serious risk of turning out to be false. If one or more of them is false, then the project loses much of its initial attractiveness. In the following selection, I will set out a brief catalog of these dubious assumptions. The second part of my critique is much more general, and I'll be after much bigger game. What I propose to argue is that for most people, neither the neo-Goodmanian program nor any alternative program that proposes to analyze or explicate our presystematic notions of epistemic evaluation will be of any help at all in deciding whether and how their own cognitive processes or those of others might be improved. But here I am getting ahead of myself. Let me get back to the neo-Goodmanian and his dubious empirical presuppositions.

4.5 Some Questionable Presuppositions of the Neo-Goodmanian Project

Let me begin with a fairly obvious point. The neo-Goodmanian, as I have portrayed him, retains his allegiance to the idea of reflective equilibrium. We last saw him heading back to his study to seek a more adequate elaboration of this notion. But nothing the neo-Goodmanian has said encourages us to expect that reflective equilibrium or anything much like it plays a role in our procedure for assessing the justification of a cognitive process. So even if it is granted that we have good reason to work hard at characterizing our justification-assessing procedure, we may find that the notion of reflective equilibrium is simply a nonstarter. Confronted with this objection, I think the only move open to the neo-Goodmanian is to grant the point and concede that in trying to patch the notion of reflective equilibrium he is simply playing a hunch. Perhaps it will turn out that something like reflective equilibrium plays a central role in our assessments of justification. But until we have an accurate characterization of the assessment process, there can be no guarantees.

Two further assumptions of the neo-Goodmanian program are that we ordinarily invoke only *one* notion of justification for inferential processes and that this is a *coherent* notion for which a set of necessary and sufficient conditions can be given. But once again these are not matters that can be known in advance. It might be that different people mean different things when they call a cognitive process "justified," because there are different notions of justification in circulation. These different meanings might cluster around a central core. But then again, they might not. There are lots of normatively loaded terms that seem to be used in very different ways by different individuals or groups in society. I would not be at all surprised to learn that what I mean by terms like 'morally right' and 'freedom' is very different from what the followers of the Reverand Falwell or the admirers of Colonel Khadafi mean. And I wouldn't be much more surprised if terms of epistemic evaluation turned out to manifest similar interpersonal ambiguities.

Even discounting the possibility of systematic interpersonal differences, it might be that in assessing the justification of a cognitive process we use different procedures on different occasions and that these procedures have different outcomes. Perhaps, for example, our intuitive notion of justification is tied to a number of prototypical exemplars, and in deciding new cases we focus in some context-sensitive way on one or another of these exemplars, making our decision about justification on the basis of how similar the case at hand is to the exemplar on which we are focusing. This is hardly a fanciful idea; recent work on the psychological mechanisms underlying categorization suggests that in *lots* of cases our judgment works in just this way.[17] If it turns out that our judgments about the justification of cognitive processes are prototype or exemplar based, then it will be a mistake to look for a property or characteristic that all justified cognitive processes have. It will not be the case that there is any single test passed by all the cognitive processes we judge to be justified. I am partial to a reading of the later Wittgenstein on which this is just what he would urge about our commonsense notion of justification, and I am inclined to suspect that this Wittgensteinian story is right.[18] But I don't pretend to have enough evidence to make a convincing case. For present purposes it will have to suffice to note that this *might* be how our commonsense concept of justification works. If it is, then the neo-Goodmanian program is in for some rough sledding.

A final difficulty with the neo-Goodmanian program is that it assumes, without any evidence, that the test or procedure we use for assessing the justification of cognitive processes exhausts our concept of inferential justification and thus that we will have characterized the concept when we have described the test. But this is hardly a claim that can be assumed without argument. It might be the case that our procrustean concept of justification is an amalgam composed in part of folk epistemological theory specifying certain properties or characteristics that are essential to justification and in part of a test or cluster of tests that folk wisdom holds to be indicative of those properties. Moreover, the tests proposed might not always (or ever!) be reliable indicators of the properties. I don't have any compelling reason to believe that our commonsense notion of justification will turn out like this. But I wouldn't be much surprised. Though our understanding of the mechanisms underlying commonsense concepts and judgments is still *very* primitive, as I read the literature it points to two important morals. First, the mental representation of concepts is likely to turn out to be a very messy business. Second, it is no easy job to separate commonsense concepts from the folk theories in which they are enmeshed.[19] All of this bodes ill for the neo-Goodmanian who hopes that the analysis or explication of our concept of justification will yield some relatively straightforward elaboration of the reflective equilibrium test.

4.6 Against Analytic Epistemology

The problems posed in the previous section shared a pair of properties. They all turned on empirical assumptions about the nature of our ordinary concept of justification, and they were all targeted fairly specifically at the neo-Goodmanian project.[20] In the current section, I want to set out a very different sort of argument—an argument that, if successful, will undermine not only reflective equilibrium theories but also the whole family of epistemological theories to which they belong.

4.6.1 What Is Analytic Epistemology?
To give some idea of the range of theories that are in the intended scope of my critique, it will be helpful to sketch a bit of the framework for epistemological theorizing suggested by Alvin Goldman in his recent book, *Epistemology and Cognition.*[21] Goldman notes that one of the major projects of both classical and contemporary epistemology has been to develop a theory of epistemic justification. The ultimate job of such a theory is to say which cognitive states are epistemically justified and which are not. Thus, a fundamental step in constructing a theory of justification will be to articulate a system of rules or principles evaluating the justificatory status beliefs and other cognitive states. These rules (Goldman calls them *justificational rules* or *J-rules*)

will specify permissible ways in which a cognitive agent may go about the business of forming or updating his cognitive states. They "permit or prohibit beliefs, directly or indirectly, as a function of some states, relations, or processes of the cognizer."[22]

Of course, different theorists may have different views on which beliefs are justified or which cognitive processes yield justified beliefs, and thus they may urge different and incompatible sets of J-rules. It may be that there is more than one right system of justificational rules, but it is surely not the case that all systems are correct. So in order to decide whether a proposed system of J-rules is right, we must appeal to a higher criterion which Goldman calls a "criterion of rightness." This criterion will specify a "set of conditions that are necessary and sufficient for a set of J-rules to be right."[23]

But now the theoretical disputes emerge at a higher level, for different theorists have suggested very different criteria of rightness. Indeed, as Goldman notes, an illuminating taxonomy of epistemological theories can be generated by classifying theories or theorists on the basis of the sort of criterion of rightness they endorse. Coherence theories, for example, take the rightness of a system of J-rules to turn on whether conformity with the rules would lead to a coherent set of beliefs. Truth-linked or reliability theories take the rightness of a set of J-rules to turn in one way or another on the truth of the set of beliefs that would result from conformity with the rules. Reflective equilibrium theories judge J-rules by how well they do on their favored version of the reflective equilibrium test. And so on. How are we to go about deciding among these various criteria of rightness? Or, to ask an even more basic question, just what does the correctness of a criterion of rightness come to; what makes a criterion right or wrong? On this point Goldman is not as explicit as one might wish. However, much of what he says suggests that, on his view, *conceptual analysis* or *conceptual explication* is the proper way to decide among competing criteria of rightness. The correct criterion of rightness is the one that comports with the conception of justifiedness that is "embraced by everyday thought or language."[24] To test a criterion, we explore the judgments it would entail about specific cases, and we test these judgments against our "pretheoretic intuition." "A criterion is supported to the extent that implied judgments accord with such intuitions, and weakened to the extent that they do not."[25] Goldman is careful to note that there may be a certain amount of vagueness in our commonsense notion of justifiedness, and thus there may be no unique best criterion of rightness. But despite the vagueness, "there seems to be a common core idea of justifiedness" embedded in everyday thought and language, and it is this common core idea that Goldman tells us he is trying to capture in his own epistemological theorizing.[26]

The view I am attributing to Goldman on what it is for a criterion of rightness itself to be right is hardly an idiosyncratic or unfamiliar one. We saw earlier that a very natural reading of Goodman would have him offering the reflective equilibrium story as an explication or conceptual analysis of the ordinary notion of justification. And many other philosophers have explicitly or implicitly adopted much the same view. I propose to use the term *analytic epistemology* to denote any epistemological project that takes the choice between competing justificational rules or competing criteria of rightness to turn on conceptual or linguistic analysis. There can be little doubt that a very substantial fraction of the epistemological writing published in English in the last quarter century has been analytic epistemology.[27] However, it is my contention that if an analytic epistemological theory is taken to be part of the serious normative inquiry whose goal is to tell people which cognitive processes are good ones or which ones they should use, then for most people it will prove to be an irrelevant failure.

4.6.2 The Analytic Epistemologist's Response to Cognitive Diversity

I think the most intuitive way to see this point is to begin by noting how the specter of culturally based cognitive diversity lends a certain urgency to the question of which cognitive processes we should use. If patterns of inference are acquired from the surrounding culture, much as language or fashions or manners are, and if we can learn to use cognitive processes quite different from the ones we have inherited from our culture, then the question of whether our culturally inherited cognitive processes are good ones is of more than theoretical interest. If we *can* go about the business of cognition differently, and if others actually *do*, it is natural to ask whether there is any reason why we should continue to do it our way. Even if we cannot change our cognitive processes once we've acquired them, it is natural to wonder whether those processes are good ones. Moreover, for many people the absence of a convincing affirmative answer can be seriously disquieting. For if we cannot say why our cognitive processes are any better than those prevailing elsewhere, it suggests that it is ultimately no more than an historical accident that we use the cognitive processes we do or that we hold the beliefs that those processes generate, just as it is an historical accident that we speak English rather than Spanish and wear trousers rather than togas.

Consider now how the analytic epistemologist would address the problem that cognitive diversity presents. To determine whether our cognitive processes are good ones, he urges, we must first *analyze* our concept of justification (or perhaps some other commonsense epistemic notion like rationality). If our commonsense epistemic notion is not too vague or ambiguous, the analysis will give us a criterion of rightness for justificational rules (or perhaps a cluster of closely related criteria). Our next step is to investigate which sets of justificational rules fit the criterion. Having made some progress there, we can take a look at our own cognitive processes and ask whether they do in fact accord with some right set of justificational rules. If they do, we have found a reason to continue using those processes; we have shown that they are good ones because the beliefs they lead to are justified. If it turns out that our cognitive processes don't accord with a right set of justificational rules, we can try to discover some alternative processes that do a better job and set about training ourselves to use them.

I submit that something has gone very wrong here. For the analytic epistemologist's effort is designed to determine whether our cognitive states and processes accord with our commonsense notion of justification (or some other commonsense concept of epistemic evaluation). Yet surely the evaluative epistemic concepts embedded in everyday thought and language are every bit as likely as the cognitive processes they evaluate to be culturally acquired and to vary from culture to culture.[28] Moreover, the analytic epistemologist offers us no reason whatever to think that the notions of evaluation prevailing in our own language and culture are any better than the alternative evaluative notions that might or do prevail in other cultures. But in the absence of any reason to think that the locally prevailing notions of epistemic evaluation are superior to the alternatives, why should we care one whit whether the cognitive processes we use are sanctioned by those evaluative concepts? How can the fact that our cognitive processes are approved by the evaluative notions embraced in our culture alleviate the worry that our cognitive processes are no better than those of exotic folk, if we have no reason to believe that our evaluative notions are any better than alternative evaluative notions?

To put the point a bit more vividly, imagine that we have located some exotic culture that does in fact exploit cognitive processes very different from our own and that the notions of epistemic evaluation embedded in their language also differ from ours. Suppose further that the cognitive processes prevailing in that culture accord quite well with *their* evaluative notions, while the cognitive processes prevailing in our culture accord quite well with *ours*. Would any of this be of any help at all in deciding which cognitive processes we should use? Without some reason to think that one set of evaluative notions was preferable to the other, it seems clear that for most of us it would be of no help at all.

4.6.3 Conceptual Analysis, Intrinsic Value, and Instrumental Value

Since the point of the previous section is an enormously important one, I want to try to state it a bit more systematically. I'll begin by rehearsing some conventional wisdom. People value many things. In some cases the value is instrumental, in the sense that the thing valued is valued because it is believed to facilitate the achievement of other goals. Money is the standard example here. In other cases the thing valued is valued *intrinsically*, or "for its own sake." There is a dispute, near enough coeval with philosophy itself, about whether people intrinsically value many things or only one. Monists, those who think that only one thing is intrinsically valuable, generally urge that it is happiness or desire satisfaction or some kindred mental state. I am inclined to think that pluralism about intrinsic value is vastly more plausible than monism and will assume that people can and do intrinsically value a variety of things. As far as I can see, however, this assumption plays no substantive role in my arguments. It's worth noting that if pluralism about intrinsic value is correct, then it is possible that some things may be valuable both intrinsically and instrumentally, since some things may be both valuable in themselves and lead to other things which are also intrinsically valuable.

The analytic epistemologist proposes that our choice between alternative cognitive processes should be guided by the concepts of epistemic evaluation that are "embedded in everyday thought and language." But this proposal is quite pointless unless we *value* having cognitive states or invoking cognitive processes that accord with these commonsense concepts. And it is my contention that when they view the matter clearly, most people will not find it intrinsically valuable to have cognitive states or to invoke cognitive processes that are sanctioned by the evaluative notions embedded in ordinary language. Nor is there any plausible case to be made in favor of the instrumental value of beliefs or cognitive processes that are justified or rational.

Let's consider intrinsic value first. Here, of course, there is little prospect of providing a conclusive argument. If a person genuinely and clearheadedly insists that she finds it intrinsically valuable to have cognitive states that accord with the standards embedded in her language, there is little more that can be said. However, in my experience such people are few and far between. For those who think they are tempted in that direction, a pair of considerations will often suffice to persuade them otherwise.

The first is the one stressed in the previous section—that other languages and other cultures certainly could and probably do invoke concepts of cognitive evaluation that are significantly different from our own, just as they invoke different conceptions of etiquette. For many people—certainly for me—the fact that a cognitive process is sanctioned by the venerable standards embedded in our language of epistemic evaluation, or that it is sanctioned by the equally venerable standards embedded in some quite different language, is no more reason to value it than the fact that it is sanctioned by the standards of a religious tradition or an ancient text, unless, of course, it can be shown that those standards correlate with something more generally valued or obviously valuable. Unless one is inclined toward chauvinism or xenophobia in matters epistemic, it is hard to see why one would much care that a cognitive process one was thinking of invoking (or renouncing) accords with the set of evaluative notions that prevail in the society into which one happened to be born.

The second consideration is another way of underscoring the fact that we might well have had quite different concepts of epistemic evaluation, and the concepts we have are, in some ways, quite arbitrary and idiosyncratic. The central point is that if the most sophisticated recent attempts to analyze our local notions of cognitive evaluative are even roughly on the right track, those notions occupy a small area in a large space of alternative concepts. And there is no obvious virtue that distinguishes our concepts from the alternatives, apart from the fact that we happen to have inherited them.

Consider, for example, Goldman's analysis of our local common-sense notion of justification, the one putatively embedded in late twentieth-century English. On Goldman's "reliabilist" account of justification, the rightness of a system of justificational rules is determined by the percentage of true beliefs that would be produced using the psychological processes sanctioned by those rules. J-rule systems are right if the psychological processes they permit "would result in a truth ratio of beliefs that meets some specified high threshold (greater than .50)."[29] But this account leaves unspecified the nature of the world in which the sanctioned processes are operating.

> Is the rightness of a rule system determined by its truth ratio in the *actual* world, and in that world only? Or should the performance of the rule system also be judged by its performance in other possible worlds?. . . Obviously, a given rule system could perform well in one possible world—say the actual world—and poorly in another. Which possible worlds are relevant to the

rightness of a rule system, and ultimately to the justifiedness of a belief formed in compliance with the system?[30]

There are, as Goldman notes, a variety of alternatives. One account of justification could relativize the criterion of rightness to the world in which the system is operating, while another could have rightness conceptually tied to the actual world. Still another cluster of alternatives have rightness conceptually linked to worlds with certain specified characteristics, whether or not those characteristics happen to obtain in the actual world or the world in which we imagine the system to be operating. On Goldman's view, the account that "best accords with our intuitions"[31] falls in this latter category. "Our concept of justification," Goldman maintains, "is constructed against the backdrop of . . . a set of normal worlds," where *normal worlds* are defined as those that comport with our "general beliefs about the sorts of objects, events and changes that occur in it."[32]

Given our current concerns, it is of no great importance whether Goldman is right about which set of worlds forms the backdrop for "our ordinary conception of justifiedness." What is important is that if Goldman is even close to being right, then *our* concept of justification occupies a small region in a large space of more or less similar concepts that can be generated by altering the specification of possible worlds in which the reliability of cognitive processes is to be assessed. Moreover, by varying other parameters of Goldman's account, a much larger space of justificationlike concepts can be generated. There is, however, nothing *prima facie* preferable about the region of this space in which *our* concept falls. It is not at all apparent why anyone would choose to have *justified* beliefs, rather than beliefs which, though not justified, are sanctioned by one or another of the many alternative justificationlike notions to be found in this space.

The fact that our notion of justification is but one idiosyncratic member in a large family of more or less similar notions does not, of course, make it impossible for a person to find having justified beliefs to be intrinsically valuable. There is nothing logically incoherent about that sort of epistemic chauvinism. However, it has been my experience that once the arbitrariness and idiosyncrasy of our own concept of justification is clearly understood—once it is seen that the notion we happen to have inherited is but one among many possible alternative notions—most people are not much inclined to say that they find having justified beliefs to be *intrinsically* valuable. Since our notion of justification is just one member of a large and varied family of concepts of epistemic evaluation, it strikes most people as simply capricious or perverse to have an intrinsic preference for justified beliefs.[33]

Let's turn now to the instrumental value of justified beliefs. Is it the case that having justified beliefs is likely to be conducive to achieving some other state of affairs that people find intrinsically valuable? Here there is little prospect of finding a general argument for a negative conclusion, particularly if we are pluralists about intrinsic value. But to sustain my critique of analytic epistemology, no such general argument is needed. In light of the idiosyncratic nature of our notions of epistemic evaluation, and the existence of a wide range of possible alternative notions, the burden of argument is surely on those who maintain that cognitive states and processes sanctioned by our notions are more instrumentally valuable than cognitive states and processes sanctioned by any of the alternatives. I know of only two lines of argument aimed at supporting such a conclusion. What I propose to argue is that neither of them is at all persuasive.

A first line of argument for the instrumental value of beliefs sanctioned by our ordinary notions of epistemic evaluation appeals to the evolution of those notions. The very fact that we have complex, highly evolved intuitive notions of justification and rationality, it is urged, is good reason to think that justified or rational beliefs are instrumentally valuable in achieving something worth having. For, the argument continues, it is plausible to suppose that our intuitive concepts of epistemic evaluation and the cognitive systems that subserve them are the product of many years of social and biological evolution. During the long process of conceptual evolution, many evaluative notions were likely tried and rejected in favor of alternatives that did a better job of facilitating people's interactions with their fellows, and thus ultimately contributing to their survival and thriving. Since our current concepts of epistemic evaluation are the result of a long evolutionary culling process, they almost certainly do an excellent job of fostering survival and thriving. One can almost hear, in this argument, the ghost of J. L. Austin who held that there is much traditional wisdom and experience distilled into the categories and distinctions embedded in ordinary language.

I am often quite amazed at how many clever people find themselves attracted to this sort of evolutionary argument for the instrumental value of one or another traditional or intuitively sanctioned category or practice. For when subjected to even a bit of scrutiny, such arguments crumble very quickly. The case at hand is no exception. The argument presupposes that evolution, over the long haul, can be counted on to locate and retain what will foster survival and thriving and to reject what will not. But, as we saw in the previous chapter, when the evolution in question is biological evolution, this is a hopelessly Panglossian assumption. There are many factors in addition to natural selection that drive biological evolution, including genetic drift, pleiotropy, meiotic drive, and others, and each of these is capable of leading evolution away from an optimal phenotype. Moreover, even when natural selection is the only force at work, it cannot be counted upon to select the best option among those available. Nor can it be taken for granted that the best option *available* is the best *possible* option—or even that it is a particularly *good* option.[34]

Of course, when the evolution of concepts is at issue, it is likely that the processes involved are more social than biological. We have only a very primitive understanding of the processes at work in social evolution, but what little we do know hardly supports the suggestion that cultural products always or typically evolve in an instrumentally efficacious direction. One would be hard put to make a serious case for generally increasing adaptiveness or utility in the evolution of clothing styles, manners, religious practices, syntactic structures, or political systems, to mention just a few. Moreover, the literature on people's intuitive capacity to detect covariation—and thus to discern which of the various practices, policies, or concepts in use at a given time leads to the best results—does little to encourage the hypotheses that our forebears carefully culled successful concepts of epistemic evaluation and abandoned the less successful ones. What the literature does suggest is that only very large differences in the success of alternative notions are likely to be noted and that even this will occur only under favorable conditions.[35]

The obvious conclusion to be drawn here is that neither biological nor social evolution can be relied upon to produce the best of all possible options, or even one that is close to the best. So the fact (if it is a fact) that our intuitive notions of epistemic evaluation are the product of an extended process of social and/or biological evolution does not make it plausible that they are more conducive to survival or thriving (or anything else) than any of the alternative notions of epistemic evaluation that might be invoked instead. Moreover, even if it could be shown that having the intuitively sanctioned notions of epistemic evaluation is especially conducive to survival and thriving, this would still not be enough to show that *having justified beliefs* is more instrumentally valuable than having beliefs sanctioned by some nonintuitive notion of epistemic evaluation. To establish this latter claim, it would have to be shown that the reason having intuitive notions of justification is conducive to survival and thriving is that it fosters having justified beliefs. And the argument at hand does not even begin to support that contention. It seems hard to avoid the conclusion that the evolutionary argument for the instrumental value of justified belief is a hopeless nonstarter.

A second strategy for trying to establish the instrumental value of cognitive states sanctioned by our intuitive notions of cognitive evaluation focuses on *truth*. It begins with the claim that while having *justified* beliefs may not be intrinsically valuable, having *true* beliefs surely is. The next step is to argue that justified beliefs are in fact more likely to be true than unjustified ones. There are, of course, notorious problems in forging the link between justification and truth, and in one guise or another the project has been central to epistemology from Descartes and Hume to Popper and the present. Just how daunting the problems are will depend in large measure on the analysis of the concept of justification. If justification is unpacked along reliabilist (or "truth-linked") lines, as suggested by Armstrong, Goldman, Nozick, and others, then there is at least a *prima facie* reason to think that justified beliefs are likely to be true. For nonreliabilist accounts of justification, the connection between justification and truth is much harder to defend. But even the reliabilists have more than a few problems on their hands, since reliabilist accounts of justification rarely count a belief as justified simply in virtue of having been produced by a process that is likely to produce true beliefs in the world the believer inhabits. That sort of bare bones reliabilism classifies as justified lots of beliefs that intuition does not. And there is a strong inclination to add bells and whistles in an effort to do a better job of capturing intuitions. Goldman's relativization of justification to the class of "normal worlds" is one among many illustrations. Typically, however, these embellishments on bare bones reliabilism, though they may do a better job at capturing intuitions, will do a worse job at linking justification to truth. If it's truth we're after, then we should exploit processes that are likely to produce truth in *our* world, not in *normal* worlds.

There is lots more that might be said about the prospects of demonstrating that justified beliefs are likely to be true, and little of it would be encouraging. But I don't propose to wade any deeper into these venerable controversies, since as I see it, there is a quite fundamental problem with this strategy for establishing the instrumental value of justification. The strategy assumes that having true beliefs is something to be valued. But as I shall argue in the following chapter, for most people that assumption is very dubious indeed. If I can succeed in casting doubt on the claim that having true beliefs is valuable, then even if it could be shown that justified beliefs are likely to be true, this will provide no reason to think that having justified beliefs will be instrumentally valuable.

4.7 Conclusions and Connections

We began this chapter by asking what it is that separates good systems of cognitive processes from bad ones and, more generally, how normative standards for cognition might be discovered and defended. Much of the work of the chapter has been aimed at establishing a pair of negative conclusions. First, reflective equilibrium is not the touchstone for normative principles about cognitive processes. Second, when it comes to deciding among alternative systems of cognitive processes, the fact that a system accords with the standards embedded in everyday thought and language is not likely to be of much interest to anyone but an epistemic chauvinist. The fact that a system of inferences or cognitive processes, or the body of beliefs they give rise to, happens to be sanctioned by our intuitive notions of rationality or justification—or, to put it in the "material mode," the fact that certain inferences are rational and certain beliefs are justified—is not a state of affairs that many of us find intrinsically valuable. Nor is there much to be said for the view that it is instrumentally valuable to have justified beliefs or to invoke rational cognitive processes. Certainly, the mere fact that our concepts of cognitive evaluation have evolved over many centuries gives little support to the thesis that they must be instrumentally valuable.

Though it may sound radical to suggest that justification and rationality are of no value, the view I am defending is really just a generalization of a point made long ago by Salmon, Skyrms, and a number of other authors.[36] In his much-discussed solution to the problem of induction—a solution that has more than a passing similarity to Goodman's—Peter Strawson argued that the rationality or reasonableness of inductive reasoning was easy to demonstrate, since being supported by inductive inference is part of what we *mean* when we say that an empirical belief is *reasonable*.[37] In reply, Salmon noted that if Strawson is right about the meaning of 'reasonable', then it is not at all clear why anyone should *want* to be reasonable. What most of us do care about, Salmon notes, is that our inferential methods are those "best suited to the attainment of our ends. . . . If we regard beliefs as reasonable simply because they are arrived at inductively and we hold that reasonable beliefs are valued for their own sake, it appears that we have elevated inductive method to the place of an intrinsic good."[38] At the core of my case against analytic epistemology is an entirely parallel complaint. For the analytic epistemologist, the standards against which competing cognitive processes are to be judged are the concepts of epistemic evaluation embedded in ordinary thought and language. But this is quite absurd unless we think that being within the extension of our ordinary terms of epistemic evaluation is an intrinsic good or is instrumentally valuable. And for most of us, neither of these alternatives has much to be said for it. By contrast, most of us *do* care whether the cognitive processes we invoke are "best suited to the attainment of our ends."

At this point, however, I suspect that Salmon and I part company. For, along with most other authors, he seems to suppose that attaining true beliefs is one of the ends of cognition and that having true beliefs is itself either intrinsically or instrumentally valuable. My project in the following chapter is to challenge those assumptions.

Chapter 5

Do We Really Care Whether Our Beliefs Are True?

5.1 Getting Started

What I propose to argue in this chapter is that once we have a clear view of the matter, most of us will not find any value, either intrinsic or instrumental, in having true beliefs. If this is right, a number of consequences follow. First, those who urge reliabilist analyses of justification, rationality, or kindred notions of cognitive evaluation will not be able to appeal to truth in explaining why rational cognitive processes or justified inferences are valuable. Much the same difficulty will confront those who eschew conceptual analysis altogether and offer truth-linked accounts of what it is to reason well, without any claim that such accounts of inferential goodness capture our ordinary concepts of epistemic evaluation.

A rather more startling consequence follows if we accept the traditional view that *knowledge* is justified true belief. For if that is what knowledge is, and if neither truth nor justification is valuable, then the value of knowledge itself is brought into question.[1] This is not a theme I propose to dwell on in this chapter, but it is certainly not a conclusion I am much inclined to resist. For more than two millennia philosophers have been concerned to rebut the skeptic who argues that, for one reason or another, people cannot gain real knowledge. But the alarm philosophers have felt in the face of the skeptic's challenge, and the urgency that has imbued their responses, can be traced in large measure to the conviction that having knowledge is very important. On my view, the best way to deal with the skeptic is to challenge that conviction. If the skeptic claims that we cannot have the special sort of justified true belief that counts as knowledge, the right move to make first is to ask why we should care.

It has been my experience that when they first hear the thesis being defended in this chapter, many people assume I must be joking, or propounding silly skeptical puzzles. To these people it seems *obvious* that true beliefs are valuable and preposterous to suggest that they are not. So perhaps it would be best to begin by trying to soften up the conviction that true beliefs are *obviously* valuable. It is my suspicion that part of the explanation for the fact that people take true beliefs to be of obvious value lies in a cluster of philosophical metaphors that have long ago become part of the fabric of commonsense wisdom. According to these metaphors, people's beliefs constitute their *picture* of the world, their internal *mirror* of reality. Or, to alter the image slightly, our beliefs are *maps* by which we steer.[2] If beliefs are like pictures or mirrors or maps, then true beliefs are like pictures that *resemble* their subject, or like *undistorted* mirrors, or like *accurate* maps. And surely we'd prefer to have veridical pictures of the world and undistorted mirrors. Surely we're better off steering our way around the world with accurate maps. If having true beliefs is like having a good picture of the world or an accurate map of reality, it seems simply perverse to suggest that having true beliefs is not a situation to be valued.

All of this begins to unravel, however, when we recognize that talk of beliefs as pictures or maps is *just* a metaphor, and one which cannot be easily unpacked. If one is a materialist, then beliefs must be located somewhere in the material universe—presumably in the brain. But there are no pictures or mirrors or maps in the brain, not literally. I believe that Oswald shot John Kennedy and that Interstate 5 runs from Solana Beach to La Jolla, but there is nothing in my brain that looks like John Kennedy being shot, nor is there anything that has the shape of the southern California freeway system. Even if one rejects materialism, the metaphor of beliefs as pictures or maps of extramental reality is all but impossible to unpack, as both Berkeley and Kant knew all too well. Consider:

> I believe that there are exactly four prime numbers between ten and twenty.

> I believe that if Robert Kennedy had not been assassinated, he would have been elected President of the United States.

> I believe that considerations drawn from the theory of evolution cannot support the view that normal people are generally rational.

> I believe that we do not now have a good theory about the nature of consciousness.

For each of these beliefs, and for countless others, it seems to make no sense at all to suppose there might be a map or a picture of what is believed. The contents of these beliefs are just not the sorts of things that can be pictured. The moral I would draw here is that the metaphor that beliefs are pictures or maps or mirrors is both obscure and profoundly misleading. The conviction that true beliefs are valuable cannot be sustained by the analogy between true beliefs and accurate maps, or between true beliefs and portraits that resemble their subjects, since when pushed those analogies quickly come unglued.

5.2 Belief and Truth

All right, then, beliefs are not much like pictures, and true beliefs are not much like accurate maps. But before considering whether having true beliefs is valuable, we will have to say something about what beliefs are and what it is for them to be true. That is a project that poses some serious difficulties, however, since both of these issues have been the focus of a great deal of philosophical dispute, and radically different views abound. My strategy for dealing with this rather untidy situation will be to start, in this section and the two to follow, by sketching what I take to be one of the more plausible positions about what beliefs are and what it is for them to be true. In 5.5, I will argue that if the account of true belief that I've presented is on the right track, then few of us will find having true beliefs to be intrinsically valuable. I'll also explore some of the obstacles to be overcome by those who would argue that true beliefs are instrumentally valuable. Of course, even if you're convinced by everything in 5.5, I will not have established that it's not valuable to have true beliefs. Rather, what I will have shown is that this conclusion follows *if* you accept the account of beliefs and what it is for them to be true developed in 5.2–5.4. Thus, in 5.6 I'll try to generalize the argument by showing that the essential features of the account of true belief developed in 5.2–5.4 will be shared by any plausible alternative account.

Now, what about belief? The theory I'll be using as a backdrop for my arguments assumes that beliefs are real psychological states, not explanatory fictions like the lines in a parallelogram of forces. Thus the theory rejects the sort of instrumentalism about belief that Daniel Dennett has made popular of late.[3] The theory embraces the so-called token-identity hypothesis, which claims that each instance (or token) of a belief is identical with some neurophysiological state or other, though it does not endorse the type-identity hypothesis, which holds that the same belief type in different individuals is always identical with the same neurophysiological state type. Subtleties aside, what these assumptions amount to is the claim that belief-state tokens are brain-state tokens.

Unlike most brain states, however, and unlike most everything else in the universe, beliefs have semantic properties. They are true or false. How can this be? What is it for a brain-state token—a neuro-physiological state or happening—to be true or false? One familiar framework in which an answer can be developed posits the existence of a function that maps certain brain-state tokens (including beliefs and perhaps some others) onto entities that are more naturally thought of in semantic terms, entities like propositions, or content sentences, or specifications of truth conditions. A variation on this idea posits a function that maps brain states onto entities like possible facts, or states of affairs, or subsets of the set of all possible worlds. An account of what it is for a belief token (i.e., a certain brain-state token) to be true can then be given in terms of the entity to which it is mapped: the belief is true if and only if the proposition (or content sentence) to which it is mapped is true; or, if and only if its truth condition obtains; or, if and only if the possible state of affairs to which it is mapped is actual; or, if and only if the actual world is one of the possible worlds to which the belief is mapped.

At this point, it might be protested that this kind of story could hardly be a complete explanation of what it is for a belief to be true, since it presupposes the notion of a proposition (or content sentence) being true, or of a truth condition obtaining, and so forth. And these notions are every bit as puzzling as the truth of a belief. Still worse, on some accounts, the semantic properties of nonpsychological entities like sentences are themselves to be explained by appeal to the semantic properties of psychological states like beliefs. If these accounts are right, then our story about what it is for a belief to be true may well be going in a circle. On my view, both of these complaints are justified. They are, moreover, indicative of a problem that is endemic in thinking about whether truth is a cognitive virtue. Problems that putatively have been solved are like the bump in the carpet that keeps cropping up somewhere else. But ultimately those bumps will *have* to be smoothed out. Unless we have some coherent story about what it is for a proposition or content sentence to be true, the mere fact that we can map beliefs to propositions or content sentences in some well-motivated way will not tell us what it is for beliefs to be true. And without an account of what it is for beliefs to be true, it is all but impossible to think clearly about whether we value having true beliefs. However, having noted my sympathy with those who want to know more about the "metaphysical" side of the story—the side that explains what determines whether a proposition is true or whether a truth condition obtains, I propose to ignore these problems in most of what follows. For argument's sake, I will simply grant that some completely unproblematic story can be told about propositions and what makes them true, or about truth conditions and when they obtain, and so forth. My doubts about the value of having true beliefs will be focused on the "interpretation function" that pairs psychological states with propositions, or truth conditions, or their kin.

Let us now consider just what determines the mapping of brain states to propositions or truth conditions. What can be said about the interpretation function? Here again, I'm afraid, the answer is, too much. There are lots of different theories around about the nature of the interpretation function. As advertised, what I propose to do is sketch one of the more plausible of them and then develop my arguments against the background of that theory. But before setting out the theory, a word is in order about what standards a theory of interpretation aspires to meet. What are the constraints that govern how this game is played? There are, I think, two very different answers that might be given to this question though, for reasons to be noted, few theorists bother to tell us which answer they endorse.

The first answer is that in developing a theory of interpretation, we are attempting to explicate and explain a well-entrenched preexisting intuitive concept or capacity. We do, after all, ascribe content to people's psychological states all the time. And in lots and lots of perfectly ordinary cases, the man or woman in the street can offer a spontaneous intuitive judgment about the conditions under which someone's belief would be true. To the extent that explication is viewed as an essential element in building a theory about the interpretation function, it is crucial that any proposed theory agree, by and large, with the judgments of the man or woman in the street about what content sentences or truth conditions get paired with the ordinary beliefs of ordinary folk. Thus any theory of interpretation that assigns to all of my beliefs truth conditions pertaining to events in the Crimean War, or to events in my own brain, would be immediately ruled out of court if what the theory is supposed to do is explicate the intuitive ability that underlies our ordinary judgments about content or truth conditions.

A very different answer to the question of what constraints govern theorizing about the interpretation function is implicit in the work of those theorists whose main aim is to construct a function that will play a role in some broader scientific or philosophical project. For example, a number of writers have maintained that a psychological theory aiming to predict and explain people's behavior should incorporate an interpretation function. Others have urged that an interpretation function will play an essential role in a metaphysical or semantic theory explaining how thought and language relate to the world. Still others might view an interpretation function as an intrinsic part of an epistemological theory. And, of course, various combinations of these doctrines are possible. Typically, philosophers who see theoretical work to be done by an interpretation function also hope that the function that will do the job will be just the one that an explication of our ordinary interpretative activities will provide, or at worst a relatively minor departure from it. But there can be no a priori guarantee that things will work out so conveniently. In building our psychological or metaphysical or epistemological theory, it *may* happen that the intuitive interpretation function proves to be theoretically awkward and that a function which departs in significant ways from commonsense practice will make for a smoother or more powerful or more elegant theory. And under those circumstances, the theorist must decide which is to be master—the theory or commonsense practice. If a theorist is prepared to allow the needs of the theory to override the dictates of intuitive judgment and everyday practice to whatever extent necessary, the constraints he recognizes are very different from those recognized by the theorist who insists that any adequate interpretation function *must* cleave reasonably closely to commonsense intuition and practice.

I have gone to lengths to draw this distinction because one side—the explicative side—is going to loom large in the pages to follow. For my arguments to work, it is going to be important that the interpretation function invoked in an account of truth conditions for beliefs is constrained in a fairly serious way by commonsense intuition. I am inclined to think that if an interpretation function does not cleave reasonably closely to commonsense practice, it is hard to see why what the function is characterizing deserves to be considered a *truth* condition. But I don't propose to push the point, since it runs the risk of leading to a dreary debate about who gets to use the word 'truth'. Instead, I will simply stipulate that my skepticism about the value of true beliefs is restricted to accounts that assign truth conditions largely compatible with commonsense intuition.

5.3 The Interpretation Function: A Sketch of a Theory

The story about the semantic properties of mental states that I propose to use as a backdrop for my arguments is a familiar and justifiably popular one. It combines insights drawn from a variety of sources including Tarski's theory of truth, the Putnam-Kripke causal theory of reference, and functionalism in the philosophy of mind. The account was first suggested by Hartry Field and has been elaborated with considerable sophistication by Ned Block, Michael Devitt, William Lycan, Colin McGinn, Kim Sterelny, and others.[4] I'll call it the causal/functional theory, and since it is so widely known I'll keep my exposition to a bare minimum.

The story starts with Tarski, who showed how to build an axiomatic theory about a language that will specify a truth condition for each of the infinitely many well-formed sentences, of the language.[5] That is, the theory will entail an infinity of theorems of the form:

(1) S is true if and only if p

where 'S' is replaced by a structural descriptive name of a sentence in the language and 'p' is replaced by a metalanguage sentence specifying the conditions under which the named sentence is true. There are, however, two conspicuous limitations to Tarski's achievement.

First, the languages to which Tarski's strategy can be straightforwardly applied are limited to a narrow range of connectives and quantifiers. A great deal of effort has been devoted to developing Tarski-style truth theories for languages that employ non-truth-functional connectives, nonstandard quantifiers, modals, adverbs, propositional attitude verbs, and various other puzzling constructions.[6] However, there remains great controversy both about the success of these efforts and about what constitutes success. Underlying much of this controversy is the fact that the notion of an adequate or acceptable truth condition is itself far from clear. It is, presumably, not sufficient that the sentence replacing 'p' in (1) have the same truth value as the sentence whose name replaces 'S', since if this were sufficient, '1 + 1 = 2' would be an adequate truth condition for all the truths of logic and mathematics. Indeed, if merely having the same truth value is all that is required, then '1 + 1 = 2' would be an adequate truth condition for *any* true sentence. Though no one has seriously proposed that '1 + 1 = 2' is an adequate truth condition for, say, 'Socrates is wise', there are lots of proposals that invoke possible worlds, situations, event-entities, and other products of the philosophical imagination in specifying the truth conditions for sentences like 'The killer couldn't have seen that the policeman was driving away slowly' or 'Most large chihuahuas like snow.'[7] Without a well-motivated general account of what it is for a specification of truth conditions to be adequate or acceptable, it is not clear how these various proposals are to be evaluated, nor how to decide among them.

The second limitation to Tarski's achievement is that in order for the project of building a truth theory for a given language to get off the ground, it must begin with a substantial list of axioms—the so-called base clauses of the recursive truth definition—specifying the semantic properties of the language's noncompound predicates and names. So, for example, a truth theory for a fragment of English might begin with long lists of axioms like:

(2a) (x) x satisfies 'is red' iff x is red

(2b) (x) x satisfies 'is wise' iff x is wise

...

(3a) 'Socrates' denotes Socrates

(3b) 'Plato' denotes Plato

....

Despite the appearance to the contrary engendered by using a meta-language that contains the object language, there is nothing trivial about these axioms. To see the point, we need only try to specify a parallel set of axioms for a newly discovered language. The fact that these axioms are nontrivial, that they make strong and substantive claims about a language, is hardly a defect in Tarski's project. What generates a problem is that Tarski tells us too little about what it is to get these axioms right. He does not tell us what sort of relationship must obtain between a name and a person if the former is to denote the latter. Nor does he tell us what relation must obtain between a predicate and a satisfaction condition if the former is to be satisfied by (and only by) things that fit the latter.

   It is just here that the causal theory of reference fits into our story. What we need is some general account of what it is for an arbitrary name or predicate in an arbitrary language to refer to a particular object or a particular class of objects. And this is just what the causal theory proposes to provide. Though the details are sketchy and controversial, the basic idea of the causal theory is that a token of a name denotes an individual if and only if the appropriate sort of causal chain extends from an original use or dubbing to the current production of the name token in question. A broadly similar account can be given for natural kind predicates. Just how the causal framework should handle predicates like 'pencil', 'popular', or 'democratic', which clearly are not natural kind terms, remains very controversial, though some theorists urge that these can be defined in terms of the more basic predicates that are themselves tied on to the world with causal ropes.[8]

   We need not dwell on the details of the causal story, since they will play little role in the argument set out below. But it is important to note that both the basic argument in favor of the causal theory of reference and the detailed working out of the theory rely heavily on commonsense intuition and the commonsense concepts or practices that underlie them. In arguing against description-theoretic accounts of names, for example, the causal theorist's central move is to point out that the description theory gets things intuitively wrong.[9] In the case where most of a speaker's claims of the form 'Aristotle was Φ' turn out to be false of the historical Aristotle but true of some long-forgotten ancient, description theories typically end up claiming that in uttering 'Aristotle' the speaker is referring to the long-forgotten ancient. But, the argument for the causal theory continues, this is intuitively unacceptable.

Intuitions on who a person's utterance is about play a similarly central role in working out the positive details of causal theories. There are, after all, endless varieties of causal chains in the world linking all sorts of events in all sorts of ways. So for my tokening of 'Aristotle' to refer to the great philosopher, it is not enough that there be *some* causal chain linking my utterance to Aristotle's baptism; it has to be the right sort of causal chain. Typically, a theorist will try to show that his account of the relevant sort of causal chain is correct by showing how the implications of the account comport with intuition. If our utterances are linked by the theorist's favored causal chain to people or objects that intuition insists we are not talking about, it is generally concluded that the theorist's account of the causal chain required for reference is defective.

Thus far the theory I have been sketching has been an account of how sentences in a natural language get their truth conditions. But our concern is with the semantics of mental states, not the semantics of natural language sentences. To bridge the gap, the causal/functional account adopts the simple expedient of putting the language inside the head. A bit less flippantly, the idea is that beliefs are complex psychological states which, like sentences, can be viewed as built up out of simpler components. So by mapping the elements out of which beliefs are constructed to the symbols of some uninterpreted formal language, in a way that preserves well-formedness, we can associate belief tokens with well-formed formulas in that language. Indeed, we can view belief tokens as neurally encoded inscriptions of the relevant well-formed formulas. To have a belief, then, is to have a token of a well-formed formula stored appropriately in one's brain. The question of how beliefs get their semantic properties can now be rephrased as a question about how we can assign truth conditions to these cerebral inscriptions. As we saw in 2.1.1, Stephen Schiffer has suggested a particularly vivid way of capturing this idea. Suppose that when we looked inside a person's head we saw a little box labeled "Beliefs," in which there was a large and evolving collection of what appeared to be inscriptions in a language we did not understand. The job of the interpretation function is to specify truth conditions for the sentences in the Belief Box.[10]

That job would be done if we could identify certain of the words out of which belief inscriptions are built as names or predicates, to which appropriate denotations or extensions can be assigned, and the rest as connectives or quantifiers amenable to a Tarski-style truth theory. In favorable cases, this would seem to be a job that is fairly easy to do. The names and predicates can be paired with the appropriate denotation or extension by tracing their causal ancestry in the way suggested by the causal theory of reference. Indeed, sophisticated versions of the causal theory of reference for public language terms typically route the reference-fixing causal paths through hypothetical wordlike brain states of speakers. So if we suppose that we have a causal theory of reference for public language, no further work is needed to explain how mental word tokens get their reference. For the connectives, the causal/functional theory maintains, it is the pattern of interactions among belief inscriptions that is essential. If the pattern of interactions manifested by sentences of the form 'P * Q' approximates the pattern one would expect if '*' were the symbol for the material conditional, then '*' *is* the symbol for the material conditional. Similarly for the rest of the connectives and quantifiers. We should not expect that people are logically flawless in their inferences, of course, and thus some slippage must be allowed between the inferences sanctioned by logic and the interactions manifested by mental inscriptions. This raises sticky questions about how much error undermines a proposed intentional interpretation. But these are details that we need not pursue here.[11] What is important is the idea, inspired by functionalism, that mental sentence inscriptions have the logical form they do in virtue of the pattern of causal interactions they manifest with other mental-state inscriptions.

5.4 The Limits and Idiosyncrasies of Causal/Functional Interpretation

In the previous section I gave a fast sketch of the causal/functional story about how mental states get paired up with their truth conditions. In the current section I want to draw out two of the implications of this story—implications that, as we shall see in 5.6, are shared by many other accounts of the relation between beliefs and their truth conditions. I am inclined to think that these implications go a long way toward undermining the widespread conviction that truth is something to be valued in one's beliefs. But I won't try to argue for that until the next section.

The first consequence of the causal/functional account of interpretation that I want to draw attention to is that the interpretation function it favors is a very partial function. The belieflike mental states for which it provides a specification of truth conditions constitute a small subset of the possible belieflike mental states that a human or other organism might have. There are two distinct reasons why the interpretation function is sharply limited in its domain, one turning on the causal account of the reference of simple names and predicates, the other turning on the functional story about logical form. On the causal side, the point is simply that any plausible specification of the kinds of causal chains required to fix the reference of mental words (or concepts) will entail that these chains are far from ubiquitous. On any account that comports even roughly with commonsense intuition, the reference-fixing causal chains are going to cut a relatively narrow swath through the space of empirically possible causal histories of mental words. Thus, there will be all sorts of ways in which a mental word can end up as part of a speaker's mental lexicon, though it is not tied to anything in the world by the special kind of causal rope that the causal theory requires for reference. These mental words may, of course, stand in a variety of other causal relations to a variety of extramental objects or kinds. But the causal account entails that they will not refer to any of these objects or to anything else. And since these mental words have no referents, the mental sentences in which they occur will have no truth conditions assigned by the causal/functional interpretation function.

The way in which the functional account of logical form restricts the domain of the causal/functional interpretation function is a bit less obvious, though no less important. The tip of the iceberg was already noted in my brief remarks on the limitations of Tarskian truth theories, where it was pointed out that there is only a very limited class of constructions for which we know how to give a Tarski-style account of how the truth conditions or referential properties of compounds depend on the referential properties of their components. Once we get beyond the truth functional constructions and standard quantifiers and attend to modal or adverbial or counterfactual constructions, it is not even clear what would count as getting the semantics right. For, as Scott Soames and Robert Stalnaker have noted, we simply do not have for connectives, quantifiers, and other constructions anything like the causal theory of reference for names and kind terms.[12] We have nothing that will tell us whether a proposed account of the recursive rules governing such constructions is correct or incorrect.

Since the point is both important and little noticed, let me elaborate a bit. In his seminal paper, "Tarski's Theory of Truth,"[13] Hartry Field argued that Tarski had not provided a physicalistically acceptable account of truth because Tarski's truth definitions begin with "base clauses," which are simply *lists* specifying the denotation or satisfaction conditions for each of the noncompound names or predicates in the language. What Tarski did not provide was any general account of what it is was for a name to denote an object or for a predicate to have a certain extension. Thus Tarski did not explain what it was to get the base clause lists *right*, and without such an account we could not even begin to apply Tarski's strategy to a newly discovered language. Field's proposal, of course, was that the causal theory of reference is just what is needed to fill the gap. The causal theory tells us what it is for an arbitrary name (or kind term) in an arbitrary language to denote a thing (or class of things): the name denotes the thing if the two are linked by the appropriate sort of causal chain. However, as Soames and Stalnaker have pointed out, an entirely parallel problem arises for the quantifiers and connectives of a language. In Tarski's paradigm theories the "recursive clauses" simply *list* quantifiers and connectives and specify, for each, how the satisfaction conditions of the constructions built from them depend on the satisfaction conditions of the parts of those constructions. Faced with a new construction that is not on the list, and with a proposed recursive clause telling us how satisfaction conditions of compounds using the construction depend on the satisfaction conditions of their parts, we have no way to judge whether the recursive clause is correct, since Tarski provides no general account of what it is to get the recursive clauses right. To make matters worse, there is nothing even roughly analogous to the causal theory of reference to step into the breach. One upshot of this problem is that even when supplemented with an otherwise unproblematic causal theory of reference for names and general terms, Tarski's work provides no physicalistically acceptable general account of the notion of truth. More relevant to our current concerns is the fact that without some general account of what it is to get the recursive clauses in a truth definition right, the only compound mental sentences in the domain of the causal/functional theorist's interpretation function will be those built from the very limited number of constructions whose projective semantic properties are relatively well understood and for which we already have the requisite recursive clauses.

Now it might be thought that the problem I have been belaboring, though real enough, is largely a matter of ignorance, and ignorance of a fairly technical sort. No one has yet been sufficiently clever to produce a general account of what it is to get the recursive clauses in a truth definition right. But when someone succeeds in doing for the recursive clauses in a truth definition what the causal theory of reference has done for the base clauses, the problem will disappear. It is important to see that this response seriously underestimates the scope of the problem. Even if we did have a plausible general account of what it is to get recursive clauses right, there will be endlessly many sorts of mental sentences that will be outside the domain of the causal/ functional interpretation function, because there are endlessly many sorts of constructions for which there simply *are* no adequate truth theoretic recursive clauses.

To see why this is so, we need to assemble a number of points. First, recall that the project of providing an account of the interpretation function is an exercise in explication that must ultimately be responsive to our intuitive judgments about content or truth conditions. Next, note that in individuating the "constructions" from which mental sentences are built, the pattern of causal interactions that they manifest plays a central role. What makes a mental sentence a conjunction is the fact that it interacts with other sentences in ways that mirror, by and large, what logic permits. Similarly, we could identify modal, counterfactual, and other sorts of constructions in a mental language (whether or not we have a suitable truth definition for such constructions) by noting that the patterns of inference they exhibit largely accords with what is intuitively logically permissible. But, and this is the central point, there are indefinitely many possible patterns of formally specifiable causal interactions among mental sentences and thus indefinitely many possible mental sentence constructions, which admit of no intuitively plausible semantic interpretation at all. *Most purely formal, syntactically characterizable patterns of interaction among sentences or well-formed formulas have no intuitively plausible semantics.* Consider, for example, the one-place construction '#p' which a system derives from any finite sequence of premises, provided that each prime numbered member of the sequence is 'p'; or consider '#$_2$p' which is derived if every second prime numbered member of the sequence is 'p', and so forth. Or consider the construction 'p {} q' which a system derives from any pair of premises 'p' and 'q' if and only if either 'p' contains more tokens of '&' than 'q' or 'q' contains fewer tokens of 'v' than 'p', or both 'p' and 'q' begin with the symbols '(($\exists$'. Each of these, and endlessly many other formal patterns of symbolic interaction, are entirely unproblematic as syntactically characterized production or derivation rules. However, the constructions implicitly defined by these rules have no intuitively natural semantic interpretation. The space of formally (or syntactically) possible productions or computations vastly outruns those that our intuitive semantics is prepared to interpret.

What I have been arguing thus far is that the causal/functional account of the interpretation function portrays it as having a domain that is a very restricted subset of the space of mental formulas. There are many possible systems of mental states to which no interpretation will be assigned, either because the elements out of which those states are constructed are not hooked on to the world by the appropriate sort of causal chain or because the formal patterns of interaction the compounds manifest admit of no intuitive semantic interpretation. What I propose to argue now is that the causal/functional interpretation function is not only limited, it is also highly idiosyncratic. Even in the domain where it specifies interpretations, there are lots of other functions that map mental states to truth conditions (or propositions or states of affairs, etc.), and there is nothing obviously superior or preferable about the one sanctioned by commonsense intuition.[14]

The point about the existence of alternatives hardly needs an argument. A function is just a mapping, and if the items in one set can be mapped to the items in another set in one way, they can be mapped in many ways. To see the idiosyncratic nature of the causal/functional mapping, we need to look a bit closer at how causal theorists go about specifying the sort of causal chain that fixes reference. Typically, these stories divide into two parts, one part focusing on the process of "grounding" or "reference fixing," whereby a name or predicate is introduced into a language to designate an object or class of objects, the other part focusing on the process of social transmission whereby the name or predicate is passed from one user to another, preserving the reference that was fixed when the term was introduced. In each part, the task for a serious causal theorist is to specify the kinds of events or processes that count as legitimate groundings or legitimate transmissions. And, as ever, an important part of the criterion of legitimacy is how well the resulting story accords with intuition.

When one looks at the sorts of accounts of grounding and transmission that emerge, it appears that in each category the allowable events are a mixed bag having at best only a loosely knit fabric of family resemblances to tie them together. Nor is it at all surprising that things turn out this way. Proper names and nicknames get affixed to all sorts of things—babies, popes, battleships, breakfast cereals, islands, wars, and tyrants, to mention just a few—and the baptismal processes typically involved differ markedly from one sort of object to another. It is hard to believe that they constitute anything like a natural kind. The heterogeneity of intuitively acceptable groundings grows even more extreme when we consider the ways in which predicates come to be paired with their extensions. 'Gold', 'helium', 'asteroid', 'electron', 'kangaroo', and 'superconductivity' are, presumably, all natural kind terms, but their groundings are sure to have been very different from each other in all sorts of ways. The processes of reference-preserving transmission are comparably diverse. None of this, I hasten to add, is intended as a criticism of the causal theory as an explication of our pretheoretic views about how words in a public language or a mental language are related to what they designate. My point is simply that any plausible elaboration of the causal story will specify *lots* of allowable causal patterns. The causal chains linking my mental tokens of the names of my children to the appropriate young people are very different from the causal chain linking my mental token of 'Socrates' to Socrates. And both of these chains are notably different from the one linking my token of 'water' with water and from the one linking my token of 'quark' with quarks. What ties all these causal chains together is not any substantive property that they all share. Rather, what ties them together is that commonsense intuition counts them all as reference-fixing chains.

But now if it is indeed the case that common sense groups together a heterogeneous cluster of causal chains, then obviously there are going to be lots of equally heterogeneous variations on the commonsense theme. These alternatives will depart from the cluster favored by common sense, some in minor ways and some in major ways. They will link some mental words, or many, to objects or extensions different from those assigned by commonsense intuition. In so doing, they will characterize alternative notions of "reference"—alternative word-world links—which we might call REFERENCE*, REFERENCE**, REFERENCE***, and so on. And the only obvious complaint to lodge against many of these alternative schemes for nailing words on to the world is that they do not happen to be the scheme sanctioned by our commonsense intuitions.

An example or two may make this a bit more vivid. Causal theorists have argued persuasively that reference, construed along the lines of commonsense intuition, is possible even in the face of massively mistaken belief about the person or object referred to. Even if all the juicy bits in the biblical story of Jonah are myth, 'Jonah' still may refer to a real, historical person about whom tall tales were told as historical facts were forgotten. However, causal theorists generally also insist that we must retain at least some true beliefs about the general category of things to which the referent of a name belongs. If the biblical legend of Jonah had a long history that began with someone overhearing a conversation about the number 17 and mistakenly thinking it was a person being spoken of, it would not be the case that 'Jonah' denoted 17. In this case, causal theories and the intuitions that guide them decree that 'Jonah' is an empty name, denoting nothing. One way in which we might modify the intuitively sanctioned notion of reference would be to expand the range of cases in which false information undermined reference. We might, for example, imagine a hybrid between familiar causal stories and the description-cluster story championed by Searle and others. Let REFERENCE* be a word-world relation just like reference save for the fact that if the majority of the (nontrivial) descriptions a speaker associates with the name actually apply to no one, then the name is empty. Thus, if there was a historical person about whom legend gradually developed, 'Jonah' refers to this person though 'Jonah' REFERS* to no one. Another variation on the commonsense theme—REFERENCE**—might give descriptions a somewhat different role in determining the reference of proper names, so that 'Jonah' might end up REFERRING** to some long-forgotten ancient who actually did survive three days in the belly of an aquatic creature. And REFERENCE*** might be designed so that 'water' includes in its EXTENSION*** not only H_2O but also the famous stuff that looks and tastes just like it, XYZ. Obviously these three alternatives are just the beginning; it would be a trivial exercise to think up endlessly many more. Alternatives of a slightly different sort can be generated by varying the allowable patterns of transmission which preserve reference as a word is passed from one speaker to another.

What makes the existence of all these alternative word-world relations relevant to our current concerns is that each of them provides an alternative set of base clauses on which we can build an alternative to the causal/functional interpretation function favored by intuition. If there was a historical figure about whom piscine legends gradually developed, then on the intuitively sanctioned account, the belief that I might express by saying 'Jonah was a Moabite' would be mapped to the proposition that is true if and only if that historical figure was a Moabite. But if we base our interpretation function instead on the REFERENCE** relation, then the same belief would be mapped to the proposition that is true if and only if a certain long-forgotten ancient who spent three days in the belly of a great fish was a Moabite. Similarly, the "standard" causal/functional interpretation function would map the belief that I express by saying 'There is no water on the sun' to the proposition that there is no H_2O on the sun, while the interpretation function based on REFERENCE*** would map that belief to the proposition that there is no H_2O or XYZ on the sun. These alternative interpretation functions are not the ones sanctioned by our intuitive judgments. They strike us as wrong or inappropriate. But there is no reason to think that we could not retrain our intuitions or bring up our children to have intuitions very different from ours. And having done so, interpretations based on reference would strike us as inappropriate while interpretations based on REFERENCE* or one of the others would seem intuitively natural. There is, in short, no reason to think that these alternative interpretation functions might not be the intuitively plausible ones for other people or for our own future selves. And there is no reason, or at least no obvious reason, to think that people whose intuitions diverged from ours in these ways would be any worse off. It is in this sense that the causal/functional interpretation function is not only limited but also *idiosyncratic*. It is one interpretation function among many that stands out among its fellows principally because it is the function favored by local, contemporary commonsense intuition and the largely unknown psychological processes that underlie that intuition.

This would be a good place to reflect briefly on where the discussion has taken us, and how. I began by announcing my intention to question the widespread conviction that having true beliefs is something to be valued. And I proposed that we approach the issue by first focusing on a plausible cluster of views about the nature of beliefs and what it is for them to be true. On beliefs, I opted for a realistic construal in the spirit of the token identity theory. Belief tokens, I have been assuming, are neural state tokens. What distinguishes beliefs (and other "intentional" mental states) from the many neural states that do not have truth values is the existence of a function—the interpretation function—that maps beliefs to truth conditions (or propositions, or possible states of affairs). In 5.3, I sketched the popular causal/functional story about how the interpretation function works. And in 5.4, I argued that the causal/functional interpretation function is both partial and idiosyncratic. There are lots of alternatives to the intuitively sanctioned causal/functional interpretation function, and these functions map mental states to truth conditions in many different ways. Nor is there any reason to suppose that the intuitive function is any better or more natural than many of the alternatives. Each of these alternative interpretation functions provides an alternative specification of the truth conditions for beliefs. So while the interpretation function based on the intuitively sanctioned notion of reference might specify that a certain belief token of mine is true if and only if there is no H_2O on the sun, an interpretation function based on REFERENCE*** would specify that the same belief token is true (or, better, TRUE***) if and only if there is no H_2O or XYZ on the sun.

One consequence of all of this is that when it comes to deciding what we really value in our doxastic states and in the processes that generate them, truth has lots of competition. Any given set of belief tokens that I might have will contain a certain percentage, say n, of true beliefs. The but same set will also contain a certain percentage, n^*, of TRUE* beliefs, a certain percentage, n^{**}, of TRUE** beliefs, and so on for indefinitely many variations on the intuitively favored semantic theme. Moreover, in general $n \neq n^* \neq n^{**}$. . . . So it will often be the case that when we increase our percentage of true beliefs, we will decrease our percentage of TRUE* (and/or TRUE**, and/or TRUE***. . .) beliefs. If we really value true beliefs, presumably we won't much care about giving up TRUTH* or TRUTH**. But do we? That is the question we are now ready to tackle.

5.5 True Belief, Intrinsic Value, and Instrumental Value

As we saw in 4.6.3, discussions of epistemic value can be conveniently organized under a pair of headings: intrinsic value, the sort of value that something has for itself, and instrumental value, the sort that something has in virtue of leading to something else. Let's begin by asking whether we should view the holding of true beliefs to be intrinsically valuable.

It might be thought that on the issue of intrinsic value very little argument is possible, since if a person tells us that she accords intrinsic value to having true beliefs, she is saying that she values them for their own sake and not because they are conducive to something else. Since she does not claim that true beliefs will facilitate the achievement of other values, we can hardly argue that her expectations about the consequences of believing the truth are mistaken. However, as we saw in the previous chapter, there is another kind of consideration that might be efficacious in persuading someone that she should not, or does not really, accord intrinsic value to the having of true beliefs. Rather than dwelling on the consequence of having true beliefs, we can try to be sure that she sees clearly the real nature of what she values—that she appreciates what having true beliefs comes to. And it is just here that the conclusions of the previous section can be brought to bear. What we saw there was that if the function pairing beliefs with their truth conditions is the one outlined by the causal/functional theory, then it is both partial and idiosyncratic. And, in rather different ways, both of these facts entail that valuing true beliefs is a profoundly conservative thing to do.

Consider first the fact that the interpretation function has a very limited domain. What this means is that there is a huge space of possible systems of mental computation and storage whose component states have no truth conditions and thus cannot be true. No doubt many of the systems in this semantics-free space are useless and chaotic. But there is certainly no reason to suppose that they all are. A much more likely possibility is that in this huge space there are systems that would vastly increase their user's power or happiness or biological fitness, systems that would lead to substantial reductions in the amount of suffering in the universe, and systems that would significantly reduce the probability that we will bomb ourselves into oblivion along with much of the biosphere. As Paul Churchland is fond of observing, our current cognitive processes are a tiny island in a vast, unexplored computational space, a space that we may reasonably suppose to contain riches beyond imagining. But almost all of that space is beyond the reach of the causal/functional interpretation function; it is a domain in which there is neither truth nor falsity. Those who would accord intrinsic value to the holding of true beliefs may well be reluctant to explore that vast space and will resist adopting what may be found, since we know in advance that it contains no true beliefs. But theirs is a profoundly conservative normative stand. For what they value in the end products of cognition must be semantically interpretable, and what is semantically interpretable cannot depart too radically from current patterns of reasoning or from familiar ways of causally tying mental states to extramental reality. To value true belief is to resolve that in matters cognitive, one will not venture very far from where we are now.

One further image may help to make the point. The vast space of mental storage and computation systems might be thought of as a surface on which peaks are occupied by systems that excel in some virtue, like increasing their user's power or fostering happiness or increasing biological fitness, and the valleys correspond to systems that do poorly in that regard. If we insist that the system we adopt must be in the limited domain of the causal/functional interpretation function, the best we are likely to do is find a local maximum—a modest peak lying relatively close to our current position. There may well be vastly higher peaks farther afield. But if we take truth to be precious, we will not find them.

The conservatism entailed by the idiosyncratic nature of the interpretation function is of a rather different kind. There are endlessly many functions mapping mental states to truth conditions (or propositions or possible states of the world). In this bristling infinity of functions there is one that is singled out by common sense as providing the "real" truth conditions for mental states, in contrast with the TRUTH* CONDITIONS, the TRUTH** CONDITIONS, and all the other variations on the theme. But if, as we have been assuming, it is the causal/functional interpretation function that is sanctioned by intuition, then it is not a particularly simple or natural function. Rather, it is something of a hodgepodge, built from a more or less heterogeneous family of strategies for fixing the reference of terms and another family of strategies for transmitting reference from one speaker to another. What distinguishes acceptable groundings and transmissions is not that they share some common natural property but simply that they are found to be acceptable by commonsense intuitions.

Now let us reflect on just where these intuitions themselves come from. Why do we have these particular intuitions rather than those that would sanction REFERENCE*, REFERENCE**, or one of the others? The short answer, of course, is that no one knows in any detail just how these intuitions arise. But it's a good bet that, like other complex systems of intuitions such as those concerning grammaticality or morality or politeness, the intuitions in question are themselves culturally transmitted and acquired by individuals from the surrounding society with little or no explicit instruction. Another possibility, though I am inclined to think it is vastly less likely, is that the intuitions are innate and coded in our genes. And, of course, it is entirely possible that both genetic and cultural factors are involved. Whatever the explanation, it is clear that our intuitions do not result from a systematic and critical assessment of the many alternative interpretation functions and the various virtues that each may have. One way or another, we have simply inherited our intuitions; we have not made a reflective choice to have them. Those who find intrinsic value in holding true beliefs (rather than TRUE* ones, or TRUE** ones, . . .) are accepting unreflectively the interpretation function that our culture (or our biology) has bequeathed to us and letting that function determine their basic epistemic value. In so doing, they are making a profoundly conservative choice; they are letting tradition determine their cognitive values without any attempt at critical evaluation of that tradition.

Now of course nothing that I have said comes even close to a knockdown argument against according intrinsic value to having true beliefs. Indeed, traditionalists who are inclined toward extreme conservatism in matters epistemic might well find their attachment to truth reinforced by the realization that it is so very conservative a value. However, there are many people, and I am among them, who are not much inclined to value what is traditional and familiar for its own sake in matters epistemic. And for them the fact that true beliefs must be within the domain of the interpretation function, the fact that the domain of the interpretation function is limited to systems of cognitive storage similar to our own, and the realization that the function is an idiosyncratic hodgepodge bequeathed to us by our cultural and/or biological heritage may well be reason enough to decide that they do not really value true beliefs intrinsically. For those whose reflective epistemic values run along these lines, true beliefs may still turn out to be valuable, but their value will be instrumental. They will have to be good for something. So let us now ask how strong a case can be made for the instrumental value of true beliefs.

To explore the instrumental value of true beliefs is to ask whether having true beliefs will lead to something else that is valued, where the *something else* may itself be valued either instrumentally or intrinsically. Since people probably value many things intrinsically, and surely value many things instrumentally, I'll make no attempt to argue that having true beliefs *could not be* instrumentally valuable. For to demonstrate this would require showing that true beliefs don't facilitate *anything* that people might sensibly value. I have no idea how one might argue for so sweeping a conclusion, and my goal is much more modest. It is widely believed that the instrumental value of true belief is obvious—that having true beliefs is clearly good for lots of things. However, it is my contention that this doctrine is anything but obvious. It requires some serious argument of a sort that, so far as I know, no one has even begun to provide. In support of this contention I'll make three points, the first aimed at clarifying what is at issue, the second aimed at short-circuiting one argument that seems to tempt a fair number of people, and the third sketching a general difficulty that any argument for the instrumental value of truth must overcome.

It might be thought that to ask whether truth is instrumentally valuable is to ask whether having true beliefs would increase the likelihood of some other valued goal being attained. But posing the question in this way is seriously misleading, for it does not specify what the instrumental value of true beliefs is to be compared with. In the absence of such a specification, it would be easy to suppose that the relevant comparison was between true beliefs and *false* ones and that our question was whether having true beliefs is more instrumentally valuable than having false beliefs. But showing that the answer to this question is 'yes', though hardly trivial, is not nearly enough. What really needs to be shown is not just that true beliefs are more conducive to some independently desirable goal than false beliefs but also that true beliefs serve us better than TRUE* ones or TRUE** ones, or any of the other categories of belief picked out by interpretation functions that don't happen to be favored by intuition and tradition. For surely if TRUE* beliefs are more conducive to the goal in question than true ones, then, other things being equal, it is the TRUE* ones rather than the true ones that we really want to have. Moreover, it will not always be the case that TRUE**. . .* beliefs which aren't true will be false. For some of the mental states to which TRUTH**. . .* CONDITIONS are assigned may have no truth conditions at all. So there will be TRUE**. . .* beliefs that are neither true nor false. Thus showing that true beliefs are better at achieving some goal than false ones does not come close to establishing that true beliefs are more instrumentally valuable in pursuit of that goal than TRUE**. . .* ones.

Let me now proceed to the argument that many seem to find tempting. The very fact that we have a complex body of intuitions concerning the truth conditions of a wide range of mental states, it is urged, is a good reason to think that truth is instrumentally valuable in achieving something worth having. For, the argument continues, it is plausible to suppose that those intuitions and the cognitive system subserving them are the product of many years of social and biological evolution. During the long process of evolution, many alternative strategies of interpretation—alternative mappings from mental states to propositions—were likely tried and rejected in favor of alternatives that did a better job in facilitating people's interactions with their fellows and thus ultimately contributing to their survival and thriving. Since our current intuitive theory of interpretation is the result of a long evolutionary culling process, it almost certainly does a very good job of fostering survival and success.

It would not be surprising if, after a sentence or two, this argument began to sound very familiar to you, since it is entirely parallel to the "evolutionary" argument for the instrumental utility of beliefs sanctioned by our ordinary notions of epistemic evaluation, as set out in 4.6.3. And my response to this "evolutionary" argument is exactly the same. For reasons set out in 4.6.3, neither biological nor social evolution can be relied upon to produce the best of all possible options, or even one that is close to the best. So the fact (if it is a fact) that our intuitive interpretation function is the product of an extended process of biological or social evolution does not make it plausible that it is more conducive to survival or thriving (or anything else) than any of the nonintuitive functions that characterize alternative notions of TRUTH*. . .*. Moreover, even if it could be shown that using the intuitively sanctioned interpretation function is especially conducive to survival or success, this would still not be enough to show that *having true beliefs* is more instrumentally valuable than having TRUE*. . .* ones. To show this, it would presumably have to be shown that the reason the intuitively sanctioned interpretation function is conducive to success is that it fosters believing the truth. And the "evolutionary" argument does not even begin to support that contention. Here, as before, the evolutionary argument for instrumental value is a hopeless nonstarter.

The final point I want to make under the heading of the instrumental value of true belief is that in many cases, we already know that having true beliefs would not be the *best* way to achieve our more fundamental goals. Consider survival. Is true belief *always* more conducive to survival than false belief? Clearly the answer is no. To see the point, we need only reflect on the plight of poor Harry who believed that his flight left at 7:45 a.m. He wrote it down, ordered a cab the night before, and asked his wife to be sure he was out of bed by 6:30. Harry's belief was true, and he got to the airport just on time. Unfortunately, the flight crashed, and Harry died. Had Harry falsely believed that the flight left at 8:45, he would have missed the flight and survived. So true belief is sometimes less conducive to survival than false belief. Now it might be protested that this is an illusion, since Harry had some other false beliefs that contributed to his death. On arriving at the airport, he no doubt believed, falsely, that the plane would not crash. If he had a true belief on this matter, he would never have boarded the plane. This protest misses the point, however. For the question at hand is not whether omniscience would foster survival but whether more true beliefs are always better than fewer. In the case of Harry it is clear that if he had had one more false belief and one fewer true one, and if everything else in his cognitive life had remained as much the same as possible, his life would have been longer.

Another way to view the matter is to consider the nonstandard mapping of mental states to propositions that is just like the standard mapping, save in this respect: The belief that Harry would express by saying 'My flight leaves at 7:45' is mapped to the proposition that his flight leaves at 8:45, and the belief Harry would express by saying 'My flight leaves at 8:45' is mapped to the proposition that his flight leaves at 7:45. This function does not map mental states to their truth conditions; it maps them instead to what we may call their TRUTH**** CONDITIONS. What the sorry tale of Harry shows is that sometimes having TRUE**** beliefs is more conducive to survival than having true ones. Harry's belief about the departure time was true; it was also FALSE****. Had he had a different mental state, one that was TRUE**** (and also false), he would not have perished in the crash. Are true beliefs always more conducive to survival than TRUE**** ones? Clearly the answer is no. Equally clearly, this sort of argument will generalize to lots of other goals that people may take to be desirable or valuable. True beliefs are not always optimal in the pursuit of happiness or pleasure or desire satisfaction, nor are they always the best beliefs to have if what we want is peace or power or love, or some weighted mix of all of these. It might be claimed that although there are special circumstances in which TRUTH**** is more conducive to survival, and other circumstances in which TRUTH***** is more conducive to love, nonetheless one would still be better off seeking plain old uncapitalized truth, since it did a better job *in general*, or *in the long run*. Well perhaps it does. But to show this requires an *argument*, and as far as I know, no one has any inkling of how that argument might go.

In this section I have tried to make plausible a pair of claims. The first is that most of us will not embrace a system of epistemic values which takes the holding of true beliefs to be intrinsically valuable, once we see clearly how conservative, limiting, and idiosyncratic this would be. The second is that the instrumental value of true belief is far from obvious. It is surely not the case that having true beliefs is *always* the best doxastic stance in pursuing our goals, and it would be no easy matter to show that believing the truth is *generally* (or even occasionally!) instrumentally optimal. The argument in this section has been carried on against the background assumption that the causal/functional interpretation function is the right one—that it is the best way of explicating and making more precise our intuitive strategy for assigning truth conditions to mental states. In the following section I'll explore how our arguments fare if we abandon this assumption and allow that some other interpretation function may be closer to the mark.

5.6 *Generalizing the Argument to Other Interpretation Functions*

What I hope to establish in this section is that the conclusions of the previous section are not hostage to the assumption that the causal/functional interpretation function is the right one. Rather, I shall argue, there is reason to think that *any* plausible account of how mental sentences get paired with propositions (or content sentences or truth conditions) can be plugged into the arguments of the previous section, with the result being no less persuasive. My strategy will be to focus on those features of the causal/functional account that were essential to the arguments in 5.5 and to argue that any plausible alternative story about the interpretation function is likely to share those features. I'll start where we left off, with instrumental value.

My arguments about the instrumental value of true beliefs were not aimed at establishing that true beliefs are not instrumentally valuable. The goal was more modest. What I wanted to show was that the instrumental value of true beliefs is far from obvious, and thus those who think that true beliefs are instrumentally valuable owe us an argument that is not going to be easy to provide. In support of that conclusion, I offered three observations. The first was that it is not enough to show that true beliefs are instrumentally preferable to false ones. What must be shown is that true beliefs are superior to the indefinitely many alternative categories of belief (TRUE*, TRUE**, and the rest) that are built on alternative accounts of REFERENCE and TRUTH CONDITIONS—accounts that are not sanctioned by commonsense intuition. The causal/functional account of truth conditions facilitated the argument by making vivid the existence of vast numbers of alternative, nonintuitively sanctioned mappings from beliefs to truth conditions or propositions. However, once the point has been made, it will stand no matter what account of the interpretation function a theorist proposes. Whatever function it is that best explicates commonsense intuition, there will be heaps of alternative functions that *don't* best explicate commonsense intuition, and the functions defining TRUTH* CONDITIONS, TRUTH** CONDITIONS and TRUTH**. . .* CONDITIONS will be among them. On any account of the interpretation function, to make a case for the instrumental value of true beliefs requires showing not just that they are better than false ones but also that they are better than TRUE* ones, TRUE**. . .*, ones and all the rest.

The second point in my discussion of instrumental value was that evolutionary considerations can't be used to show that beliefs mapped to true propositions by the intuitively sanctioned interpretation function will be instrumentally optimal or even close to optimal. The argument on that point turned on the nature of biological and social evolution and made no use of the details of the causal/functional theory. So it should apply, without change, no matter what account of the interpretation theory a theorist may offer.

My third point on instrumental value was that we already know there are some circumstances in which true beliefs are less efficacious than, say, TRUE**** ones. Here again the argument will work with any plausible account of the interpretation function. Recall that for an account of the interpretation function to be in the running, it must match up with commonsense intuition, at least most of the time. Thus, to be plausible, an interpretation function had better map poor Harry's belief to the proposition that the plane will leave at 7:45, since that's what common sense says he believes. Actually, that is a bit too strong. In the spirit of conservative explication, an interpretation function might override commonsense intuition in this case and map Harry's belief to some other proposition. But there are going to be *lots* of cases like Harry's, and any interpretation function that gives all of them counterintuitive interpretations will not be doing an acceptable job at explicating the intuitive notion of truth conditions.

Let's turn now to the arguments for intrinsic value. My central theme there was that those who imbue true belief with intrinsic value are opting for a deeply conservative normative epistemology, which most of us are likely to find very unattractive. In setting out the argument, two features of the causal/functional interpretation function loomed large. The first was the very *partial* nature of the function—the fact that its domain includes only a relatively small subset of the possible systems of mental storage and computation, a subset whose members are relatively close to the system (or systems) we now employ. Thus, those who insist on the intrinsic value of true belief, when that notion is explicated along causal/functional lines, are resolving that in matters cognitive they will cleave close to the status quo. It should be clear that exactly the same point can be made for any plausible alternative to the causal/functional interpretation function. For to be plausible, an interpretation function must more or less match commonsense intuition, at least most of the time. And, as we've seen, there is abundant evidence that our intuitions about the content or truth conditions of cognitive states begin to fall silent when directed at systems of cognitive storage and computation that are significantly different from our own.[15] So any account of the interpretation function that systematically assigns truth conditions in the huge space of mental storage systems falling outside the domain of the causal/functional interpretation function will depart quite radically from the commonsense intuitions that any acceptable interpretation function must respect.

The second feature of the causal/functional account that played a role in our discussion of intrinsic value was the *idiosyncratic* nature of the mapping it generated. Three facts contribute to this idiosyncrasy. The first is that there are *lots* of alternatives to the causal/functional mapping, some of which differ in minor ways while others may differ quite radically. Each of these alternative mappings defines an alternative notion of TRUTH CONDITIONS. The second is that our culturally inherited intuitions play a central role in selecting among these alternatives, and those intuitions have little to be said for them apart from the fact that they have the sanction of tradition. The third is that the causal/functional interpretation function does not pick out any simple or natural relation between mental states and truth conditions. It is a jerry-built contraption combining a heterogeneous family of strategies for grounding reference with an equally heterogeneous family of strategies for transmitting reference from one speaker to another. These three together make the preference for true belief look like a very conservative preference indeed, since, when compared with TRUTH CONDITIONS*, TRUTH CONDITIONS**, and the rest, the only thing that makes truth conditions special is that they have the sanction of tradition.

Two of the three facts contributing to the idiosyncrasy of causal/ functional mapping will clearly obtain with any alternative mapping.

No matter which mapping does the best job in explicating the commonsense notion of content or truth conditions, there are bound to be lots of alternatives. And the choice among them will be guided and constrained by a system of intuitions that have been inherited from our culture. The third fact, the hodgepodge nature of the causal/functional mapping, is a rather different matter. It is entirely possible that someone may find a much smoother, simpler, more natural, and less disjunctive function that does a good job at explicating our ordinary notion of content or truth conditions. And since this is possible, we cannot know in advance that any proposed alternative to causal/functional interpretation will be equally quirky and baroque. But merely finding some neat and natural relation which captures our intuitions about how cognitive states are to be interpreted won't be enough to persuade most of us that we really value true beliefs. To see the point, we need only suppose that in addition to the neat, natural, intuitively sanctioned function there is also some other mapping, which is less neat and less natural and does a less good job at capturing commonsense intuitions. This messier mapping will define a notion of TRUTH^{-m} CONDITIONS, which can in turn be used to define a notion of TRUE^{-m} beliefs. Suppose further that people whose cognitive systems tend to produce TRUE^{-m} beliefs generally lead happier, healthier, more rewarding lives than people whose cognitive systems tend to produce true beliefs. If all of this were the case, it is hard to see why anyone would think that the greater neatness, naturalness, and intuitiveness of the (uncapitalized) truth condition relation would lend any intrinsic value to the holding of true beliefs.

Chapter 6

A Pragmatic Account of Cognitive Evaluation

The last two chapters have been motivated by concerns about the evaluation of alternative cognitive systems. We began chapter 4 by asking just what it was for a system of cognitive processes to be a good one or for one such system to be better than another. And we have now come to reject two broad categories of answers—those associated with the tradition of analytic epistemology and those that tie cognitive evaluation to the generation of true beliefs. Though the arguments of chapters 4 and 5 are largely negative in tone, they also contain the seeds of a much more promising proposal on how to go about evaluating cognitive systems, a proposal that is in the spirit of pragmatism. My goals in this chapter are to sketch this pragmatic alternative (in 6.1), to defend it against some of the more obvious complaints that might be lodged against it (in 6.2 and 6.3), and to explore some of its implications (in 6.4). In saying that I propose to *sketch* a pragmatist account of cognitive evaluation, I choose my words carefully. For the story I have to tell in 6.1 is very much a preliminary sketch, leaving many questions unanswered and much work to be done. Some further details will be added in the sections to follow, in the course of answering objections and putting the theory to work. But even when the chapter and the book have come to an end, there will still be much to say about how the details of a pragmatist account should be developed. I'll note a number of these lacunae in passing and say a bit about why I have chosen to leave them as open questions. In general, of course, the reason is simply that I don't know what to say. That is one of the reasons I've chosen to describe the book as a *Preface* to a Pragmatic Account of Cognitive Evaluation.

6.1 Toward Pragmatism

Let me begin with a brief reminder of just why it was that the analytic and truth-generating accounts of cognitive assessment came to grief. In each case, I think, there is a lesson to be learned about how a more successful account can be developed. In chapter 4, we rejected the research program that proposes to choose among competing accounts of cognitive assessment by determining which of them best accords with commonsense concepts or practices of cognitive evaluation—the concepts and practices "embedded in everyday thought and language." At bottom, the argument against this analytic program was that, on reflection, being sanctioned by those concepts and practices is of no particular value to most of us. For even if it should turn out that our own evaluative notions are reasonably coherent, systematic, and stable, they mark only one spot in a rich and varied space of possible (and probably actual) alternatives. If the principal reason that our evaluative epistemic concepts, concepts like rationality and justification, stand out from the crowd is that they happen to be the evaluative notions passed on by our language and culture, it's hard to see why anyone but an epistemic chauvinist would much care whether his cognitive processes were sanctioned by those notions. Yet if the appeal of local, culturally inherited concepts won't lead a clear headed nonchauvinist to prefer one system of cognitive processes over another, what will?

A natural suggestion is that rather than looking at how high alternative systems of cognitive processes rank on some evaluative standard embedded in our language, we attend instead to the *consequences* of employing one alternative or the other—more specifically, to the likelihood that use of one system or the other will lead to something we value. Just as I don't much care whether the cognitive system I use does better than some proposed alternative on a standard that might be extracted from venerable texts, so too I don't much care whether it does better on a standard that may happen to have been bequeathed by my culture. But I do care whether my cognitive system does a better job than a proposed alternative at bringing about consequences that I value. Nor do I take myself to be at all unusual here. For most people who see the issue clearly, what will really be important in choosing among cognitive systems will be the consequences to which they lead. So the moral I would extract from the failure of the analytic strategy is that our account of cognitive virtue should be a *consequentialist* account.

But now what sort of consequences are going to be relevant for the evaluation of cognitive strategies? Truth, or true beliefs, is the obvious answer, since truth is widely held to be the appropriate goal of cognition. However, the moral I would draw from the arguments of chapter 5 is that, despite being both venerable and intuitively plausible, for most of us this is exactly the wrong answer. It is the wrong answer because in order to avoid the "who cares" complaint that scuttles the analytic program, a consequentialist account must take as the relevant consequences something that people actually value. And the burden of the argument in chapter 5 is that for most of us true belief just won't do, once we see how limited and idiosyncratic the notion of true belief is. Without some reason for thinking that true beliefs stand us in better stead than TRUE* ones, TRUE** ones, and all the rest, it is hard to see why anyone would care whether his beliefs are true rather than, say, TRUE****. Moreover, if you don't care whether your beliefs are true rather than TRUE****, if you attach no greater value to having true beliefs than to having TRUE***** ones, you're not likely to care whether your cognitive processes lead to true beliefs rather than TRUE***** ones.

At this juncture one might begin to worry that we have painted ourselves into a corner. If our account of cognitive evaluation is going to be a consequentialist account, and if truth is not the relevant consequence, what is? What else could possibly be viewed as a value that is relevant to the assessment of cognition?

The first step toward the answer I would urge is to adopt a perspective on cognition that grows out of the pragmatist tradition. Cognitive processes, pragmatists will insist, should not be thought of primarily as devices for generating truths. Rather they should be thought of as something akin to tools or technologies or practices that can be used more or less successfully in achieving a variety of goals. Viewing cognitive processes as akin to technologies suggests an obvious answer to the question of what goals or values we might appeal to in assessing them. The consequences that may be considered in deciding whether to adopt a given technological innovation are as rich and varied as the things that people find intrinsically valuable. Some of these things, like health, happiness, and the well-being of one's children, we are probably biologically predisposed to value, and thus they are likely to be valued by large numbers of people. Other things may be valued only in a more limited cultural environment; and still others may be valued by only a few idiosyncratic individuals. If, as I am urging, we view systems of cognitive processes as analogous to tools or technologies, then they too are to be evaluated by appeal to the rich and varied class of things that people take to be intrinsically valuable.

Here, then, is a first pass at a pragmatic account of cognitive evaluation. In evaluating systems of cognitive processes, the system to be preferred is the one that would be most likely to achieve those things that are intrinsically valued by the person whose interests are relevant to the purposes of the evaluation. In most cases, the relevant person will be the one who is or might be using the system. So, for example, if the issue at hand is the evaluation of Smith's system of cognitive processes in comparison with some actual or hypothetical alternative, the system that comes out higher on the pragmatist account of cognitive evaluation is the one that is most likely to lead to the things that Smith finds intrinsically valuable. In contrast with the analytic and truth-generating accounts, there is no mystery about why Smith should care about the outcome of this evaluation.[1]

This, as advertised, is only a sketch of the sort of pragmatic account of cognitive evaluation that I would recommend. In drawing the sketch, I have helped myself to unanalyzed notions, invoked undefended assumptions, and tucked some substantive problems under the rug. Moreover, at this point I have neither analyses nor defenses nor solutions to offer. But I will say a little about each of these shortcomings and about work that still needs to be done.

Perhaps the most obviously problematic notion that I am invoking is the idea of a person intrinsically valuing something. The textbook story about intrinsic valuing is that intrinsically valued things are the things a person values for their own sake, not because he believes they will lead to other things. And any well-trained undergraduate philosophy major should be able to come up with a blue book full of quibbles with that story.[2] The textbook story about valuing—about what it is for a person to value something—is near enough the Louis Armstrong story: "If you gotta ask, you ain't ever gonna get to know." Plainly, at some point in the elaboration of a pragmatic theory of cognitive evaluation, a careful and empirically well-grounded examination of the concepts of valuing and intrinsic valuing will be in order. And I would not be surprised if, in the light of such an examination, the pragmatic story itself may be seen to need some substantial reworking.[3] Still, I am inclined to think that for many purposes the intuitive notion of valuing and the textbook account of intrinsic valuing are solid enough to work with. Neither the discussion of objections to pragmatism in the following two sections nor the applications of the pragmatic account in the section after that are much hampered by the lack of a detailed account of the nature of intrinsic valuing.

In discussing what people may intrinsically value, I have persistently presupposed an exuberant pluralism. People, I have claimed, can and do intrinsically value a great diversity of things, with some of these values being widely shared while others are local or idiosyncratic. There is, of course, a long philosophical tradition that takes the opposite view. Monists about what is intrinsically valued maintain that there is only one thing (typically happiness, pleasure, or some similar commodity) that anyone could possibly value intrinsically. This is, by my lights, a wildly implausible view supported by notoriously unpersuasive arguments. But in the present context there is no need to defend my value-pluralism, since this sort of pluralism only makes things more difficult for the brand of epistemic pragmatism I advocate. As we'll see in the next section, value-pluralism entails that the pragmatic account of cognitive evaluation is relativistic in a way that truth-generating accounts are not. And since relativism is widely viewed as a liability, I am doing myself no favor by assuming value-pluralism.

Actually, the fact that value-pluralism engenders relativism is not much of a concern for me since, as I'll argue in 6.2.2, relativism in cognitive evaluation is itself nothing to worry about. A more unsettling fact about value-pluralism is that if it is true, it may considerably complicate the pragmatist's calculation of consequences. To see the point, let's go back to the analogy between cognitive systems, on the one hand, and technologies, on the other. How would someone with consequentialist leanings go about assessing the relative merits of a pair of technological options. Perhaps the simplist idea is to use a sort of "cost-benefit analysis" that is a straightforward generalization of the basic utilitarian strategy. For each option we construct a list of possible outcomes and try to determine the probability that the option in question will lead to each of those outcomes. We then must make some assessment of the value of each outcome and express that value as a cardinal number. Having done all this, we can determine the "expected value" of an option by multiplying the value of each outcome by the probability that the option will lead to that outcome and then summing the numbers that result. The option to be preferred is the one with the greatest expected value.[4]

It has long been recognized that one of the difficulties facing a policy maker who would assess technologies in this way is the fact that the "outcomes" whose values must be assessed are typically complex states of affairs whose components may be very hard to compare. For example, one possible outcome of a given technological option might be the state of affairs in which 1000 new jobs will be generated in an economically depressed area. Another possible outcome might be a state of affairs that is similar to the first except that, in addition to creating the new jobs, one worker a year will be killed in an industrial accident. Obviously, the value assigned to the second outcome should be lower than the value assigned to the first. But how much lower? To answer the question requires that we have some fairly specific quantitative assessment of the comparative value of lives and economic benefits. And such assessments are notoriously hard to make.

Suppose, now, that we take this "expected value" approach to technology assessment as our model in pragmatic cognitive evaluation. To assess the comparative merits of a pair of cognitive systems that a person might exploit requires that we compute the expected value of adopting each system. To do that, we must try to determine the probability of each option leading to various possible outcomes and then multiply those probabilities by cardinal number indices of the values we have assigned to the outcomes. The consequences that are important for a pragmatic evaluation will be things that the person in question takes to be intrinsically valuable. And if value-pluralism is true, the outcomes to which numbers must be assigned will often be conjunctive states of affairs combining various different intrinsically valued elements. Thus, in making the assignments we must find some way of weighing a person's intrinsic values against one another. And often that will be no easy task.

The simple expected value approach to technology assessment is, of course, not the only one that has been proposed. The assumptions—about coherently ordered values and discoverable probabilities—needed to make this approach work are very strong ones. And in many cases, they seem hopelessly unrealistic. These difficulties have given rise to a large, sophisticated literature exploring alternative decision strategies, many of them clearly consequentialist in spirit, which relax some of the implausible assumptions of the expected value approach.[5] The existence of these alternative approaches poses something of a problem for my rough-and-ready account of how an epistemic pragmatist would evaluate competing cognitive systems. For according to that account, the cognitive system to be preferred is the one best suited to the attainment of what we intrinsically value. But it now appears that there are various rather different ways of unpacking this idea and no overriding reason why the pragmatist should take the simple expected value approach as his model rather than one of the alternatives.

Clearly this is another area where the epistemic pragmatist has more work to do. And much of this work will have to be done in collaboration with psychologists, anthropologists, economists, and others who are trying to get an empirically plausible account of the nature of human value systems. This sort of integration of empirical and normative investigations is a hallmark of the pragmatic tradition in epistemology. We'll see some further examples of it in 6.4.

6.2 Pragmatism and Relativism

It is a virtue of the sort of pragmatic evaluation of cognitive processes sketched in the previous section that it provides an obvious answer to the question of why we should care how such an evaluation turns out. Though it's hard to see why anyone but an epistemic chauvinist would be much concerned about rationality or truth, we can count on people caring about the pragmatic evaluation of their cognitive processes because that evaluation is tied to goals that they themselves take to be intrinsically valuable. Offsetting this positive point about pragmatic evaluation, however, are a number of *prima facie* deficits. Among these, the one that many people seem to find the most worrisome is that pragmatic evaluation is blatantly and floridly relativistic. What I propose to do in the current section is first to explain the various ways in which a pragmatic account of cognitive evaluation may give rise to relativism. I will then go on to ask a question that has, in my experience, been asked all too infrequently: What's so bad about epistemic relativism? I will propose a pair of answers that, I think, together account for much of the disquiet that people feel about relativism. I'll then go on to argue that this disquiet is largely unjustified, since the first of the alleged nasty consequences of relativism is not a consequence at all, while the second is nothing much to worry about.

6.2.1 How Pragmatism Leads to Relativism

Before setting out the various ways in which pragmatism gives rise to relativism, we'd do well to get a bit clearer on just what relativism, as I use the notion, comes to. And to do that, we'll have to back up a bit and remind ourselves of some terminology set out in chapter 1. In that chapter, I introduced the label *normative cognitive pluralism* for the thesis that there is no uniquely good system of cognitive processes— no single system that people ought to use. Rather, the normative cognitive pluralist insists, there may be various systems of cognitive processes that are significantly different from each other, though they are all equally good. One way in which this situation might arise—a thoroughly nonrelativistic way—would be for our account of what it is for a cognitive system to be a good one to turn on intrinsic (perhaps formal) features of the system. If the story about cognitive virtue were told in the right way, it might happen that two or more substantially different systems each have the specified intrinsic virtues to just the same extent and thus come out tied for first.

There is also a very different way in which the situation envisioned by the normative cognitive pluralist might arise. Suppose that our account of what makes one system of cognitive processes better than another involves relational features of the systems being evaluated, where one of the elements in the relation is the person or group using the system, or some property of that person or group. If systems of cognitive processes are evaluated in this user-relative way, then in general it will not make sense to ask whether one system is better than another (full stop). Rather, we must ask whether one system is better than another for a given person or group; and it may well turn out that one system is best for one person or group, while another system is best for another person or group. I take this possibility to be the hallmark of relativism in the assessment of cognitive processes. An account of cognitive evaluation is relativistic if the assessments of cognitive systems it offers are sensitive to facts about the person or group using the system.[6]

Given this characterization of relativism, a pragmatic account of cognitive evaluation is going to be relativistic for two quite different reasons. The most obvious source of relativism is the plurality of values to which a pragmatic assessment must be sensitive. A somewhat less obvious source is the consequentialist character of pragmatic evaluation. Let me take these up in turn.

The pragmatic account urges that we assess cognitive systems by their likelihood of leading to what their users value. If, as I have been supposing, people can and do intrinsically value a wide variety of things, with considerable variation from person to person and culture to culture, then pragmatic assessments of cognitive systems will be sensitive to highly variable facts about the users of those systems. Moreover, given the diversity of goals and values, it is all but certain that different systems of cognitive processes will be pragmatically preferable for different people. Indeed, pragmatic assessment will even distinguish between people who share the same values but who differ in the relative importance they attach to them.

While it is no surprise that pragmatic evaluations must be relativized to people's varying values, it is perhaps less obvious that pragmatic assessment is also relativistic for a quite different reason. Epistemic pragmatism urges a consequentialist account of inferential virtue— the goodness or badness of a system of cognitive processes depends on the likelihood of the system leading to certain consequences. And consequentialist evaluations will typically be relativistic, since the likelihood of a given system leading to a certain consequence will generally depend on the environment in which the system is operating. If we keep the goals constant, the probability that a given system of cognitive processes will lead to those goals is going to depend, to a significant extent, on the circumstances of the person using the system.

Though not often emphasized, this sort of relativism is as much a feature of truth-generating accounts of inferential virtue as it is of pragmatic accounts. Whether a given system of cognitive processes is likely to produce truths depends on the environment of the person using the system.[7] Perhaps the easiest way to see the point is to invoke a variation on the Cartesian evil demon theme. Imagine a pair of people who suddenly fall victim to such a demon and are from that time forward provided with systematically misleading or deceptive perceptual data. Let's further suppose that one of the victims has been using cognitive processes quite like our own and that these have done a pretty good job of generating truths and avoiding falsehoods, while the other victim's cognitive processes have been (by our lights) quite mad, and have produced far more falsehoods and far fewer truths. In their new demon-infested environment, however, the sane system of cognitive processes—the one like ours—will yield a growing fabric of false beliefs. The other system, by contrast, may now do a much better job at generating truths and avoiding falsehoods, since what the evil demon is doing is providing his victims with radically misleading evidence—evidence that only a lunatic would take to be evidence for what actually is the case. So on a truth-generating, consequentialist account of cognitive evaluation, our system would be preferable in one environment, while the mad system would be preferable in another environment. And clearly an entirely parallel tale could be told if the goal being sought were not truth but some other more pragmatic commodity.

We have just seen that consequentialism in cognitive evaluation is capable of bringing relativism in its wake. But my invocation of evil demons to make the point might suggest that this is a very peripheral phenomenon, one not worth worrying about except in Cartesian nightmares. I think that would be a serious mistake. For whether it is truth we want our cognitive processes to produce, or whether we have other goals whose desirability is less problematic, the chances of success are going to depend on features of the environment that are much less exotic than infestation by evil demons. Consider, for example, the effects of the commonsense world view prevailing in the culture that surrounds a person in his formative years—the fabric of socially shared beliefs, concepts, and distinctions (both explicit and tacit) about matters physical and metaphysical, cosmological, theological, psychological, and social. It is plausible to speculate that most people internalize a fair amount of this socially shared Weltanschauung very uncritically and very early on, in the course of language acquisition and acculturation.[8] But now consider how a consequentialist account of cognitive evaluation would assess the cognitive processes underlying the assimilation of a world view. If such matters as theology, folk geography, folk cosmology, and folk medicine are included in the domain of these assimilative processes, then plainly the consequentialist's assessment is going to vary significantly with the surroundings in which the assimilative processes are working. The folk wisdom my children acquired on these topics contains vastly more that is true and (for some purposes at least) vastly more that is useful than the folk wisdom acquired by Thales's children. Indeed, from the perspective of a consequentialist whose single goal is truth, Thales's children might have been better served by a system of assimilative processes that systematically distorted the socially provided input in the direction of a world view more like our own. Given other goals, of course, processes of world view assimilation that systematically distort the input might serve their users less well. If Thales's children had ended up with the folk wisdom of contemporary California kids, they might have become great leaders; but it is more likely that they would have been social outcasts, taken to be mad. The moral here is that if the output of a cognitive process depends heavily on the social environment in which it is functioning, then consequentialist evaluations of that process are typically going to be highly environment-relative.

Nor is this the only way in which consequentialist accounts of cognitive virtue give rise to relativism. Suppose for a moment that the members of a given group—the community of scientists, perhaps—each has as a high priority goal the group's discovering and coming to accept important truths of nature. Suppose, further, that within the group there is considerable variability in the amount of evidence it takes to dislodge conviction in an accepted theory and launch off along some new line of inquiry. The cognitive processes of investigators at one end of the spectrum lead them to hang on to prevailing theories or paradigms until the evidence against them is overwhelming, while the cognitive processes of investigators at the other end of the spectrum may lead them to reject the prevailing doctrines and commit themselves to new ideas while the preponderance of evidence still clearly favors the established view. And between these two extremes, there is a variety of intermediate positions. Given that the shared goal of the community is the discovery and acceptance of important scientific truths, which of these cognitive processes should a scientist have; which is the best? The answer is that there may be no answer—that the question itself is badly posed. For the question presupposes that there is a single optimal spot along the spectrum described, a cognitive system such that if everyone in the scientific community were to share it, the community would stand the best chance of achieving its goal. However, as Philip Kitcher has shown, there are many circumstances in which this presupposition is simply untenable.[9] In these circumstances the probability of achieving the community's goal is maximized by a mixed strategy in which some investigators are very conservative in giving up received doctrines, while others do so much more readily. This is not the place to recount the sophisticated mathematical models that support Kitcher's conclusion. However, the point should be intuitively plausible even without a detailed proof. If we assume that investigators typically invest their energy attempting to elaborate and support the theory they accept, then it will often be best to have the community's allegiance divided, with the bulk of the effort going into the established (and presumably the best-supported) theory, while some effort is devoted to exploring new ideas and long shots. Moreover, when the established theory is seriously threatened, it will often be best to have some substantial number of residual defenders trying to shore it up, rather than to have everyone jump ship more or less simultaneously.

What makes all this important for our purposes is that it points to another potential source of relativism in consequentialist accounts of cognitive assessment. Consider the situation of a single investigator in the inquiring community. Should she be conservative in her attitude toward the received theory, or would it be better if she were more of a radical, more willing to reject the community's favored theory? The answer, of course, is that it depends on what the rest of the community is doing. If the community is already oversupplied with conservatives, then their shared goal would be best served if her cognitive processes tend in the radical direction. While if radicals abound, she ought to be a conservative. What is more, exactly the same conclusion follows if, instead of assuming that our investigator values the communal discovery of truth, we suppose instead that her goal is getting tenure, developing a new and useful technology, or winning a Nobel Prize. The likelihood that one's cognitive processes will lead to these goals will often be partly determined by what others in one's community are doing, since the expected payoff of exploring unpromising domains will often decline if one has too much company. Whether it is truth or fame or technological prowess we want, there is no saying which cognitive system is best (full stop); the evaluation of a system must be relativized to the setting in which it is used.[10]

Though I won't attempt an exhaustive inquiry into the various ways in which consequentialism in cognitive evaluation gives rise to relativism, I am inclined to think that the few illustrations I've provided are just the very small tip of a very large iceberg. Whether the goal is truth or some cluster of things whose desirability is easier to understand, it is my bet that a consequentialist evaluation of cognitive processes is going to be acutely sensitive to the cultural, technological, and epistemic setting in which the processes are to function. The likelihood that one system of cognitive processes will do a better job than another at securing just about any plausible goal will, I suspect, depend on such factors as the existence of a system of writing, the existence and the structure of disciplinary communities, and the relation of those communities to the political and economic arrangements of the wider society. It will also often depend on the level of conceptual, mathematical, scientific, and technological sophistication that has been achieved. It's not implausible to suppose that there are strategies of thought that will lead to a dead end in a community where geometry is unknown, others that will lead to a dead end without the calculus, or probability theory, or powerful computers, and still others that will be pragmatically powerful only in environments where the distinction between velocity and acceleration has been clearly drawn, where the basic idea of evolution by natural selection is widely accepted, or where the expectation that things have final causes has been rejected. If these conjectures are right, it follows that pragmatic accounts of cognitive or epistemic evaluation will have a certain post-Hegelian historicist flavor. There will be no one ideal method of inquiry, no cognitive system that excels in all historical settings. Rather, we can expect that the assessment of a cognitive system will vary as its historical setting varies and that, just as with technologies (and indeed with genes), it will sometimes happen that a successful system will undermine its own success by changing the environment in such a way that competing systems will now be more successful. There are people, and I am one of them, who find something refreshing, even liberating, in the thought that there may be no final, ultimate, best way of going about the business of cognition. But, among philosophers at least, the sort of relativism that a pragmatic epistemology engenders is more often a source of dread than of celebration. So the next item on my agenda will be to explore why it is that many people find relativism so ominous a view, and to see what can be said to quiet these qualms.

6.2.2 Is Epistemic Relativism Really Worrisome?

It is an easy matter to find evidence for the widespread abhorrence of relativism among contemporary philosophers. Indeed, it sometimes seems that many of my philosophical acquaintances can barely bring themselves to utter the word without embedding it in an epithet. "The specter of relativism" is a phrase that comes naturally to many. It is, however, a much more difficult matter to find any serious effort to justify this negative attitude—to show that relativism is a bad thing, or that it would lead to ominous consequences. What I propose to do in this section is to sketch the two lines of argument that have most often emerged in conversation when I have asked philosophers to support the view that epistemic relativism is an ominous or unwelcome doctrine. In the first case my reply will be that the danger is imaginary—that it rests on a misunderstanding of what relativists, particularly pragmatic relativists, claim. The second argument will require a longer discussion. For, in that case, I think the accusation leveled against relativism can likely be made to stick. However, if the arguments elaborated in the previous chapter are successful, only those whose intrinsic values are epistemically chauvinistic should find the accusation worrisome. Perhaps there are other, more plausible reasons to find epistemic relativism worrisome. But if so, I don't know what they are.

6.2.2.1 The first charge against relativism, and the easiest to dispatch, is that it is nihilistic, that it simply gives up on the project of distinguishing good cognition from bad and embraces a Feyerabendian cognitive libertinism—the doctrine that "anything goes." I am not at all certain that Feyerabend would really endorse the view that there is no distinction between good and bad ways of going about the business of cognition, or that he would be serious about it if he did.[11] But however this may be, it is quite clear that the "anything goes" slogan is singularly inappropriate for epistemic pragmatism or the relativism it engenders. Pragmatism does not give up on the project of assessing cognitive processes. Quite the contrary. Epistemic pragmatism offers an account of cognitive evaluation that is both demanding and designed to produce assessments that people will care about. For a given cognitive agent in a given historical setting, it will typically be the case that a pragmatic evaluation will rank one cognitive system higher than another. Occasionally perhaps a pair of cognitive systems may come out ranked equally. But it will near enough never be the case that pragmatism ranks all contenders on a par.

It is sometimes supposed that epistemic relativists must be wimps when it comes to evaluating the cognitive doings of other people or other cultures—that they must condone whatever they find. But clearly no such consequence follows from pragmatism. The fact that a given system of cognitive processes prevails in a culture does not even begin to show that that system is the best one for that culture. The pragmatist is perfectly prepared to find that people in some other culture would be doing a better job of cognition if they were to replace their own cognitive processes with ours. But he is also prepared to find that people in another culture are doing quite a good job of cognition, given their goals and circumstances, even though their system of cognitive processes would be a disaster for us. (Indeed, in the assessment of the cognitive practices of premodern science, I'd not be surprised if this turned out to be just the right thing to say.) Pragmatism in the assessment of cognition is no more nihilistic than pragmatism in the assessment of alternative technologies. In both cases, the evaluations proposed are going to depend on the goals of the users and on the situations in which they find themselves. But in neither case does pragmatism entail that anything goes.

6.2.2.2   A second complaint against relativism in epistemology is that it threatens the connection between cognitive inquiry and truth. To see the point, it helps to go back to Descartes and the very beginnings of modern epistemology. In the *Meditations*, Descartes sketches the method of clear and distinct ideas that, he urges, is the correct strategy of inquiry—the right way to go about the business of cognition. Having set out the method, Descartes goes on to ask what guarantee it provides. Why should we suppose that if we use the method diligently, we must ultimately arrive at the truth? Descartes's answer, which appeals to the goodness of God, runs roughly as follows. *If this, the best of methods, were to fail, then we might end up with false beliefs despite doing the best we could. But having done the best we could, our error would not be our fault; it would be God's. Moreover, if God built the world in such a way that we could not help being deceived despite doing the best we could, then God is a deceiver. And that we know to be impossible, since it is incompatible with His goodness.*

This answer is notoriously unconvincing. But if Descartes's answer was a nonstarter, his question certainly was not. Epistemologists from his time onward have been preoccupied with the relation between good thinking or good methods of inquiry, on the one hand, and truth, on the other. What reason do we have to believe that if we do a good job of cognition, the beliefs we end up with will be any closer to the truth than they would be if we reasoned poorly? The last four centuries have seen no shortage of attempts to answer this question. They have also seen more than a few skeptical arguments aimed at showing that an answer is impossible. And it is just here that relativism enters the picture. For it might well be thought that if epistemic relativism can be sustained, then the skeptics will have won the day.

A first pass at an argument to this effect might run something like this:

> *Suppose the epistemic relativist is right. Then there may be a pair of people whose cognitive systems are very different from one another, though the systems are equally (and even optimally) good. But if their cognitive systems are really very different from one another, we can expect that, on being exposed to essentially the same data, they will generally end up with very different sets of beliefs. When this happens, it can't be the case that both sets are true; at least one set of beliefs must be substantially mistaken. Since at least one of our hypothetical people will end up*

with false beliefs, and since ex hypothesis *they are both using optimally good cognitive systems, it can't be the case that good cognition guarantees truth. Indeed, it can't even be the case that good cognition has a high probability of producing the truth. For our story might just as well have been told with fifty people as with two. If relativism is right, these fifty people could have fifty different cognitive systems, all equally good. But, at most, one is going to end up with the truth.*

Now, as it stands, this argument is hardly ironclad. One possible objection turns on the assumption that alternative sets of beliefs generated by alternative cognitive systems cannot both be true. This assumption would surely be defensible if there were some reason to think that the alternative belief sets must be logically incompatible with one another. But nothing the relativist says commits him to that. Perhaps alternative cognitive systems produce alternative beliefs that are not logically incompatible but rather logically "incommensurable" in some way. One might, for example, imagine them stored in alternative dialects of mentalese whose concepts and constructions, and the mental sentences built from them, are not intertranslatable.

Confronted with this objection, those who are tempted by the argument sketched above have a number of options. One option would be to accept the objection and modify the conclusion the argument aims to establish. Rather than showing that relativism severs the connection between good thinking and truth, what the argument shows is that relativism severs the link between good thinking and the whole truth. If two people can each exploit good cognitive processes in a given environment and end up with very different sets of beliefs, then even if both sets are true it is still the case that neither person can get at the whole truth. So relativism seems to lead us to a doctrine of separate truths. The users of alternative, equally good cognitive systems each have a perspective on reality from which the other is excluded. But, for two reasons, this seems a less-than-promising path for those who would argue that epistemic relativism is a bad thing. First, it requires that we make some sense of the idea that mental sentences or cognitive states can have truth conditions and truth values despite being "incommensurable" with our own beliefs. Second, even if some sense can be made of the idea of beliefs that are true but incommensurable, it's far from clear why this new accusation is a problem for relativism. Many theorists are anxious to show that good reasoning will get us closer to the truth. But not even Descartes thought that by pursuing proper strategies of reasoning we could come to know *everything* that is true.

A second option, for those who would press the complaint against relativism, and by my lights a far more promising one, would be to challenge the suggestion that incommensurable systems of belief could possibly both be true. Those who pursue this line can grant that there may be systems of belieflike cognitive states that are incommensurable with our beliefs—systems of mental sentences perhaps that are built from significantly different concepts and constructions. But, they would insist, the very fact that they are incommensurable entails that these cognitive states have no truth conditions, and thus they are neither true nor false. It would, of course, require a fair bit of additional argument to shore up this response and show just why it is that systems of cognitive states incommensurable with our own have no truth conditions. But I am inclined to think that a plausible case might be made along these lines. Indeed, our discussion of truth in the previous chapter provides a good beginning, since we saw there that one of the more promising and well-articulated accounts of what it is for a mental state to have a truth condition entails that there will be a large space of belieflike cognitive states which do not have truth conditions. We also saw why any plausible alternative account of the interpretation function is likely to lead to the same conclusion. So I am prepared to concede, for argument's sake at least, that some suitably elaborated version of the argument displayed above does in fact go through, and thus that if epistemic relativism is right, there is no hope of showing that good reasoning leads to the truth.

But my mention of the results of the previous chapter will perhaps suggest why I am unfazed by this complaint. A central thesis of that chapter is that there is an enormous space of head-world relationships among which the one picked out by the socially transmitted, intuitively sanctioned notion of truth has no unique advantages. Apart from epistemic chauvinists, it is hard to see why any clearheaded person would care whether her beliefs were true—why she would prefer true beliefs to TRUE* ones, TRUE** ones, and so on. It is harder still to see why a clearheaded person would prefer cognitive processes that typically yield true beliefs over cognitive processes that are pragmatically sanctioned. For the latter, in contrast with the former, have an obvious connection with what the person wants and values. So to the complaint that relativism would sever the connection between good cognition and truth, my answer is as follows. Perhaps that's right; perhaps it would. But this is no reason to *worry* about relativism unless we have some reason to want our beliefs to be true, some reason to care whether they are true rather than TRUE*, TRUE**, and so on. Without some reason to prefer truth to the infinite variety of alternative head-world relationships, we should be no more concerned about the fact that good reasoning may not lead to truth than we are about the fact that good reasoning may not lead TRUTH*****—or, for that matter, about the fact that good reasoning may not lead to beliefs sanctioned by some ancient text.

The epistemological tradition that begins with Descartes is built on the unquestioned assumption that there is some unique, special, intrinsically desirable relationship—the truth relationship—in which cognitive states should stand to nature. Much of the work in that tradition is fueled by the fear that this relation may be in jeopardy. But on my view—and here I think I echo a central thesis in the history of pragmatism—the entire Cartesian project is ill conceived. There is no unique, intrinsically desirable head-world relationship to which all cognitive agents should aspire. And since there is no universally desirable endpoint of cognitive activity, there is no point in fretting over the fact that if relativism is right, good thinking won't get us there.[12]

6.3 Pragmatism and Circularity

The previous section was motivated by the worry that the relativism implicit in my pragmatic account of cognitive evaluation might count as a deficit for that account. My response was that, though pragmatism does indeed lead to a kind of epistemic relativism, for most of us this relativism should be no cause for concern. In this section I want to consider another putative deficit that might be thought to encumber a pragmatic epistemology. In this case, the charge is circularity. But, I shall argue, when we see just what this accusation comes to, it turns out that in this case too the alleged defect is not worth worrying about. Since pragmatic accounts of cognitive evaluation have not been center stage in the philosophical literature, the charge that they are somehow viciously circular has not been debated in any detail. However, that charge has been repeatedly leveled at various truth-linked accounts of cognitive evaluation, and in ways that invite straightforward extension to pragmatic accounts. So I will begin my discussion of the circularity objection by reworking what I take to be the most cogent version of the complaint, taking pragmatic rather than truth-linked theories as the target.[13] That done, I will set out a series of replies, most of which are themselves adapted from parallel moves that have been made in defense of truth-linked accounts.[14] Taken together, these replies should suffice to show that the putative circularity does pragmatism no damage.

The best of the arguments alleging that truth-linked accounts of cognitive evaluation involve some sort of vicious circularity focus on the situation that arises when we attempt to apply these accounts. So in building the parallel case against epistemic pragmatism, let's consider where circularity might be thought to lurk in the application of the theory. According to the pragmatic account, one system of cognitive processes is better than another if it is more likely to achieve those things that are intrinsically valued by the relevant person. Let us suppose that in a given instance I am the relevant person, and I am trying the determine whether my own system of cognitive processes is better than some alternative system that has been proposed. In order to do that, I must study both systems and attempt to determine the likelihood of various consequences that might follow if I used one system or the other. But, of course, in order to do this I must do some thinking; I must *use* my cognitive system. And, the critic protests, it is just here that we confront a vicious circularity. For suppose that as a result of my inquiry I conclude that my own system of cognitive processes is indeed better than the proposed alternative. In coming to that conclusion, I have used the very system whose superiority I claim to have established. Moreover, it may well be the case that had I used some other system of cognitive processes (perhaps even the system whose merits I am comparing with mine), I might have ended up with just the opposite conclusion; I might have concluded that the proposed alternative is better than mine. Since in establishing the superiority of my own system of reasoning I have made essential use of that very system, the critic concludes that my effort has been viciously circular. I am trying, in vain, to pull myself up by my own bootstraps.

The argument just sketched is a variation on a venerable and very influential theme in the history of philosophy. Similar arguments can be found in writers as diverse as Sextus Empiricus, Montaigne, and Roderick Firth.[15] But despite its long history and its enormous influence, I find the argument singularly unpersuasive. Whether aimed at truth-linked or pragmatic accounts, it is very hard to see why the sort of circularity on which the argument turns is anything other than benign. To make the point, I'll assemble a number of replies.

First, it is important to recognize that the outcome in the story imagined by the critic is not the only possible outcome. In the critic's story, I use my cognitive system to reach the conclusion that it is itself better than some proposed alternative. However, it is entirely possible that the inquiry could come out just the other way and that, while using my cognitive system, I might reach the conclusion that the alternative system is in fact the better one. Were this to happen, I might contrive to rerun the inquiry using the proposed alternative (perhaps after doing a bit of cognitive retooling) and discover that,

that way too, the alternative comes out best. This would be a prime example of the sort of "bootstrapping" imagined by those who view the project of cognitive assessment as part of a larger project whose goal is cognitive improvement. And plainly there is no vicious circularity lurking in this scenario. Similarly, there will be no hint of unwelcome circularity if the assessment is run by both my system and the alternative, and they both end up with the conclusion that mine is better. The only case in which there is even a *prima facie* danger of begging the question is the one in which my system ends up with the conclusion that it is better, and the alternative ends up with the opposite conclusion. But obviously not all attempts at pragmatic cognitive assessment need turn out this way, nor is there any reason to think that such cases are going to be particularly common. So my first reply is that the circularity the critic fears will not be found in all attempts to apply a pragmatic account of cognitive evaluation. It may turn out to be quite rare.

My second reply is that, even in the *prima facie* problematic cases, there is no formal fallacy being committed. For an argument to beg the question, or be viciously circular, it must take as one of its premises the very conclusion that it purports to establish. But the pragmatic cognitive assessment imagined by the critic involves no such formal begging the question. The conclusion of that assessment is that my cognitive system is more likely than the alternative to achieve those things that I intrinsically value. To establish that conclusion, I will need to detail the workings of the two systems and to explore how they are likely to interact with my physical and social environment. But at no point in this inquiry am I going to assert the conclusion as a premise. To see this more clearly, it may help to compare the pragmatic assessment of a pair of cognitive systems with the pragmatic assessment of a pair of noncognitive tools. In both cases I am trying to determine which alternative is more likely to achieve what I value. And in both cases, of course, I must use my cognitive system in the process of coming up with an answer. But in assessing tools, there is plainly no need to invoke a premise about the efficacy of the cognitive system I am using. Nor is there any need to do so in assessing cognitive systems.

At this point, the critic may protest that, while the conclusion is not explicitly asserted in arguments for the superiority of our own cognitive system, it is tacitly presupposed. To make this objection stick, however, the critic will have to tell us a lot more about his notion of presupposition and about the principles that determine which propositions are presupposed by a given argument. This promises to be no easy matter, since the principle that seems to underwrite the critic's charge of tacit circularity quickly leads to absurdity. To see this, consider the case at hand in a bit more detail. We are supposing we have before us an empirical argument to the conclusion that our cognitive system is pragmatically better than a proposed alternative. (Let's call the alternative System A, and the conclusion Proposition A). It is claimed that because we are using our cognitive system in constructing and assessing the argument, the argument must tacitly presuppose Proposition A. But, of course, we use our cognitive system in all our reasoning. So if the mere fact that we use our cognitive system in constructing and assessing an argument entails that the argument presupposes Proposition A, then all our arguments presuppose Proposition A, even those that have nothing to do with the comparative merits of cognitive systems. Moreover, since proposition A is hardly unique, this is just the beginning of the critic's list of ubiquitous presuppositions. Consider the claim (call it Proposition B) that our cognitive system is better than some other alternative, System B. Presumably, the critic would claim that in using our cognitive system to construct arguments for Proposition B, we tacitly presuppose Proposition B. But, once again, if the mere fact that we use our cognitive system in constructing an argument entails that the argument presupposes Proposition B, then all our arguments presuppose Proposition B. And so on, for Proposition C, Proposition D, and indefinitely many more. Yet surely there is something more than a bit absurd about any view entailing that all our arguments have infinitely many presuppositions. To summarize, my second reply runs as follows: In applying the pragmatic account there will be no explicit circularity, and the critic who insists that there is a tacit circularity owes us some account of the notion of presupposition that does not lead to absurd consequences.

For argument's sake, let's ignore the problems with the notion of presupposition and grant that in some cases there will be a tacit circularity in applying the pragmatic account of cognitive evaluation. Against the background of these concessions, my third reply is that this circularity is no special problem for the pragmatic account, since an entirely parallel circularity will beset attempts to apply any other account of cognitive evaluation. What motivates the charge of circularity in applying the pragmatic account is simply that we are using our cognitive system in the process of showing that it is pragmatically better than some proposed alternative. But now suppose that we reject the pragmatic account in favor of some different account that says system A is better than system B if and only if A has property P and B doesn't. For any P that is even remotely plausible, we are going to have to use our cognitive system in order to determine whether our system has it and the alternative does not. And if that use of our cognitive system is all it takes to convict an account of cognitive evaluation of circularity, then any remotely plausible alternative to pragmatism is going to be circular, too. So the "circularity problem" gives us no reason to reject the pragmatic account in favor of some other account of cognitive evaluation.

The fact that the circularity argument is equally threatening to all accounts of cognitive evaluation should be no surprise, since the historical prototypes for the argument were skeptical in intent, aimed at undermining all efforts to show that our beliefs are justified. Taking a cue from that skeptical heritage, the critic might respond to my third reply by granting the broad applicability of the circularity argument and urging that in fact all accounts of cognitive evaluation are circular. To this move, I offer a fourth, and last, reply. Suppose we agree with the critic that pragmatism, along with all other accounts of cognitive evaluation, are "tacitly circular" when we attempt to apply them. Why is this circularity supposed to be a defect? The critic's answer, presumably, is that we should want something more from an account of cognitive evaluation; we should want an account that can be applied without this sort of circularity. But let's think a bit more carefully about this. The "tacit circularity" arises simply in virtue of the fact that we use our cognitive system in assessing cognitive systems. So according to the critic, what we should want is an account of cognitive evaluation that can be applied without any cognitive activity at all. Surely, at this juncture, the right reply to make is that this is a perfectly preposterous thing to want. The "defect" that the critic has discovered in the pragmatic account (and all the others) is simply that we can't apply it without thinking. And that, I submit, is not a defect that any sensible person should worry about.

6.4 Interpreting Psychological Studies of Reasoning: Pragmatism Applied

The reader who is favored with an unusually robust memory may recall that my concern with the evaluation of alternative strategies of cognitive processing was originally provoked by some striking experimental findings and by a question about how those findings were to be interpreted. The findings indicated that in quite ordinary and unthreatening environments, many normal subjects exhibited curious and unexpected patterns of reasoning—patterns which inclined some experimenters to conclude that the subjects were reasoning very poorly. The question was raised by critics who acknowledged the findings but challenged the experimenters' conclusion: Are the subjects really doing a bad job at the business of reasoning? This question leads very quickly to some more general ones: What is it to reason well or poorly? What constitutes doing a good job at the business of cognition? Much of the work of chapters 4, 5, and 6 has been devoted to undermining some widely endorsed answers to these questions and to laying the groundwork for a pragmatic alternative. It seems appropriate to end the volume by exploring how the pragmatic account of cognitive evaluation that I have endorsed might be used in answering the questions that have been raised about the implications of the experimental findings. What does the pragmatic account say about those troubling results in the psychological study of cognition? Is it the case that people are indeed reasoning badly when they exhibit belief perseverance, neglect base rates, make judgments on the basis of biased samples, or exploit one of the other suspect patterns of reasoning?

Perhaps the least controversial lesson to be drawn from the arguments of chapters 4 and 5 is that this last question is in need of some serious glossing before we try to answer it. In asking whether a pattern of reasoning, or the system of cognitive processes that underlies it, is good or bad, there are lots of things the questioner might have in mind. She might, for example, be asking whether the cognitive processes in question are rational, or whether they are the sort that give rise to justified beliefs, where the concepts of rationality or justification are presumed to be implicit in our ordinary thought and language. If this is the question being asked, then there is an obvious way to go about trying to answer it. The first step is to analyze or explicate the concepts of rationality or justification embedded in everyday thinking. The next step is to do some psychology in order to discover in sufficient detail just what the cognitive processes at hand are like. The final step is to determine whether the cognitive processes that have been described fall within the extension of the concept that has been explicated. None of this is likely to be easy, of course, and it may even prove to be impossible. For, as we noted in chapter 4, there is no guarantee that the concepts of rationality or justification underlying ordinary usage are sufficiently coherent and well behaved to sustain a usable explication. Moreover, even if things go well on this score, there is a serious worry about why anyone should much care how the whole project comes out, since, absent some further argument, the local evaluative concepts that drive the project have no more going for them than local notions of etiquette. But my current purpose is not to refight the battle over "analytic epistemology." Rather, it is to stress that questions about the goodness or badness of cognitive systems admit of a variety of interpretations. To tackle such questions without first thinking long and hard about how we propose to understand them is an open invitation to confusion. It is a mug's game to ask whether someone is reasoning well without some clear idea of what it is we really want to know and how we might go about finding out.

It's been my contention that questions about the evaluation of cognitive processes are most productively understood as pragmatic questions—that in most cases what we really want to know is how well the cognitive systems at issue will do at achieving what the people using them value. But most of what I have said about the pragmatic assessment of cognitive systems has focused on the comparative assessment of two or more systems, and this comparative account does not directly address the question of whether a given system is a good one, or whether people using that system are reasoning well. So let us ponder how the comparative pragmatic account might serve as the basis of a plausible pragmatic interpretation for those noncomparative evaluative questions.

One thought that might seem tempting is to count a particular cognitive system as a good one (for a specified person, in a specified context) if it is at least as good, from the pragmatic point of view, as any logically possible alternative. But, for a pair of closely related reasons, I am more than a bit dubious about this proposal. The first reason is that if we take it literally, the proposal seems to stack the deck in favor of a negative evaluation of our own cognitive system. No matter how pragmatically successful our cognitive system might turn out to be, it is hard to believe there isn't some logically possible alternative that won't do a bit better. Moreover, and this is the second reason, when we set out to evaluate a cognitive system—our own or someone else's—it is not clear that we are really very interested in knowing whether it reaches the ideal standard of being at least as successful as any logically possible alternative. For, given almost any plausible set of values that might be plugged into a pragmatic evaluation, that standard is likely to be vastly beyond anything that could even be approached by a creature with a brain like ours. And it is implausible to suppose that in debating whether people are reasoning well, what we are concerned about is whether they are living up to a standard that beings like us cannot even remotely approach. Since the point is an important one, and since the gap between our biological capacities and the idealized standard of what is logically possible all too often goes unappreciated, I think we would do well to consider a number of examples.

The first is drawn from Cherniak's fascinating work on the epistemological implications of complexity theory, a branch of computer science concerned with assessing the computational feasibility of various classes of algorithms.[16] Among the surprising results in this area is the demonstration that many quite familiar algorithms—including some that would likely be of considerable pragmatic utility to any cognitive system that could compute them easily—require immensely more computational power than could be packed into a human skull. Consider, for example, the *prima facie* pragmatically desirable project of testing one's beliefs from time to time for truth-functional consistency. One familiar way to do this is to use the truth table method. But, it turns out, this is not only unfeasible for a human brain, it is unfeasible even for what we might suppose to be the ideal, physically buildable computer. Here is how Cherniak makes the point:

> Suppose that each line of the truth table for the conjunction of all [of a person's] beliefs could be checked in the time a light ray takes to traverse the diameter of a proton, an appropriate "supercycle" time, and suppose that the computer was permitted to run for twenty billion years, the estimated time from the "big-bang" dawn of the universe to the present. A belief system containing only 138 logically independent propositions would overwhelm the time resources of this supermachine.[17]

Cherniak goes on to note that, while it is not easy to estimate the number of atomic propositions in a typical human belief system, the number must be vastly in excess of 138. It follows that, whatever its practical benefits might be, the proposed consistency-checking algorithm is not something a human brain could even approach.[18] Thus, it would seem perverse, to put it mildly, to insist that a person's cognitive system is doing a bad job of reasoning because it fails to periodically execute the algorithm and check on the consistency of the person's beliefs.

For a second illustration, consider the phenomenon of belief perseverance, in which a belief persists despite the fact that the subject no longer accepts the evidence from which the belief has been inferred.[19] Though the details would no doubt be a long story, and not an easy one to tell, it is *prima facie* plausible to suppose that (in most settings and for most values) belief perseverance will occasionally get you in pragmatic trouble. Thus, some logically possible cognitive system that does not exhibit perseverance will be pragmatically preferable to systems like ours that do. But, as Harman has noted, to build such a nonperseverating system would require placing extraordinary demands on memory, since the system would have to remember all of the evidence (including, presumably, all of the perceptual beliefs) on which each of its beliefs is based.[20] Plainly, our brains do not work in this way. And, though we do not know enough about the mechanisms of human memory to give a conclusive argument for the point, I would not be much surprised if it turned out that for a brain built like ours to store that much information, it would have to be the size of a bathtub, or perhaps a battleship. Suppose this is right. Are we then prepared to say that our own cognitive system is reasoning badly in this domain, because there are logically possible alternatives that would not exhibit belief perseverance and that would thus do a pragmatically better job? Plainly, that would be very odd.

For my final illustration, I once again borrow from Cherniak, this time his work on memory compartmentalization.[21] To begin, consider a pair of anecdotes that Cherniak recounts.

> At least a decade before Fleming's discovery of penicillin, many microbiologists were aware that molds cause clear spots in bacteria cultures, and they knew that such a bare spot indicates no bacterial growth. Yet they did not consider the possibility that molds release an antibacterial agent.[22]

> Smith believes an open flame can ignite gasoline . . . , and Smith believes the match he now holds has an open flame . . . , and Smith is not suicidal. Yet Smith decides to see whether a gas tank is empty by looking inside while holding the match nearby for illumination. Similar stories appear often in newspapers; this is approximately how one of Faulkner's characters, Eck Snopes, dies in *The Town*.[23]

The point Cherniak is illustrating with these examples is that it is "part of the human condition" that we "fail to 'make the connections' sometimes in a web of interconnected beliefs."[24] The explanation for this failure, Cherniak suggests, is that human long-term memory is organized into separate files or compartments and that typically only a small number of these compartments are actively searched in the course of dealing with a given cognitive problem. When a salient bit of information is stored in a memory compartment that has not been searched, the subject will not retrieve it and will fail to "make the connection." Moreover, Cherniak argues, the fact that human memory is organized into separately searchable compartments "is not just an accident of human psychology."[25] For, given the large size of the typical adult memory, the fact that memory search takes time, and the fact that there are serious time constraints on much of our cognitive activity, particularly when it involves practical matters, it would often be unfeasible, indeed fatal, to attempt an exhaustive search of memory. Compartmentalization makes it possible for the system to search quickly through those files that promise to be most relevant, though as Cherniak's two anecdotes show, there will sometimes be a pragmatic price to be paid for this efficiency. It is, of course, easy to imagine a logically possible cognitive system whose pragmatic performance is better than ours, because its search speed is so fast that it doesn't need to compartmentalize its memory. But, once again, it seems perverse to conclude that our system is doing a bad job at the business of cognition simply because such an alternative system is logically possible.

The point I have been belaboring with these examples is that in many areas there is going to be an enormous gap between what brains like ours can do and what would be done by the best logically possible cognitive systems. The conclusion I would draw is that in looking for a plausible pragmatic interpretation of what we want to know when we ask whether a person's cognitive system is a good one, it won't do to insist that the system be at least as good (or even almost as good) as any logical possible alternative. But if that's not the question we're asking, what is?

In all three of the examples, the pragmatically superior cognitive system was for one reason or another completely unfeasible for us. It was not something that creatures with brains like ours could hope to approach. And because the best alternative was not something we could even get close to, it seemed inappropriate to conclude that people are doing a bad job of reasoning simply because such an alternative is logically possible. This suggests that when we ask whether subjects are reasoning well, perhaps what we really want to know is whether their cognitive system is at least as good as any *feasible* alternative, where an alternative is feasible if it can be used by people operating within some appropriate set of constraints. This is, I think, a step in the right direction. But it leaves us with the problem of saying just which constraints we are going to count as appropriate. And here there is a danger of going too far in the constraints we take into account.

That danger was driven home to me by a conversation with Donald Norman in which (perhaps just as the devil's advocate) he defended the view that there is no such thing as bad or irrational reasoning. He was, of course, perfectly prepared to concede that in some cases we can describe patterns of reasoning that are better than the ones subjects actually exhibit. But, he insisted, these alternatives are irrelevant since they are not alternatives that the subjects could have used. In some cases, the subjects couldn't use them because they had never learned them; in other cases, they couldn't use them because they didn't remember them; in still other cases, there may have been environmental or internal stimuli that caused the subjects' cognitive systems to react as they did. In all of these cases, the subjects are reasoning and behaving within a rich structure of historical, psychological, and environmental constraints. And, Norman argued, when all of those constraints are taken into account, the subjects are doing as well as they can.

There is one point in Norman's argument that I think we should be prepared to concede. Given all the constraints under which subjects are operating, it may well be that their cognitive processes are completely determined. So, if we take all of those constraints as given, the subjects could do no better (and no worse). But the moral I would draw here is quite different from the one Norman proposed. Rather than concluding that bad reasoning is impossible, I think the right conclusion is that when we ask whether a subject has reasoned well, we do not take all of these constraints to be relevant to our question. What we really want to know is whether there are pragmatically superior cognitive systems that are feasible in the sense that the subject might have used them if some, but not all, of the constraints that actually obtained had been relaxed. This gets us back to the question of which constraints are appropriate.

One way to tackle this questions would be to hunt for a single set of constraints, and thus a general notion of feasibility, that will capture our intentions whenever we raise questions about the quality of a person's reasoning. But I think it is clear that this approach is doomed to failure for the very simple reason that there is no single set of intentions lying behind all questions about the goodness or badness of a person's reasoning. Rather, I suggest, there are many different reasons why we might ask whether a person's cognitive system is a good one. The question may be raised as part of different projects with different goals, and when asking the question there may be many different things we want to know. These varying projects impose a variety of interpretations on the notion of feasible alternatives for a given cognitive system, and thus the question, Which constraints are appropriate? admits of no general answer. My proposal (and here again I am following in the footsteps of the pragmatists) is that in deciding which constraints are relevant, or which alternative cognitive systems we will count as feasible, we must look to our purposes in asking the question. Or, as William James might put it, we must ask what the "cash value" of the question is—what actions might we take as the result of one answer or another. A consequence of this proposal is that there is yet another sort of relativism lurking in our questions about the goodness or badness of reasoning, a relativism that turns on the purpose of the inquiry. Another consequence is that to the extent that we do not have a clear purpose in asking whether people are reasoning well or poorly, the question itself is obscure and ill defined. I think there is good reason to suppose that much debate over the normative standing of one or another experimentally observed inferential strategy has been carried on without any well-focused idea about the purpose of the inquiry and thus without any clear understanding of what was being debated.[26]

Among the various purposes one might have in asking whether people's reasoning in a given domain is good or bad, there is at least one that is of obvious relevance to traditional epistemological concerns. From Bacon and Descartes to Mill and Goldman, epistemologists have aspired not simply to evaluate reasoning but to improve it. This same goal looms large for a number of the psychologists whose studies of reasoning have proved so unsettling. So let us stipulate that for present purposes the cash value of questions about the quality of reasoning is to be found in the steps we might subsequently take to help people reason better. Against this background, finally, we can ask how studies in the psychology of reasoning should be interpreted. Are the psychologists who see these studies as having "bleak implication for human reasoning" right? Do the studies indicate that the subjects are reasoning badly? The answer I propose to defend is that in just about every case the critique of ordinary inference has been premature. When the question is unpacked along the lines I have suggested, it is *far* from clear that the subjects are doing a bad job at the business of reasoning.

In order to sustain the charge that subjects in a given experiment are reasoning badly, we must show that there is some alternative to the cognitive system that the subjects are currently using that is both pragmatically superior and feasible. When our goal is to help people do a better job of reasoning, a feasible alternative will be one that we could actually get people to employ. So, given current purposes, a feasible alternative cognitive systems is one we have some effective method or technology for imparting. And for the time being at least, educational strategies of various sorts are the only candidates we need to take seriously. What we need to ask, then, is whether there are teachable strategies that are pragmatically superior to the ones subjects currently use. To answer this question in detail will, of course, require careful empirical exploration of the effects that can be achieved by various educational strategies. And, as it happens, some of the researchers who earlier uncovered curious patterns of reasoning have, in more recent work, turned their attention to the question of what reasoning strategies can and cannot be taught with various techniques.

To date, the results of those studies have been tentative and controversial, and the studies themselves have examined only a handful of teaching strategies. But even before considering those results, we should note that in some cases those who drew bleak implications from experiments on reasoning were obviously too hasty. Studies of belief perseverance are a good example here. The experimental results make it clear that people do perseverate and that the phenomenon is widespread and robust. But if the goal is amelioration then, as our recent reflections have shown, these findings by themselves are not adequate to establish that people are reasoning poorly. To support that conclusion, we must also show that there are pragmatically superior feasible alternatives—alternatives that can be taught and learned. As Harman has argued, an alternative cognitive system that keeps track of *all* its evidence for *all* of its beliefs is almost certainly not one that could be learned, because it imposes such extraordinary demands on memory. So, even if it is granted that nonperseverating systems would be pragmatically superior to ours, it still does not follow that we are reasoning badly when we hold on to a belief after rejecting the evidence on which the belief is based. Of course, it need not be the case that a cognitive system must avoid belief perseverance altogether in order to be better than ours. It may be that a modest reduction in perseverance has a significant pragmatic payoff and that we can learn how to reduce perseverance to a certain degree. But so far as I know, the feasibility of such alternatives has not yet been explored. Thus it is an open question whether people who perseverate are reasoning badly. Much the same conclusion follows about people who fail to eliminate all inconsistencies in their beliefs and about people who fail to use all the relevant information they have available.

Recent research on teaching strategies of reasoning suggests that even after a course devoted to the topic, people are generally very bad at using purely formal or syntactic principles of inference of the sort that are usually encountered in traditional formal logic. However, it is much easier to get people to use various strategies of statistical reasoning, including in particular those that exploit the "law of large numbers."[27] With a relatively modest amount of instruction, it seems that people can be gotten to grasp the notion that, in populations that are not likely to be homogeneous, predictions based on a small sample are likely to be much less reliable than predictions based on a larger sample. Moreover, what people learn is typically utilized in dealing with topics and tasks quite different from those on which they are trained. Thus, there are feasible alternatives to those cognitive systems which readily generalize from small samples in nonhomogeneous populations. But, of course, this result by itself is not sufficient to show that people whose reasoning regularly flouts the law of large numbers are doing a bad job of reasoning. We must also show that one or another of the alternatives they might learn would be pragmatically superior. And to do this, we must know enough about their values and about the environments in which they operate to show that if they were to adopt one of the learnable alternative systems, it would serve them in better stead. There is no shortage of anecdotes in the literature illustrating how reasoning that ignores the law of large numbers can lead to frustration—or worse. But there is a considerable gap between such anecdotes and a systematic demonstration that an alternative cognitive system is pragmatically superior for a given person or group. Thus, I submit, even in these cases a bleak assessment of ordinary reasoning would be premature.

This cautious conclusion should not, however, be mistaken for an endorsement of commonsense reasoning, nor should it give much encouragement to those Panglossian optimists who think that in matters cognitive we live in (or near) the best of all possible worlds. For even if current membership is sparse in the set of alternative cognitive systems that are both feasible and known to be pragmatically superior, there is no reason to think that this situation will not change dramatically as we learn more about what makes cognitive systems useful and develop more powerful technologies for modifying the systems that nature and culture have provided. Cognition, for the pragmatist, is an activity that plays a central role in the pursuit of a variety of ends. Viewed from this perspective, it is no more likely that there is a best way of going about the business of cognition than that there is a best means of transportation, or of communication. A pragmatic epistemology encourages the hope that human cognitive systems may improve without limit, as we learn more about how to expand their capacities and as our physical, social, and technological environments present us with new opportunities and new challenges. Nor should we assume that all the improvements in human reasoning must follow the same path. From the pragmatist perspective it's to be expected that quite different strategies for improving cognitive processing may prove preferable for different people with different goals, different technologies, or different environments. Just as there are many good ways to prepare food, or raise children, or organize a society, so too there may be many good ways to go about the business of cognition.

Notes

Chapter 1

1. See, for example, Burtt (1932); Koyré (1956); Blake, Ducasse, and Madden (1960); Laudan (1968).
2. The paper that started it all is Gettier (1963). For a detailed review of the subsequent literature, see Shope (1983).
3. See, for example, Moore, (1959), Popkin (1968), Rescher (1980), Klein (1981), Stroud (1984).
4. For the Fords, see Lehrer and Paxson (1969); Harman (1973), chap. 8; Annis (1973); and Sosa (1974). For the barns, see Goldman (1976).
5. Stich (1988) was a pilot study for chap. 4, and a good deal of the material in chap. 4 is borrowed from that paper.
6. Nisbett and Borgida (1975).
7. For an excellent review of this literature, see Nisbett and Ross (1980). A number of important papers in the area are collected in Kahneman, Slovic, and Tversky (1982). Another useful collection of material can be found in Tweney, Doherty, and Mynatt (1981). For a survey of some more recent work, see Holland et al. (1986), chaps. 8, 9. Other good sources are Goldman (1986), chaps. 13–16, and Johnson-Laird (1983); chaps. 2–6.
8. Wason (1968a), (1968b), (1977); Wason and Johnson-Laird (1970); Johnson-Laird and Wason (1970).
9. For further discussion of these issues, see Johnson-Laird; Legrenzi, and Legrenzi (1972); Manktelow and Evans (1979); Griggs and Cox (1982); Rips (1983); Cheng and Holyoak (1985); and Holland et al. (1986), chap. 9.
10. Tversky and Kahneman (1983).
11. Smedslund (1963), Ward and Jenkins (1965).
12. Doherty et al. (1979).
13. Nisbett and Ross (1980), p. 92.
14. Ross, Lepper, and Hubbard (1975); Ross and Anderson (1982). For a good introduction to this literature, see Nisbett and Ross (1980), chap. 8.
15. For details, see 4.1.
16. Conee and Feldman (1983).
17. That account first appeared in Stich (1982a) and was reworked into chap. 4 and 5 of Stich (1983).
18. I am also grateful to the National Endowment for the Humanities, the University of Maryland, and the Andrew W. Mellon Foundation, each of which provided financial support for my year at the Center.
19. I am grateful to Francis Snare, who helped me find a perspicuous taxonomy for the various views sketched in this section.

20. See, for example, Gladwin (1964), Levi-Strauss (1966), Colby and Cole (1973), Gellner (1973), Cooper (1975). For an elegant study raising doubts about the claim that primitive folk reason differently, see Hutchins (1980).
21. Jenkins (1973).
22. See, for example, Levy-Bruhl (1966), (1979).
23. The terms 'relativism' and 'relativist' are used in a bewildering variety of ways. As I shall use the term, *cognitive relativism* is a species of normative cognitive pluralism. An account of cognitive virtue—of what makes a system of reasoning a *good* one— is *relativistic* if it entails that different systems are good for different people (or different groups of people). Not all pluralistic accounts of cognitive virtue are relativistic, since some accounts will entail that different systems of reasoning are equally good *for everyone*. For more on this, see 6.2.1.
24. This is one of the topics I managed to mangle quite thoroughly in Stich (1984a).
25. Davidson (1973–74).
26. There is a valuable critique of Stich (1985) in Feldman (1988). I think the argument developed in chap. 3 avoids all of the pitfalls Feldman points out.
27. Though not entirely; see Dennett (1981c), p. 52. (Page reference is to Dennett (1987a).)
28. Cohen (1981). See also Cohen (1979), (1982).
29. There are other possible answers. They are discussed in some detail in 4.1.
30. See Stich (1970), (1976).
31. My thinking on these matters was helped along by many extended conversations with Peter Godfrey-Smith. See Godfrey-Smith (1986).
32. See, for example, Dretske (1971), Armstrong (1973), Nozick (1981), Goldman (1986). For a useful critique, see Lycan (1988h).
33. Compare, for example, the following quote from William James's *Pragmatism*:

   Let me now say only this, that truth is *one species of good*, and not, as is usually supposed, a category distinct from good, and co-ordinate with it. *The true is the name of whatever proves itself to be good in the way of belief*. . . . Surely you must admit this, that if there were no good for life in true ideas . . . then the current notion that truth is divine and precious, and its pursuit a duty, could never have grown up or become a dogma. . . . "What would be better for us to believe!" That sounds very like a definition of truth. It comes very near to saying "what we *ought* to believe" and in *that* definition none of you would find any oddity. Ought we ever not to believe what is *better for us* to believe? And can we then keep the notion of what is better for us, and what is true for us, permanently apart? Pragmatism says no, and I fully agree with her (pp. 59–60).

34. The argument that truth-linked accounts are relativistic is set out in 6.2.1.

Chapter 2

1. Quine (1960). For the remainder of this section, page references to Quine will be given in parentheses in the text.
2. The *locus classicus* for the language of thought paradigm is Fodor (1975). For further discussion and elaboration of the view, see Fodor (1978b), (1981b), (1987) app.; Field (1978); Dennett (1982); Devitt and Sterelny (1987); Lycan (1988b); MacNamara (1986).
3. Schiffer (1981).
4. Dennett (1978), p. 20. Dennett has made much the same claim in a number of other places. See, for example, Dennett (1981b), p. 19; Dennett (1980), p. 74; Dennett (1978), p. 22. In fairness to Dennett, I should note that he sometimes denies he is

talking about ordinary, folk psychological, intentional description. When this mood is upon him, his proclaimed goal is to *replace* the folk psychological language of belief with a tidied up technical language. And it is only intentional description in this new technical jargon that requires perfect rationality. For some discussion of how Dennett is best interpreted, see Stich (1981) and Dennett's reply (1981a).

5. See Harman (1986), pp. 3–4.
6. See Dennett (1978), pp. 11, 20, 44. However, in Dennett (1981a), he seems to take it back when he writes: "First a few words on what rationality is *not*. It is not deductive closure. . . . Nor is rationality perfect logical consistency" (pp. 94–5). The view he leaves us with, in that essay, is that "the concept of rationality is . . . slippery" (p. 97). Page references are to the version of Dennett (1981a) reprinted in Dennett (1987a).
7. Hollis (1982), p. 73.
8. The fixed and floating bridgehead terminology is due to Lukes (1982), pp. 272ff.
9. See Cherniak (1981a), (1981b), (1983); Davidson (1973), (1974), (1975); Loar (1981), Lukes (1982). Loar tells me that his considered view is actually a version of the fixed bridgehead view.
10. On the role of intuition in judging these questions, see Stich (1983), pp. 51–52.
11. Stich (1981); (1983), chap. 5, sec. 4; (1985).
12. Cherniak (1986).
13. Cherniak (1981b), p. 254.
14. Davidson (1974), p. 19.
15. Ibid.
16. Grandy (1973). For the remainder of this section, page references to this article will be given in parentheses in the text.
17. For a interesting elaboration of this idea, see Gordon (1986).
18. For an elaboration of this point, see Stich (1982a).
19. Quine (1960), p. 219.
20. For more details, see Stich (1982a) and Stich (1983), chap. 5.
21. See n. 20.
22. For further evidence on this point, see Stich (1982a), Stich (1983), chap. 4, and Stich (1984c).
23. See 2.3.2.
24. For further details on this second example, see Stich (1983), p. 69ff. and Stich (1984b).

Chapter 3

1. Quine (1969), p. 126.
2. Dennett (1981b), p. 75.
3. Fodor (1981b), p. 121.
4. Here are a few more examples:

Believing truths often helps a person achieve practical goals. Realizing practical goals, such as food, shelter and mating, typically promotes biological ends. There is also plausibility in supposing that many cognitive functions subserving the attainment of true belief, or goal realization, were selected for in evolution because of their biological consequences, that is, their contribution to genetic fitness. (Goldman (1986), p. 98)

I suggest that the normative force of epistemological terms comes from the value notions explicit or implicit in design-stance psychology. What Mother Nature provides is *good design*, and it is that evaluative notion that is the ultimate source of our ordinary superficial evaluative ideas of "better expla-nation," "rational inference," and so forth. (Lycan, (1988d), p. 142)

Assuming that the capacity to form and use beliefs has survival value mainly in so far as the beliefs formed are true (or close enough), and assuming that humans currently have this capacity in part because, historically, having it had survival value, the mechanisms in us that produce beliefs, learn new concepts etc.—mechanisms, perhaps, that program other mechanisms that program still other mechanisms etc.—all have in common at least one proper function: helping to produce true beliefs. (Millikan (1984), p. 317)

Habits of thought which correspond to deductively valid steps will tend to be preserved by natural selection. Since truth conditions are identified as circum-stances in which beliefs lead to advantageous action, the teleological theory of representation implies that true beliefs are *ipso facto* biologically advantageous. And so it follows that habits of thought which generate new true beliefs from old ones will be biologically advantageous. (Papineau (1987), pp. 77–78)

5. The most detailed argument along these lines that I have found is in Lycan (1988d). However, as I'll note below, at several crucial points Lycan asserts or assumes strong empirical premises with little or no defense. There is an extended discussion of evolution and rationality in Sober (1981). But what Sober wants to establish is that rational inferential processes *could* have been produced by evolution, not that irrational ones could not.

6. See, for example, Armstrong (1973); Dretske (1969), chap. 3; Dretske (1971); and Goldman (1986).

7. In comments on an earlier version of this chapter, Peter Godfrey-Smith protested that this truth-linked analysis of rationality is much too crude to be plausible. It is not just producing *more* truths and *fewer* falsehoods that makes one system of reasoning better than another; the system must excel at producing certain kinds of truths and avoiding certain kinds of errors. This objection is surely right, as far as it goes. The problem is that it does not go far enough. It does not say *which kinds* of truths and errors are important. And without a reasonably specific answer, we can't even begin to reconstruct a serious argument for the claim that well-designed cognitive systems are rational. One easy way to say which truths and errors are important is to appeal to reproductive success: the truths to get are those that enhance fitness; the errors to avoid are those that detract from fitness. But if we adopt this suggestion, our truth-linked account of rationality will be all but indis-tinguishable from the previous account, which analyzes rationality directly in terms of fitness.

8. Sober (1981).

9. Williams (1986), p. 33.

10. Sober (1981), p. 105.

11. Sober (1984), p. 29.

12. Kimura (1983); Nei (1987). Also see Sober (1984), chap. 4; and Kitcher (1985), pp. 221–26.

13. Kitcher (1985), pp. 223–24. Lycan (1988d) claims that "the effect of nonselectional factors in the evolutionary process has not (in actual historical fact) been great enough to to deflect Mother Nature's basic strategy of maximizing cognitive effi-ciency . . ." (p. 153). However, his reasons for making this claim are neither clear nor convincing.

14. Sober (1984), pp. 104–5; Kitcher (1985), chap. 7; Lycan (1988d), p. 149; Feldman (1988), p. 220.

15. The example, along with much useful advice on these matters, was provided by Elizabeth Lloyd.

16. Thanks are due to Elizabeth Lloyd and Michael Dietrich for helpful feedback on earlier versions of this section.

17. For more on meiotic drive, see Crow (1979); and Crow (1986), pp. 191–93.

   Note that I have been assuming that the process which spreads cheating genes through a population is an instance of natural selection. This is a plausible assumption if one takes the gene to be the unit of selection. For obviously the cheating gene is more successful than the competition at getting into the next generation. However, if we assume that individuals rather than genes are the unit of selection, it might be argued that the spread of cheating genes is not an instance of natural selection at all. Those who adopt this perspective will classify meiotic drive the way we have classified genetic drift; it is a cause of evolution that is distinct from natural selection.

   My discussion of meiotic drive has benefited from some very helpful advice from Michael Dietrich and Philip Kitcher.

18. Kitcher (1985), p. 215. Cf. Templeton (1982), pp. 16–22.

19. Note that this is not an example of genetic drift. The distribution of genes among the humans who survive might well be identical to the distribution in the annihilated population. If this were the case, then, since biological evolution requires a change in gene frequency, this example would not involve biological evolution at all.

20. The assumption that there must be some innate inferential strategies is very clear in Goldman's *Epistemology and Cognition,* where innateness is used to distinguish "primary" from "secondary" epistemology. Primary epistemology focuses on "native" cognitive processes, while secondary epistemology is concerned with acquired processes. In his treatment of "primary" epistemology Goldman considers a variety of inferencelike cognitive processes. However, he offers us no reason at all to suppose that the cognitive processes he considers are innate.

   Lycan (1988d) also assumes that our "fundamental canons of theory-preference" are innate:

   > Even if our rules of theory-preference are not themselves epistemically justifiable, we must guard against supposing that we could simply see the error of our ways and stop using them. We never made a conscious choice to use those rather than others, and I doubt psychology will ever reveal that as children we make unconscious choices to use them either; *probably they are hard-wired* (pp. 138–89; emphasis added).

   But, like Goldman, Lycan gives no reason to suppose that the principles in question are "hard-wired," nor does he tell us why he doubts that children unconsciously acquire these rules.

21. For more on these matters, see Stich (forthcoming, a).

22. See Stich (1978), and (forthcoming, a); Lightfoot (forthcoming).

23. Nor is the Chomskian story about language acquisition without its critics. But that is another matter. For some discussion, see Ramsey and Stich (forthcoming).

24. For a more detailed discussion see Kitcher (1985), pp. 88–95, and the literature cited there.

Chapter 4

1. Rawls (1971), pp. 20ff.

2. Goodman (1965), pp. 66–67; emphasis is Goodman's.

3. Cherniak (1986), chap. 4; Harman (1986), chap. 2; Goldman (1986), sec. 5.1.

4. Well, I will argue it a little. Note first that according to Goodman, the only justification needed for either rules or inferences "lies in" the agreement achieved by the reflective equilibrium process. This talk of justification *lying in* the agreement strongly suggests the constitutive reading. Moreover, on the nonconstitutive reading, Goodman's doctrine would be an oddly incomplete one. It would present us with a test for justification without telling us why it was a test or giving us any account of what it is that is being tested for. On the constitutive reading, by contrast, no such problem arises. We have in one tidy package both an analysis of the notion of justification and an unproblematic explanation of the relation between justification and the process Goodman describes.

5. See, for example, Kripke (1972); Putnam (1973a), (1973b), (1975a). For a useful overview, see Schwartz (1977).

6. For more on explication see Goodman (1966), chap. 1. The notion of a conservative explication is discussed in Loar (1981), pp. 41–43.

7. For some discussion of the empirical plausibility of the notion of a psycho-logic, see Johnson-Laird (1983); Rips (1983a), (1983b); MacNamara (1986); Stich (forthcoming, b).

8. Cohen (1981), p. 321.

9. It is worth noting that Cohen does not explicitly endorse the claim that the reflective equilibrium story constitutes an analysis or explication of our ordinary notion of justification. It is possible to read Cohen as claiming that while the reflective equilibrium test is the right test for normative theories, this is not because the test follows from an analysis or explication of the concept of justification. However, if we do read him in this way, his position would be curiously incomplete, since he would be offering no defense of the claim that a normative theory "has to be based" on the data of intuition.

10. Stich and Nisbett (1980).

11. The writer was Henry Coppée (1874). Here is a brief quote: "Thus, in throwing dice, we cannot be sure that any single face or combination of faces will appear; but if, in very many throws, some particular face has not appeared, the chances of its coming up are stronger and stronger, until they approach very near to certainty. It must come; and as each throw is made and it fails to appear, the certainty of its coming draws nearer and nearer." (p. 162) Thanks are due to Arnold Wilson for having brought this passage to my attention.

12. Cohen comes close when he claims that "a different competence, if it actually existed, would just generate evidence that called for a revision of the corresponding normative theory" ((1981), p. 321).

13. Rawls (1974).

14. Daniels (1979), (1980a), (1980b).

15. Stich and Nisbett (1980).

16. As Conee and Feldman (1983) point out, the situation is actually a bit worse for the version of the expert reflective equilibrium analysis that Nisbett and I offered. On that account, different groups may recognize different people as experts. And it is surely at least possible for a group of people to accept as an expert some guru who is as bonkers as he is charismatic. But we certainly don't want to say that the followers of such a guru would be rational or justified in invoking whatever wild inferential principle might be in reflective equilibrium for their leader.

17. For a good review of the early literature in this area, see Smith and Medin (1981). For a review of more recent literature, see Smith (forthcoming).

18. The Wittgensteinian flavor of some of the empirical work on categorization is no accident. Eleanor Rosch, whose seminal work inspired much of the recent interest in categorization among psychologists, is quite explicit about her indebtedness to Wittgenstein. For some discussion of the links between Rosch and Wittgenstein, see Lakoff (1987), chap. 2.
19. For some insightful observations on the potential complexity of commonsense concepts and the ways in which intuitive tests can fail to capture the extension of concepts, see Rey (1983), (1985). For a survey of some recent work indicating how complex conceptual representation might turn out to be, see Smith (forthcoming).
20. Actually, the last three of my four objections might, with a bit of reworking, be generalized so as to apply to all of analytic epistemology, as it is defined below. But I don't propose to pursue them since, as we shall see, analytic epistemology has more pressing problems.
21. Goldman (1986).
22. Ibid., p. 60. For the reader who wants a more hands-on feel for Goldman's notion of a J-rule, the quote continues as follows: "For example, J-rules might permit a cognizer to form a given belief because of some appropriate antecedent or current state. Thus, someone being "appeared to" in a certain way at t might be permitted to believe p at t. But someone else not in such a state would not be so permitted. Alternatively, the rules might focus on mental operations. Thus, if S's believing p at t is the result of a certain operation, or sequence of operations, then his belief is justified if the system of J-rules permits that operation or sequence of operations."
23. Ibid., p. 64.
24. Ibid., p. 58.
25. Ibid., p. 66.
26. Ibid., pp. 58–59.
27. For an extended review of part of this literature; see R. Shope (1983). As Shope notes, relatively few of the philosophers who have tried their hands at constructing an "analysis" of knowledge (or of some other epistemic notion) have been explicit about their objectives. (See pp. 34–44.) However, absent indications to the contrary, I am inclined to think that if a philosophical project proceeds by offering definitions or "truth conditions" and testing them against our intuitions about real or imaginary cases, then the project should be viewed as an attempt at conceptual analysis or explication. Unless one has some rather unusual views about intuitions, it is hard to see what we could hope to gain from capturing them, apart from some insight into the concepts and psychological mechanisms that underlie them.

One philosopher who does have unusual views on intuitions is William Lycan. Like Goodman, Cohen, Goldman, and many others, Lycan takes intuitions about justifiedness and other notions of cognitive assessment to play a central role in epistemology: "Basic epistemic norms . . . are justified not by being deduced from more fundamental norms (an obvious impossibility), but by their ability to sort specific, individual normative intuitions and other relevant data into the right barrels in an economical and illuminating way." (1988d, pp. 135–36).

But for Lycan the appeal to intuition is not aimed at uncovering epistemic notions embedded in ordinary language (1988f, p. 179). Rather, he maintains, "epistemological intuitions," along with modal, moral, and metaphysical intuitions (1988g, p. 209) are *prima facie* justified. This follows from a more general principle which holds that *every* spontaneous belief is *prima facie* justified.

> I want to propose the following Principle of Credulity: "Accept at the outset each of those things that seem to be true." That is, I hold that each of the

spontaneous beliefs I have mentioned is prima facie justified. . . . (1988e, pp. 165–66).

The principle is a bit less radical than it seems, since on Lycan's view it is *"highly defeasible,* indeed . . . [it] can be defeated by almost anything" (1988e, p. 166). One might think that interpersonal and cross-cultural differences in both moral and epistemic intuitions would go a long way toward undermining what Lycan sees as the *prima facie* justifiedness of those intuitions. But Lycan seems to think that such diversity is rare or nonexistent (1988g, p. 212, n. 12).

28. Evidence on this point, like evidence about cross-cultural differences in cognitive processes, is hard to come by and hard to interpret. But there are some intriguing hints in the literature. Hallen and Sodipo (1986) studied the terms of epistemic evaluation exploited by the Yoruba, a West African people. It is their contention that the Yoruba do not have a distinction corresponding to our distinction between knowledge and (mere) true belief. The Yoruba do, however, divide beliefs into two other categories—roughly those for which a person has immediate, eyewitness evidence, and those for which he does not. In the standard Yoruba-English dictionaries, the Yoruba term for the former sort of belief, 'mo', is translated as 'knowledge' while the term for the latter sort, 'gbagbo', is translated as 'belief'. Hallen and Sodipo argue that these translations are mistaken, since 'mo' has a much narrower extension than 'knowledge'. Most of what we would classify as scientific knowledge, for example, would not count as 'mo' for the Yoruba, because it is based on inference and secondhand report. Since the Yoruba do not draw the distinction between knowledge and (mere) true belief, they have no use for our notion of epistemic justification, which earns its keep in helping to draw that distinction. Instead, the Yoruba presumably have another notion which they exploit in distinguishing 'mo' from 'gbagbo'. Hallen and Sodipo do not indicate whether the Yoruba have a single word for this notion, but if they do, it would be a mistake to translate the word as '(epistemic) justification'. Clearly, if Hallen and Sodipo are right, the Yoruba categories of epistemic evaluation are significantly different from our own.

29. Goldman (1986), p. 106.

30. Ibid., p. 107.

31. Ibid.

32. Ibid.

33. In the last few paragraphs, I have been ignoring the skeptical concerns voiced in 4.5 about the empirical feasibility of the sort of conceptual analysis that seeks to provide necessary and sufficient conditions. If it turns out that our concepts of epistemic evaluation have a prototype structure, or one of the hybrid structures suggested in 4.5, the argument I have sketched will be easy enough to adapt. All that is required to make my point is that our actual concept is one of a large family of more or less related concepts that can be generated by tinkering with parameters along a variety of dimensions.

34. For the argument on these last two points, see 3.3.3 and 3.3.2.

35. See Chapman (1967); Chapman and Chapman (1967), (1969). For an excellent overview, see Nisbett & Ross (1980), chap. 5.

36. See Salmon (1957), Skyrms (1975).

37. Strawson (1952), chap. 9.

38. Salmon (1957), pp. 41, 42.

Chapter 5

1. In the wake of Gettier's celebrated paper (1963), many philosophers have come to view the justified-true-belief account of knowledge as inadequate, because it allows in too much. However, most of these philosophers go along with the tradition in regarding justification and truth as major epistemic virtues; each is necessary for knowledge, and they are part of what makes knowledge important.
2. The map metaphor is invoked in Ramsey (1931), p. 238, and is repeated approvingly by Armstrong (1973), pp. 3–5, 71–72, and by Dretske (1988), p. 79.
3. See, for example, Dennett (1981b), (1981c), (1987b). For some critical discussion of Dennett's view, see Stich (1981) and Dennett's reply (1981a).
4. See Field (1978); Block (1986); Devitt (1981); Devitt and Sterelny (1987); Lycan (1988b), (1988c); McGinn (1982).
5. See Tarski (1956).
6. See, for example, Davidson (1967), (1968); Kaplan (1968), Clark (1970), Parsons (1972), Wheeler (1972), Burge (1974), Weinstein (1974), Loar (1976), Lycan (1984).
7. See, for example, Davidson (1967), (1968); Lewis (1973); Barwise and Perry (1983).
8. For further details, see Kripke (1972); Putnam (1973a), (1973b), 1975a); Devitt (1981); Devitt and Sterelny (1987).
9. Description theories typically claim that a name used by a speaker denotes the person who satisfies most (or a weighted most) of the descriptions that the speaker would offer of the person. Thus description theories, unlike causal theories, entail that there is a limit to how misinformed a speaker can be. If most of the assertions of the form 'Aristotle was Φ' that a speaker would accept are false of the great philosopher, then, if description theories are correct, the speaker is not expressing lots of false beliefs about the great philosopher. He is not talking about the great philosopher at all.
10. Schiffer (1981).
11. On all of these matters, compare the discussion in 2.1.3.
12. Soames (1984) and Stalnaker (1984).
13 Field (1972).
14. Much of what I have to say about the idiosyncrasy of the causal/functional interpretation function was inspired by Peter Godfrey-Smith (1986) and by our many conversations about earlier drafts of that paper.
15. For discussion of this point, see 2.1.3, 2.3.1, and 2.3.2. For further evidence, see Stich (1982) and Stich (1983), chap. 5.

Chapter 6

1. This would be a good place to record one of my more significant intellectual debts. The sort of epistemic pragmatism I advocate is species of what Rescher (1977) calls "methodological pragmatism," and my thinking about these matters has been influenced in many ways by Rescher's rich and lucid book. There are many points on which Rescher and I disagree. We could hardly be further apart in our views about the importance of truth and the prospects for showing that pragmatically sanctioned cognitive strategies will lead to truth. But whether one agrees with Rescher or disagrees, his book is essential reading for anyone interested in a pragmatic epistemology.
2. Historically, of course, pragmatists have been very suspicious of the distinction between intrinsic and instrumental values.
3. One particularly worrisome challenge to the framework of the pragmatic account is the claim that people typically do not have stable or determinate values. For a

discussion of some of the literature supporting this conclusion, see Slovic (forthcoming).

4. For further details see Stich (1982b).

5. For lucid discussions see Schick (1984) and Levi (1986).

6. This use of 'relativism' differs from the use in Stich (1984), where I did not distinguish relativism from nonrelativistic sorts of pluralism. Thanks are due to Francis Snare for helping me to think more clearly about the distinction between relativism and pluralism.

7. One writer in the reliabilist tradition who has been particularly sensitive to the fact that the environment in which a cognitive system operates will effect how well it does in producing truths is Goldman (1986). See the discussion of his notion of "normal worlds" in 4.6.3.

8. See, for example, Carey (1985).

9. Kitcher (forthcoming).

10. It's worth noting that the situation is analogous, in important ways, to the case of the hawk and dove genes, discussed in 3.6.

11. For the reader who wants to judge for him- or herself, the place to start is Feyerabend (1978a) or (1978b).

12. For some insightful observations on the pragmatists' rejection of the view that there is a single desirable way in which beliefs should relate to the world, see Rorty (1982b).

13. For some discussion of the circularity objection as it applies to pragmatism, see Rescher (1977), chaps. 2, 3, 7.

14. There is an excellent discussion of the circularity objection aimed at truth-linked theories in Goldman (1986), pp. 116–21. I've borrowed substantially from that discussion, particularly in my second and third replies.

15. Sextus Empiricus (1933), pp. 163–64; Montaigne (1933), p. 544; Firth (1981), p. 19.

16. Cherniak (1986), chap. 4.

17. Ibid, p. 93.

18. Cherniak notes that more efficient algorithms are known. But even these "still require as much time in the worst cases" (93).

19. See 1.2.1.4.

20. Harman (1986), pp. 37–42.

21. Cherniak (1983); (1986), chap. 3.

22. Cherniak (1986), p. 50.

23. Ibid., p. 57.

24. Ibid., p. 50.

25. Ibid., p. 61.

26. See, for example, Cohen (1979), (1980), (1981), (1982); Kahneman and Tversky (1973), (1979).

27. Cheng and Holyoak (1985); Fong, Krantz, and Nisbett (1986); Cheng et al. (1986); Nisbett et al. (1987). For a useful review, see Holland et al. (1986), chap. 9.

References

Annis, D. (1973). "Knowledge and Defeasibility." *Philosophical Studies* 24.

Armstrong, D. (1973). *Belief, Truth, and Knowledge*. Cambridge: Cambridge University Press.

Barwise, J. and J. Perry (1983). *Situations and Attitudes*. Cambridge, Mass.: The MIT Press. A Bradford book.

Blake, R., C. Ducasse, and E. Madden (1960). *Theories of Scientific Method: The Renaissance through the Nineteenth Century*. Seattle: University of Washington Press.

Block, N. (1980). *Readings in the Philosophy of Psychology*, 2 vols. Cambridge, Mass.: Harvard University Press.

Block, N. (1986). "Advertisement for a Semantics for Psychology." In P. French et al., eds., *Midwest Studies in Philosophy: Studies in the Philosophy of Mind*. Minneapolis: University of Minnesota Press.

Burge, T. (1974). "Demonstrative Constructions, Reference and Truth." *Journal of Philosophy* 71.

Burtt, E. (1932). *The Metaphysical Foundations of Modern Physical Science*, Rev. ed. New York: Doubleday Anchor Books.

Carey, S. (1985). *Conceptual Change in Childhood*. Cambridge, Mass.: The MIT Press. A Bradford book.

Chapman, L. J. (1967). "Illusory Correlation in Observational Report." *Journal of Verbal Learning and Verbal Behavior* 6.

Chapman, L. J., and J. P. Chapman (1967). "Genesis of Popular but Erroneous Diagnostic Observations." *Journal of Abnormal Psychology* 72.

Chapman, L. J., and J. P. Chapman (1969). "Illusory Correlation as an Obstacle to the Use of Valid Psychodiagnostic Signs." *Journal of Abnormal Psychology* 74.

Cheng, P., and K. Holyoak (1985). "Pragmatic Reasoning Schemas." *Cognitive Psychology* 17:391–416.

Cheng, P., K. Holyoak, R. Nisbett, and L. Oliver (1986). "Pragmatic versus Syntactic Approaches to Training Deductive Reasoning." *Cognitive Psychology* 18.

Cherniak, C. (1981a). "Minimal Rationality." *Mind* XC.

Cherniak, C. (1981b). "Feasible Inference." *Philosophy of Science* 48.

Cherniak, C. (1983). "Rationality and the Structure of Human Memory." *Synthese* 57.

Cherniak, C. (1986). *Minimal Rationality*. Cambridge, Mass.: The MIT Press. A Bradford book.

Clark, R. (1970). "Concerning the Logic of Predicate Modifiers." *Nous* 4.

Cohen, J. (1979). "On the Psychology of Prediction: Whose Is the Fallacy?" *Cognition* 7.

Cohen, J. (1980). "Whose Is the fallacy? A Rejoinder to Daniel Kahneman and Amos Tversky." *Cognition* 8.

Cohen, J. (1981). "Can Human Irrationality Be Experimentally Demonstrated?" *Behavioral and Brain Sciences* 4.

Cohen, J. (1982). "Are People Programmed to Commit Fallacies? Further Thoughts about the Interpretation of Experimental Data on Probability Judgment." *Journal for the Theory of Social Behavior* 12.

Colby, B., and M. Cole (1973). "Culture, Memory and Narrative." In Horton and Finnegan (1973).

Conee, E. and R. Feldman (1983). "Stich and Nisbett on Justifying Inference Rules." *Philosophy of Science* 50.

Cooper, D. (1975). "Alternative Logic in 'Primitive' Thought." *Man* 10.

Coppée, H. (1874). *Elements of Logic*, rev. ed. Philadelphia: H. Butler & Co.

Crow, J. (1979). "Genes that Violate Mendel's Rules." *Scientific American* 240.

Crow, J. (1986). *Basic Concepts in Population, Quantitative, and Evolutionary Genetics.* New York: W. H. Freeman & Co.

Daniels, N. (1979). "Wide Reflective Equilibrium and Theory Acceptance in Ethics." *Journal of Philosophy* 76.

Daniels, N. (1980a). "Reflective Equilibrium and Archmedian Points." *Canadian Journal of Philosophy* 10.

Daniels, N. (1980b). "On Some Methods of Ethics and Linguistics." *Philosophical Studies* 37.

Davidson, D. (1967). "The Logical Form of Action Sentences." In N. Rescher, ed., *The Logic of Decision and Action.* Pittsburgh: University of Pittsburgh Press.

Davidson, D. (1968). "On Saying That." *Synthese* 19.

Davidson, D. (1973). "Radical Interpretation." *Dialectica* 27.

Davidson, D. (1974). "On the Very Idea of a Conceptual Scheme." *Proceedings and Addresses of the American Philosophical Association* 47.

Davidson, D. (1975). "Thought and Talk," In S. Guttenplan, ed., *Mind and Language.* Oxford: Oxford University Press.

Davidson, D., and G. Harman, eds. (1972). *Semantics of Natural Language.* Dordrecht, The Netherlands: Reidel.

Davidson, D., and G. Harman, eds. (1975). *The Logic of Grammar.* Encino, Calif.: Dickinson Publishing Co.

Dennett, D. (1978). *Brainstorms.* Cambridge, Mass.: The MIT Press. A Bradford book.

Dennett, D. (1980). "Reply to Prof. Stich." *Philosophical Books* 21.

Dennett, D. (1981a). "Making Sense of Ourselves." *Philosophical Topics* 12. Reprinted in Dennett (1987a).

Dennett, D. (1981b). "True Believers." In A. Heath, ed., *Scientific Explanation.* New York: Oxford University Press. Reprinted in Dennett (1987a).

Dennett, D. (1981c). "Three Kinds of Intentional Psychology." In R. Healy, ed., *Reduction, Time, and Reality.* Cambridge: Cambridge University Press. Reprinted in Dennett (1987a).

Dennett, D. (1982). "Beyond Belief." In Woodfield (1982). Reprinted in Dennett (1987a).

Dennett, D. (1987a). *The Intentional Stance.* Cambridge, Mass.: The MIT Press. A Bradford book.

Dennett, D., (1987b). "Reflections: Instrumentalism Reconsidered." In Dennett (1987a).

Devitt, M. (1981). *Designation.* New York: Columbia University Press.

Devitt, M., and K. Sterelny (1987). *Language and Reality: An Introduction to the Philosophy of Language.* Cambridge, Mass.: The MIT Press. A Bradford book.

Doherty, M., C. Mynatt, R. Tweney, and M. Schiavo (1979). "Pseudo-diagnosticity." *Acta Psychologica* 43.

Dretske, F. (1969). *Seeing and Knowing.* Chicago: University of Chicago Press.

Dretske, F. (1971). "Conclusive Reasons." *Australasian Journal of Philosophy* 49.

Dretske, F. (1988). *Explaining Behavior.* Cambridge, Mass.: The MIT Press. A Bradford book.

Feldman, R. (1988). "Rationality, Reliability, and Natural Selection." *Philosophy of Science* 55(2).

Feyerabend, P. (1978a). *Against Method: Outline of an Anarchistic Theory of Knowledge.* London: Verso.

Feyerabend, P. (1978b). *Science in a Free Society.* London: New Left Bank Publishers.

Field, H. (1972). "Tarski's Theory of Truth." *Journal of Philosophy* 69.

Field, H. (1978). "Mental Representation." *Erkenntnis* 13. Reprinted in Block (1980).

Firth, R. (1981). "Epistemic Merit, Intrinsic and Instrumental." *Proceedings and Addresses of the American Philosophical Association* 55.

Fodor, J. (1975). *The Language of Thought.* New York: Crowell.

Fodor, J. (1978a). "Tom Swift and His Procedural Grandmother." *Cognition* 6. Reprinted in Fodor (1981a).

Fodor, J. (1978b). "Propositional Attitudes." *The Monist* 61. Reprinted in Fodor (1981a).

Fodor, J. (1981a). *Representations.* Cambridge, Mass.: The MIT Press. A Bradford book.

Fodor, J. (1981b). "Three Cheers for Propositional Attitudes." In Fodor (1981a).

Fodor, (1987). *Psychosemantics.* Cambridge Mass.: The MIT Press. A Bradford book.

Fong, G., D. Krantz, and R. Nisbett (1986). "The Effects of Statistical Training on Thinking about Everyday Problems." *Cognitive Psychology* 18.

Gellner, E. (1973). "The Savage and the Modern Mind." In Horton and Finnegan (1973).

Gettier, E. (1963). "Is Justified True Belief Knowledge?" *Analysis* 23.

Gladwin, T. (1964). "Culture and Logical Process." In W. Goodenough, ed., *Explorations in Cultural Anthropology.* New York: McGraw-Hill.

Godfrey-Smith, P. (1986). "Why Semantic Properties Won't Earn Their Keep." *Philosophical Studies* 50.

Goldman, A. (1976). "Discrimination and Perceptual Knowledge." *Journal of Philosophy* 73.

Goldman, A. (1986). *Epistemology and Cognition.* Cambridge, Mass.: Harvard University Press.

Goodman, N. (1965). *Fact, Fiction, and Forecast.* Indianapolis: Bobbs-Merrill.

Goodman, N. (1966). *The Structure of Appearance,* 2nd ed. Indianapolis: Bobbs-Merrill.

Gordon, R. (1986). "Folk Psychology as Simulation." *Mind and Language* 1.

Grandy, R. (1973). "Reference, Meaning, and Belief." *Journal of Philosophy* 70.

Griggs, R., and J. Cox (1982). "The Elusive Thematic Materials Effect in Wason's Selection Task." *British Journal of Psychology* 73:407–20.

Hallen, B., and J. Sodipo (1986). *Knowledge, Belief, and Witchcraft.* London: Ethnographica.

Harman, G. (1973). *Thought.* Princeton, N.J.: Princeton University Press.

Harman, G. (1986). *Change in View.* Cambridge, Mass.: The MIT Press. A Bradford book.

Holland, J., K. Holyoak, R. Nisbett, and P. Thagard (1986). *Induction.* Cambridge, Mass.: The MIT Press. A Bradford book.

Hollis, M. (1982). "The Social Distruction of Reality." In Hollis and Lukes.

Hollis, M., and S. Lukes (1982). *Rationality and Relativism.* Cambridge, Mass.: The MIT Press.

Horton, R., and R. Finnegan, eds. (1973). *Modes of Thought: Essays on Thinking in Western and Non-Western Societies.* London: Faber & Faber.

Hutchins, E. (1980). *Culture and Inference: A Trobriand Case Study.* Cambridge, Mass.: Harvard University Press.

James, W. (1907). *Pragmatism.* New York: Longmans, Green & Co.

Jenkins, H. (1973). "Religion and Secularism: The Contemporary Significance of Newman's Thought." In Horton and Finnegan, eds. (1973).

Johnson-Laird, P. (1983b). *Mental Models*. Cambridge, Mass.: Harvard University Press.

Johnson-Laird, P., P. Legrenzi, and M. Legrenzi. (1972). "Reasoning and a Sense of Reality." *British Journal of Psychology* 63.

Johnson-Laird, P., and P. Wason (1970). "A Theoretical Analysis of Insight into a Reasoning Task, and Postscript—1977." In Johnson-Laird and Wason eds. (1977).

Johnson-Laird, P., and P. Wason, eds. (1977). *Thinking*. Cambridge: Cambridge University Press.

Kahneman, D., P. Slovic, and A. Tversky (1982). *Judgment under Uncertainty: Heuristics and Biases*. Cambridge: Cambridge University Press.

Kahneman, D., and A. Tversky (1973). "On the Psychology of Prediction." *Psychological Review*. 80.

Kahneman, D. and A. Tversky (1979). "On the Interpretation of Intuitive Probability: A Reply to Jonathan Cohen." *Cognition* 7.

Kaplan, D. (1968). "Quantifying In." *Synthese* 19. Reprinted in Davidson and Harman, eds. (1975).

Kimura, M. (1983). *The Neutral Theory of Molecular Evolution*. Cambridge: Cambridge University Press.

Kitcher, P. (1985). *Vaulting Ambition*. Cambridge, Mass.: The MIT Press. A Bradford book.

Kitcher, P. (forthcoming). "The Division of Cognitive Labor." In *The Journal of Philosophy*.

Klein, P. (1981). *Certainty: A Refutation of Skepticism*. Minneapolis: University of Minnesota Press.

Kornblith, H. (1985). *Naturalizing Epistemology*. Cambridge, Mass.: The MIT Press. A Bradford book.

Koyré, A. (1956). "The Influence of Philosophical Trends on the Formulation of Scientific Theories." In P. Frank, ed., *The Validation of Scientific Theories*. Boston: Beacon Press.

Kripke, S. (1972). "Naming and Necessity." In Davidson and Harman, eds. (1972).

Kuhn, T. (1962). *The Structure of Scientific Revolutions*. Chicago: University of Chicago Press.

Lakoff, G. (1987). *Women, Fire, and Dangerous Things*. Chicago: University of Chicago Press.

Laudan, L. (1968). "Theories of Scientific Method from Plato to Mach: A Bibliographical Review." *History of Science* 7.

Lehrer, K. and T. Paxson (1969). "Knowledge: Undefeated Justified True Belief." *Journal of Philosophy* 66.

Levi, I. (1986). *Hard Choices: Decision Making under Unresolved Conflict*. Cambridge: Cambridge University Press.

Levy-Bruhl, L. (1966). *Primitive Mentality*. Boston: Beacon Press.

Levy-Bruhl, L. (1979). *How Natives Think*. New York: Arno Press.

Levi-Strauss, C. (1966). *The Savage Mind*. Chicago: University of Chicago Press.

Lewis, D. (1973). *Counterfactuals*. Oxford: Basil Blackwell.

Lightfoot, D. (forthcoming). "The Child's Trigger Experience: Degree-O Learnability." In *Behavioral and Brain Sciences*.

Loar, B. (1976). "The Semantics of Singular Terms." *Philosophical Studies* 30.

Loar, B. (1981). *Mind and Meaning*. Cambridge: Cambridge University Press.

Lukes, S. (1982). "Relativism in Its Place." In Hollis and Lukes (1982).

Lycan, W. (1984). *Logical Form in Natural Language*. Cambridge, Mass.: The MIT Press. A Bradford book.

Lycan, W. (1988a). *Judgement and Justification*. Cambridge: Cambridge University Press.

Lycan, W. (1988b). "Toward a Homuncular Theory of Believing." In Lycan (1988a).

Lycan, W. (1988c). "Representation and the Semantics of Belief Ascription." In Lycan (1988a).

Lycan, W. (1988d). "Epistemic Value." In Lycan (1988a).

Lycan, W. (1988e). "Conservatism and the Data Base." In Lycan (1988a).

Lycan, W. (1988f). "Induction and the Best Explanation." In Lycan (1988a).

Lycan, W. (1988g). "Moral Facts and Moral Knowledge." In Lycan (1988a).

Lycan, W. (1988h). "Reliabilism." In Lycan (1988a).

MacNamara, J. (1986). *A Border Dispute: The Place of Logic in Psychology.* Cambridge, Mass.: The MIT Press. A Bradford book.

Manktelow, K., and J. Evans (1979). "Facilitation of Reasoning by Realism: Effect or Non-Effect?" *British Journal of Psychology* 70.

McGinn, C. (1982). "The Structure of Content." In Woodfield (1982).

Millikan, R. (1984). "Naturalist Reflections on Knowledge." *Pacific Philosophical Quarterly* 65.

Montaigne (1933). *The Essays of Montaigne.* New York: Modern Library.

Moore, G. E. (1959). *Philosophical Papers.* London: Allen & Unwin.

Nei, M. (1987). *Molecular Evolutionary Genetics.* New York: Columbia University Press.

Nisbett, R., and E. Borgida (1975). "Attribution and the Psychology of Prediction." *Journal of Personality and Social Psychology* 32.

Nisbett, R., G. Fong, D. Lehman, and P. Cheng, (1987). "Teaching Reasoning." *Science* 238.

Nisbett, R., and L. Ross (1980). *Human Inference: Strategies and Shortcomings of Social Judgment.* Englewood Cliffs, N.J.: Prentice-Hall.

Nozick, R. (1981). *Philosophical Explanations.* Cambridge, Mass.: Harvard University Press.

Papineau, D. (1987). *Reality and Representation.* Oxford: Basil Blackwell.

Parsons, T. (1972). "Some Problems concerning the Logic of Grammatical Modifiers." In Davidson and Harman, eds. (1972).

Popkin, R. (1968). *The History of Scepticism from Erasmus to Descartes.* New York: Harper & Row.

Putnam, H. (1973a). "Explanation and Reference." In G. Pearce, and P. Maynard, eds., *Conceptual Change.* Dordrecht, The Netherlands: Reidel. Reprinted in Putnam (1975b).

Putnam, H. (1973b). "Meaning and Reference." *Journal of Philosophy* 70.

Putnam, H. (1975a). "The Meaning of Meaning." In K. Gunderson, ed., *Language, Mind and Knowledge: Minnesota Studies in the Philosophy of Science* 7. Minneapolis: University of Minnesota Press. Reprinted in Putnam (1975b).

Putnam, H. (1975b). *Mind, Language, and Reality.* Cambridge: Cambridge University Press.

Quine, W. (1960). *Word and Object.* Cambridge, Mass.: The MIT Press.

Quine, W. (1969). "Epistemology Naturalized." In *Ontological Relativity and Other Essays.* New York: Columbia University Press.

Ramsey, F. (1931). *The Foundations of Mathematics and Other Logical Essays.* London: Routledge & Kegan Paul.

Ramsey, W., and S. Stich (forthcoming). "Connectionism and Three Levels of Nativism." In *Synthese.*

Rawls, J. (1971). *A Theory of Justice.* Cambridge, Mass.: Harvard University Press.

Rawls, J. (1974). "The Independence of Moral Theory." *Proceedings and Addresses of the American Philosophical Association* 48.

Rescher, N. (1977). *Methodological Pragmatism.* Oxford: Basil Blackwell.

Rescher, N. (1980). *Scepticism*. Totowa, N.J.: Rowman & Littlefield.

Rey, G. (1983). "Concepts and Stereotypes." *Cognition* 15.

Rey, G. (1985). "Concepts and Conceptions." *Cognition* 19.

Rips, L. (1983a). "Cognitive Processes in Propositional Reasoning." *Psychological Review* 90:38–71.

Rips, L. (1983b). "Reasoning as a Central Intellective Activity." In R. Sternberg, ed., *Advances in the Study of Human Intelligence*. Hillsdale, N.J.: Erlbaum.

Rorty, R. (1982a). *Consequences of Pragmatism*. Minneapolis: University of Minnesota Press.

Rorty, R. (1982b). "Introduction: Pragmatism and Philosophy." In Rorty (1982a).

Ross, L., and C. Anderson (1982). "Shortcomings in the Attribution Process: On the Origins and Maintenance of Erroneous Social Assessments." In Kahneman, Slovic, and Tversky (1982).

Ross, L., M. Lepper, and M. Hubbard (1975). "Perseverance in Self Perception and Social Perception: Biased Attributional Processes in the Debriefing Paradigm." *Journal of Personality and Social Psychology* 32.

Salmon, W. (1957). "Should We Attempt to Justify Induction?" *Philosophical Studies* 8.

Schick, F. (1984). *Having Reasons: An Essay on Rationality and Sociality*. Princeton, N.J.: Princeton University Press.

Schiffer, S. (1981). "Truth and the Theory of Content." In H. Parret and J. Bouverese, eds., *Meaning and Understanding*. Berlin: Walter de Gruyter.

Schwartz, S. (1977). Introduction to *Naming, Necessity, and Natural Kinds*. Ithaca, N.Y.: Cornell University Press.

Sextus Empiricus (1933). *Outlines of Pyrrhonism*, vol. 1. R. G. Bury, trans. London: Heinemann.

Shope R. (1983). *The Analysis of Knowing*. Princeton, N.J.: Princeton University Press.

Skyrms, B. (1975). *Choice and Chance*. Belmont, Calif.: Wadsworth.

Slovic, P. (forthcoming). "Choice." In D. Osherson et al., eds., *An Invitation to Cognitive Science*. Cambridge, Mass.: The MIT Press. A Bradford book.

Smedslund, J. (1963). "The Concept of Correlation in Adults." *Scandanavian Journal of Psychology* 4.

Smith, E. (forthcoming). "Categorization." In D. Osherson et al., eds., *An Invitation to Cognitive Science*. Cambridge, Mass.: The MIT Press. A Bradford book.

Smith, E., and D. Medin (1981). *Concepts and Categories*. Cambridge, Mass.: Harvard University Press.

Soames, S. (1984). "What Is a Theory of Truth?" *Journal of Philosophy* 81.

Sober, E. (1981). "The Evolution of Rationality." *Synthese* 46.

Sober, E. (1984). *The Nature of Selection*. Cambridge, Mass.: The MIT Press. A Bradford book.

Sosa, E. (1974). "How Do You Know?" *American Philosophical Quarterly* 11.

Sperber, D. (1982). "Apparently Irrational Beliefs." In Hollis and Lukes (1982).

Stalnaker, R. (1968). "A Theory of Conditionals." In N. Rescher, ed., *Studies in Logical Theory*. Oxford: Basil Blackwell.

Stalnaker, R. (1984). *Inquiry*. Cambridge, Mass.: The MIT Press. A Bradford book.

Stich, S. (1970). "Dissonant Notes on the Theory of Reference." *Nous* 4(4).

Stich, S. (1976). "Davidson's Semantic Program." *Canadian Journal of Philosophy* 4(2).

Stich, S. (1978). "Empiricism, Innateness, and Linguistic Universals." *Philosophical Studies* 33(3).

Stich, S. (1981). "Dennett on Intentional Systems." *Philosophical Topics* 12(1).

Stich, S. (1982a). "On the Ascription of Content." In Woodfield (1982).

Stich, S. (1982b). "Genetic Engineering: How Should Science Be Controlled?" In T. Regan and D. VanDeVeer, eds., *Individual Rights and Public Policy.* Towota, N.J.: Roman & Littlefield.

Stich, S. (1983). *From Folk Psychology to Cognitive Science.* Cambridge, Mass.: The MIT Press. A Bradford book.

Stich, S. (1984a). "Relativism, Rationality, and the Limits of Intentional Description." *Pacific Philosophical Quarterly* 65(3).

Stich, S. (1984b). "Life without Meaning." *Proceedings of the Russellian Society* (Sydney University) 9.

Stich, S. (1984c). "Armstrong on Belief." In R. Bogdan, ed., *D. M. Armstrong.* Dordrecht, The Netherlands: Reidel.

Stich, S. (1985). "Could Man Be an Irrational Animal?" *Synthese* 64(1). Reprinted in Kornblith (1985).

Stich, S. (1988). "Reflective Equilibrium, Analytic Epistemology, and the Problem of Cognitive Diversity." *Synthese* 74.

Stich, S. (forthcoming, a). "The Dispute over Innate Ideas." In M. Dascal et al., eds., *Sprachphilosophie, Ein Internationales Handbuch Zeitgenossischer Forschung.*

Stich, S. (forthcoming, b). Review of MacNamara (1986). In *Journal of Applied Psycholinguistics.*

Stich, S., and R. Nisbett (1980). "Justification and the Psychology of Human Reasoning." *Philosophy of Science* 47.

Stove, D. (1986). *The Rationality of Induction.* New York: Oxford University Press.

Strawson, P. (1952). *Introduction to Logical Theory.* New York: John Wiley.

Stroud, B. (1984). *The Significance of Philosophical Scepticism.* Oxford: Clarendon Press.

Tarski, A. (1956). "The Concept of Truth in Formalized Languages." In A. Tarski, *Logic, Semantics, and Metamathematics,* J. H. Woodger trans. New York: Oxford University Press.

Templeton, A. (1982). "Adaptation and the Integration of Evolutionary Forces." In R. Milkman, ed., *Perspectives on Evolution.* Sunderland, Mass.: Sinaver.

Tversky, A., and D. Kahneman (1983). "Extentional versus Intuitive Reasoning: The Conjunction Fallacy in Probability Judgment." *Psychological Review* 90(4).

Tweney, R., M. Doherty, and C. Mynatt (1981). *On Scientific Thinking.* New York: Columbia University Press.

Ward, W., and H. Jenkins (1965). "The Display of Information and the Judgment of Contingency." *Canadian Journal of Psychology* 19.

Wason, P. (1968a). "Reasoning about a Rule." *Quarterly Journal of Experimental Psychology* 20:273–81.

Wason, P. (1968b). "On the Failure to Eliminate Hypotheses . . .—A Second Look." In Wason and Johnson-Laird, eds. (1977).

Wason, P. (1977). "Self-contradiction." In Johnson-Laird and Wason, eds. (1977).

Wason, P., and P. Johnson-Laird (1970). "A Conflict between Selecting and Evaluating Information in an Inferential Task." *British Journal of Psychology* 61:509–15.

Wason, P., and P. Johnson-Laird, eds. (1968). *Thinking and Reasoning.* Harmondsworth: Penguin.

Weinstein, S. (1974). "Truth and Demonstratives." *Nous* 8.

Wheeler, S. (1972). "Attributives and Their Modifiers." *Nous* 6.

Williams, G. (1966). *Adaption and Natural Selection.* Princeton N.J.: Princeton University Press.

Woodfield, A. (1982). *Thought and Object.* Oxford: Oxford University Press.

Index